Cases in Environmental Politics

Like Norman Miller's companion text, *Environmental Politics*, this casebook emphasizes the struggle for power among stakeholders in environmental politics and policymaking. Whether examining recent legislation on energy policy, air pollution, endangered species, land use, or the politics of food, each case is presented through a narrative introduction and a dozen or more primary source documents that illustrate whose interests are at stake, and how they pursue them in the policymaking process. Engaging introductions by Miller provide a narrative frame and context for the primary source documents in each chapter. Discussion questions prompt students to analyze the struggles and compromises inherent in environmental policymaking.

The primary source documents include excerpts from public hearing testimony, regulatory agency statements, journal articles, scientific reports, online briefs, and commentary in media outlets from businesses and environmental groups. Collectively, the cases in this volume cover the full spectrum of groups involved in the environmental policy arena.

Norman Miller has served on the faculties of Rutgers University, Rollins and Meredith Colleges, and North Carolina State University. He is currently a member of the Global Warming and Energy Subcommittee of the national Sierra Club and the Executive Committee of the Sierra Club's North Carolina Chapter. Previously he worked in both the legislative and executive branches of New Jersey state government in a variety of environmental policy capacities. He is also an academic member of the Society of Environmental Journalism.

Cases in Environmental Politics

Stakeholders, Interests, and Policymaking

Edited by
Norman Miller

Routledge
Taylor & Francis Group

NEW YORK AND LONDON

First published 2009
by Routledge
270 Madison Ave, New York, NY 10016

Simultaneously published in the UK
by Routledge
2 Park Square, Milton Park, Abingdon, Oxon OX14 4RN

Routledge is an imprint of the Taylor & Francis Group,
an informa business

© 2009 Taylor & Francis

Typeset in Garamond by RefineCatch Limited, Bungay, Suffolk
Printed and bound in the United States of America on acid-free
paper by Edwards Brothers, Inc.

Library of Congress Cataloging in Publication Data
Cases in environmental politics / edited by Norman Miller.—
1st ed.
p. cm.
Includes bibliographical references and index.
1. Environmental policy—Case studies.   I. Miller, Norman,
1939–
GE170.C39 2009
363.7'0561—dc22

2008015012

ISBN10: 0–415–96103–3 (hbk)
ISBN10: 0–415–96104–1 (pbk)

ISBN13: 978–0–415–96103–5 (hbk)
ISBN13: 978–0–415–96104–2 (pbk)

Brief Contents

Contents

Acknowledgements

I would be remiss if I did not publicly express my appreciation to Ryan White and Helen Marino who brought their technical and diplomatic skills to the tedious but indispensable tasks of securing the reprint permissions and text preparation necessary to bring a volume such as this to press. Both carried out their responsibilities with good humor under sometimes stringent deadlines. I am in their debt.

Permissions Acknowledgements

Alliance of Automobile Manufacturers. "Our Positions on CAFE, Energy Security and Carbon Dioxide," The Alliance of Automobile Manufacturers, http://www. autoalliance.org/fuel/fuel_whitepaper.php

American Farm Bureau Federation. "American Farm Bureau Federation Position Paper on the Farm Bill of 2007" and "Endangered Species Act Improvement," Policy Position of the American Farm Bureau Federation. Reprinted with permission.

Bonnicksen, Thomas M. "Tree-Huggers or Fire-Huggers? The Environmental Movement's Confused Forest Policy," The National Center for Public Policy Research.

Brewer, Joe. "The Coming Biofuels Disaster," Joe Brewer, Truthout.org, Guest Column. Reprinted with permission.

Bruckner, Traci. "Conservation and the 2007 Farm Bill," Center for Rural Affairs. www.cfra.org. Reprinted with permission.

Bryce, Robert. "Ethanol Is the Agricultural Equivalent of Holy Water," Robert Bryce, *The Washington Spectator*.

Cleetus, Rachael. "We Need a Well-Designed Cap-and-Trade Program to Fight Global Warming," Union of Concerned Scientists. Reprinted with permission.

Coalition on the Environment and Jewish Life. "Action Alert: Protect the Endangered Species Act". Reprinted with permission.

Defenders of Wildlife. "Partnerships for Conservation: 'The Endangered Species Recovery Act of 2006' " and "New Bush Administration Policy Limits Endangered Species Listings: Many Species Would No Longer Qualify for ESA Protection". Copyright 2008 Defenders of Wildlife, www.defenders.org. Reprinted with permission.

Earthjustice. "The Pombo Endangered Species Extinction Bill—He Wants to Pave Habitat to Put Up a Parking Lot". www.earthjustice.org. Reprinted with permission.

Engdahl, F. William. "The Great Biofuel Fraud," *Asia Times*. Reprinted with permission.

Evangelical Environmental Network. "The Academy of Evangelical Scientists and Ethicists on the Critical Importance of Conserving Endangered Species." © 2005 Evangelical Environmental Network. This article first appeared in the Summer 2005 issue of *Creation Care*. Used by permission.

Faber, Scott. "A Safety Net, Not a Security Blanket," Scott Faber, Environmental Defense.

Food First. "Immigration, the 2007 US Farm Bill, and the Transformation of our Food and Fuel Systems," Backgrounder, Food First Books. Reprinted with permission.

Friends of the Earth. "Windfalls in Lieberman-Warner Global Warming Bill: Quantifying the Fossil Fuel Industry Giveaways," October 2007. Reprinted with permission.

Glasgow, Nathan and Lena Hansen. "Setting the Record Straight on Ethanol," Position Paper of Nathan Glasgow and Lena Hansen, Rocky Mountain Institute Solutions. Reprinted with permission.

Greacen, Scott. " 'Healthy Forests Initiative': A Campaign of Severe Forest Policy Rollbacks," Environmental Protection Information Center.

Gun Owners of America. "Letter to Rep. Richard Pombo Re: 'Endangered Species Act' Reauthorization." Reprinted with permission.

Holt-Gimenez, Eric. "Biofuels: Myths of the Agro-fuels Transition," Food First Books. Reprinted with permission.

Kelderman, Eric. "Ethanol demand outgrows corn," www.Stateline.org. Reprinted with permission.

Kleit, Andrew J. "CAFE Changes, By the Numbers," *Regulation*, Fall 2002. © Cato Institute. Reproduced by permission.

Knobloch, Kevin. "House Vote Sends Landmark Energy Bill to President Bush," Statement of President Kevin Knobloch of the Union of Concerned Scientists, December 18, 2007. Reprinted with permission.

Leduc, Doug. "GM workers lobbying for less-stringent CAFE rule," *Greater Fort Wayne Business Weekly*, July 27, 2007. Reprinted with permission.

Lilley, Sasha. "Green Fuel's Dirty Secret," CorpWatch, June 1, 2006. www.corpwatch.org. Reprinted with permission.

Milloy, Steve. "Global Warming and the Supremes." Reprinted with permission.

Moberg, David. "Biofuels: Promise or Peril?" and "Whose Subsidy Is It Anyway?" David Moberg, *In These Times*. www.inthesetimes.org. Reprinted with permission.

Murray, Iain. "Cap and Trade: A System Made for Fraudsters," Competitive Enterprise Institute. Reprinted with permission.

National Family Farm Coalition. "Farm Bill Policy Statement." www.nffc.net. Reprinted with permission.

The Natural Resources Defense Council. "Issue Paper, May 2003," www.nrdc.org. Reprinted with permission.

Niskanen, William A. "Dumb, Greedy, and Ugly," The Cato Institute. © Cato Institute. Reproduced by permission.

Oko, Dan and Ilan Kayhatsky. "Fighting Fire With Logging?" Mother-Jones.com, August 1, 2002. © 2008, Foundation for National Progress. Reprinted with permission.

O'Toole, Randal. "Bush's Fire Plan Won't Work," © Cato Institute. Reprinted by permission.

Pew Center on Global Climate Change. "Statement on Reducing US Greenhouse Gas Emissions Cost-Effectively from Hon. Eileen Claussen, President, Pew Center on Global Climate Change, Submitted to the United States Senate, The Environment and Public Works Committee," November 15, 2007. Reprinted with permission.

Physicians for Social Responsibility. "Lieberman-Warner Global Warming Legislation Provides Vehicle for Important Senate Debate," December 5, 2007. Reprinted with permission.

Public Citizen. "Boosting Fuel Efficiency Can Increase Highway Safety; Public Citizen Debunks Auto Industry Safety Canard," Summary of

Testimony to the Senate Committee on Commerce, Science and Transportation, January 24, 2002. Reprinted with permission.

Renewable Fuels Association. "Ethanol Facts: Food vs. Fuel," Fact Sheet, Renewable Fuels Association. Reprinted with permission.

Ridenour, Amy and Payton Knight. "CAFE Kills, and Then Some: Six Reasons to Be Skeptical of Fuel Economy Standards," The National Center for Public Policy Research, June 19, 2007. Reprinted with permission.

Sedjo, Roger. "The Fires This Time," The Property and Environmental Research Center. Reprinted with permission.

Society of American Foresters. "Healthy Forest Bill an Important First Step."

Society of American Foresters. "Protecting Endangered Species on Private Land," Position Paper of the Society of American Foresters. Reprinted with permission.

St. Clair, Jeffrey. "Chainsaw George Bush Fire Plan: Log It All," Jeffrey St. Clair, Dissident Voice. Reprinted by permission.

Stirling, M. David (vice president and attorney, Pacific Legal Foundation). "Endangered Species Act Finally Meets the Fifth Amendment," Policy Position of the Pacific Legal Foundation. www.pacificlegal.org. Reprinted with permission.

Stoller, Matt. "The Green Civil War Needs to Begin," "The Open Left," October 17, 2007. Reprinted with permission.

Taylor, Jerry and Peter Van Doren. "Don't Raise CAFE Standards," National Review (online), August 1, 2007. © 2007 by National Review Online, www.nationalreview.com.

Union of Concerned Scientists. "Building a Better SUV," Selections from the Executive Summary of a Research Report. Reprinted with permission.

Visnic, Bill. "New CAFE: Higher Number, Same Problems," Copyright Edmunds Inc. All rights reserved. First published on www.autoobserver.com and reprinted with permission.

Wattenburg, Bill. "The 'Let Our Forests Burn Policy' is Criminal and Stupid—It Must be Re-examined by the Scientists of This Nation," Research Foundation at California State University at Chico, August 18, 1998. Reprinted with permission.

Preface

Cases in Environmental Politics is a compilation of documents that collectively constitute the political profiles of six major environmental issues. The thesis of my companion text, *Environmental Politics: Stakeholders, Interests, and Policymaking*, is that public policy stems, in large part, from the reconciliation of the competing interests that have stakes in how issues are resolved. This competition, though, does not take place in the abstract. Rather it is embodied in public testimony on proposed legislation and regulation, open letters to Congressional committees, press releases of stakeholders and institutions, regulatory agency statements, journal articles, scientific reports, online briefs, blogs, and the websites of advocacy groups that the various interests prepare and advance to influence and shape public policies.

Accordingly, this volume is a diverse collection of these primary source materials representing the broad spectrum of viewpoints and positions on *The Endangered Species Act*, Biofuels, Corporate Average Fuels Economy Regulations (CAFE Standards), the Cap-and-Trade Protocol, the *Food and Energy Security Act of 2007 (The Farm Bill of 2007)*, and *The Healthy Forest Restoration Act* and Federal Wildfire Policy. In selecting the case subjects, I have sought, first, to present as diverse a range of issue areas as possible—natural resources, energy, pollution control, and food production, while representing issues of particular concern to different geographical areas. It would have been an impossible task to illustrate in each case the full range of actors in the political process writ large, but I have attempted to highlight the perspective of as many kinds of groups as possible—Congress; regulatory agencies; state and local governments; business, science and environmental advocacy and activist groups; the media; and the courts—collectively across the volume. Second, I have sought to make these cases as timely and relevant as possible; all were extensively debated by Congress in 2007. In fact, in two of the cases, no legislative resolution was achieved as of this writing, unwittingly affording students the opportunity to follow up on future deliberations to see which interests prevailed and why.

The primary documents, from which each case is constructed, are identified in a numbered list at the beginning of each case study for readers to see at a glance what lies ahead. This numbering corresponds to the beginning of each primary source so that students can more easily identify and locate each document. In the introductory background discussions, I have sought only to set the historical and political context of the matters in dispute. Extensive summaries or structuring of the documents might well implicitly, if not explicitly, predispose readers to certain policy outcomes, and thus undermine the pedagogical value of primary sources as invaluable complements to texts that mediate, analyze, and evaluate policies and positions. While conceived as a companion to *Environmental Politics*, this Casebook can thus supplement other environmental policy texts, lectures, and teaching strategies by illustrating and exemplifying the principles and concepts presented in those texts and lectures. It also supplies a rich mine of materials for discussion, writing, and further research. Perhaps most important, it will allow students to confront policy debates directly, and encourage them to analyze and evaluate these political arguments and proposals on their own, unfiltered. The questions following each case are intended to stimulate and facilitate this critical thinking process.

Chapter I

The Endangered Species Act

Primary Documents

The Endangered Species Act

1.1. "Opening Statement on H.R. 3824, 'The Threatened and Endangered Species Recovery Act of 2005 (TESRAS)'," Rep. Richard W. Pombo, Sponsor and Chair of the House Committee on Resources Before the House Committee on Resources

1.2. "Letter to Rep. Richard Pombo Re: 'Endangered Species Act' Reauthorization," from the Gun Owners of America

1.3. "Testimony of Marc Racicot, Governor of Montana, on behalf of The Western Governors Association Before the House Resources Committee on HR 3160, Common Sense Protection of the 'Endangered Species Act'"

1.4. "Protecting Endangered Species on Private Land," Position Paper of the Society of American Foresters

1.5. "'Endangered Species Act' Improvement," Policy Position of the American Farm Bureau Federation

1.6. "'Endangered Species Act' Finally Meets the Fifth Amendment," Policy Position of the Pacific Legal Foundation

1.7. "The Pombo Endangered Species Extinction Bill—He Wants to Pave Habitat to Put Up a Parking Lot," Earthjustice

1.8. "A Letter from Biologists to the United States Senate Concerning Science in the Endangered Species Act"

1.9. "The Academy of Evangelical Scientists and Ethicists on the Critical Importance of Conserving Endangered Species"

1.10. "Action Alert: Protect the Endangered Species Act," Coalition on the Environment and Jewish Life

BACKGROUND

In 1973, the Endangered Species Act (ESA) was enacted into law by an overwhelming margin. Not incidentally, a counterpart wildlife protection measure—The Convention on International Trade in Endangered Species of Wild Fauna and Flora (CITES)—was actively promoted by the United States and agreed to by more than 80 nations that same year. Like its international counterpart, the Endangered Species Act reflected a profound concern over the increasingly precarious status of precious animals and plants, and, perhaps more significantly, a recognition of man's responsibility for jeopardizing their viability. Lawmakers were obviously mindful of, and responsive to, the biological, commercial, and ethical values inherent in these natural resources.

Notwithstanding the wide support for this conservation mandate when signed into law, the ESA has proven to be one of the most contentious environmental statutes ever enacted. The reasons are not hard to discern. Most broadly, it pits the right Americans most jealously guard—to own and utilize their property as they see fit—against what the environmental, scientific, and religious communities regard as man's most sacred obligation—to save God's most vulnerable creatures from extinction. But the political controversies it has generated are attributable largely to an essential aspect of its implementation overlooked by legislators. Protecting "threatened" and "endangered" species involves not only a prohibition on their "taking" but on guarding their habitat, which significantly expands its reach. It is habitat protection that has brought into the political fray builders, developers, and utilities whose development ambitions have had to be compromised; industries who lay claim to natural resources within these habitats; military installations that find land use prohibitions constraining; and any number of property owners who are lodging "takings" claims.

So controversial has the law been over the last 35 years that Congress has failed in several attempts to reauthorize it, notwithstanding a legislative mandate to do so, preferring instead to keep it in effect by annual appropriations. The year of writing, 2007, that stalemate appears to be broken. A bipartisan group of Senators has fashioned legislation that has garnered the support of most of the major interest groups on both sides of the controversy.

While the ESA has operated largely below the radar, its reach attracted wide public attention in two celebrated cases. In 1975, the fate of a tiny creature called a snail darter held up the construction of a major dam project in Tennessee. The case went all the way to the Supreme Court, that upheld the Fish and Wildlife Service's listing of the minnow and its preemptive effect on the Tellico Dam project. It took a subsequent act of Congress to exempt the snail darter to permit completion of the dam. And in 1990, timber interests claimed that the listing of the northern spotted owl severely impacted their industry and occasioned the closing of hundreds of mills. The "jobs v. owls" framing of the issue, like the snail darter controversy a decade and a half earlier, gained sympathy for opponents of the law, and put the environmental community, at least for a while, on the defensive. Despite such high-profile cases, opponents were not able to make significant headway. A powerful and diverse group of allies under the banner of the National Endangered Species Act Reform Coalition (NESARC), was formed in 1991 to continue the fight. NESARC counted among its members the American Farm Bureau, the American Public Power Association, the Edison Electric Institute, the National Association of Counties, the National Association of Home Builders, the National Water Resources Association, and a host of other organizations and corporations whose various building and facility projects were stalled, circumscribed, or precluded, by the ESA.

Given the breadth and economic power of the law's opponents, it may seem surprising that the ESA has withstood efforts to gut or even significantly change it. Its survival can be attributed to a combination of favorable public opinion, an aggressive Department of Interior Secretary during the late 1990s (Bruce Babbitt), and a determined campaign by the environmental, scientific, and religious communities. It's also probably fair to say that many, though by no means all, of those seeking its reform wanted just that—reform—not repeal. Many paid more than lip service to its noble goals while lamenting its failure to reach them.

As noted, the economic hardship challenge came first, to be followed by the "regulatory takings" claim. Neither prevailed. More recently, Congressman Richard Pombo of California tried to move a reform bill in 2005 principally on the grounds that the act has not made any meaningful progress toward its mission. While it was reported out of his Committee, it got no further. By his criteria, the meager number of species removed from the endangered list and confirmed recoveries since its enactment did not seem to warrant the expense—financial and administrative—of the program's implementation. But the scientific, environmental, and religious communities, acting under different standards, closed ranks to defeat his reform effort. More moderate voices wanted something less—a more stringent standard for listings and a substantial role in the nomination process. This brought the scientific community into aggressive opposition to the bill, and their steadfast support of the law as it had been implemented proved a decisive force in its survival.

But another argument has resurfaced and promises to fundamentally alter the direction of the Act's implementation. The Western governors, among others, have argued that the Act can be more successfully administered by State and local governments and private landowners, on whose property most of the endangered species, as well as their habitat, reside. It is ground that the private sector and the scientific and environmental communities can share. This forms the fundamental basis of the bill that now seems to have achieved consensus, S-700 of 2007.

It may seem odd that the apparent breakthrough legislation is not an "environmental" bill at all, but a financial one—specifically an amendment of the tax code. It provides a number of financial incentives to private landowners that, in effect, conscript them into the restoration and recovery efforts of the Federal government, making them partners, not opponents. While it is unclear whether or not this bill, if enacted, would constitute a reauthorization of the Endangered Species Act, it will certainly take much pressure off those agencies with responsibility to pursue its objectives for some time, and buy them time to show more concrete and empirically demonstrable results. Not incidentally, it comes at a time when proponents of the ESA fear that the forces for change—more substantial change—are gathering and face a business friendly Administration and Congress.

Opponents may not be satisfied. A legal policy paper issued just one month after introduction of S-700 by the Department of Interior's solicitor David Bernhardt proposes a severely limited criterion for endangered species status, limiting the reach of the ESA. Failing to achieve their goals legislatively, opponents are turning to the regulatory arena for relief, a common tactic of opponents of environmental measures. It is important to note that the current Interior Secretary is Dirk Kempthorne, an historic opponent of ESA and sponsor of reform measures years earlier. Here, however, Congress, as well as the scientific community, are aggressively challenging the proposed new policy. Excerpts from the policy paper, a question and answer rebuttal from the Defenders of Wildlife, and a letter from five influential Senators objecting to the proposed policy, together with a series of questions they pose to Interior, close out the list of documents that represent the range of interests and stakeholders that have grappled with this law.

DOCUMENTS

The sponsor of the ESA reform proposal introduced in 2005 (H.R.3824) and Chairman of the House Resources Committee to which the bill was referred, Congressman Richard

Pombo (R., CA), argues that the law has not accomplished its goals. The following testimony sets forth his justification for reforming and modernizing the 1973 Act and a brief list of the changes to that act proposed by the bill. Note the criteria upon which he bases his ESA report card; scientists and environmentalists have different criteria, or, more precisely, find that the data on its implementation history lead to opposite conclusions. (See, for example, a science community's Report Card that appeared in the June 2005 issue of Natural History.)

1.1. "Opening Statement on H.R. 3824, 'The Threatened and Endangered Species Recovery Act of 2005 (TESRAS)'," Rep. Richard W. Pombo, Sponsor and Chair of the House Committee on Resources Before the House Committee on Resources

Washington, DC Rep. Richard W. Pombo (R-CA), Chairman of the House Committee on Resources, issued the following opening statement at today's hearing on the Threatened and Endangered Species Recovery Act of 2005 (TESRA):

The Endangered Species Act was signed into law and introduced to the American public in 1973, more than three decades ago.

Right around this time, Americans were also being introduced to the first VCRs, jumbo jets, and Atari TV game consoles. In medicine, ultrasound diagnostic techniques were developed and the sites of DNA production on genes were discovered.

Since then, Americans have experienced the introduction of innovative wonders like Microsoft Windows, the Internet, cellular phones, anti-lock brakes and air bags, Nintendo Game Cube (whatever that is), the Blackberry, etc.

But most importantly for our species science, technology and the freedom of innovation have led to incredible advances in medicine. What was once a seven-day hospital stay is now a half-day outpatient visit, perhaps even just a prescription from a doctor.

America's endangered species unfortunately have not been the beneficiary of these society-wide advancements over the last three decades. America has been getting better, but for all intents and purposes the ESA is still stuck in 1973, wearing leisure suits, mood rings, and collecting pet rocks.

According to the US Fish and Wildlife Service, only ten of the roughly 1300 species on the ESA's list have recovered in the Act's history. That is a less than one percent success rate. And the Service's data on our species' progress towards recovery today isn't much better.

Yet, despite these facts, the ESA's groupies would have you believe that it is better than ever before. They defend the Act's original language from updates as if it were Shakespeare's works we were editing.

It has been 99% successful, they will tell you, because all but nine species are with us today. The official Fish and Wildlife Service data, however, tells a much different story:

39% of the Act's listed species are in "unknown" status—they have no idea—could be extinct.
21% [are] classified by the Service as declining
3% though currently on the list are believed to be extinct.
30% are classified as "stable" though for many species in this category, this is only a result of corrections to original data error, rather than actual accomplishments of the ESA.
And finally, only 6% are classified as improving.

The math just doesn't add up.

And across the board, according to the Service, 77% of all the listed species have only achieved somewhere between ZERO and one quarter of their recovery goals. In fairness, I am sure this includes the species in the "unknown" category, because if you don't know where the species is, or if it is still around, you can't accurately gage its status.

Now, we all know it takes time to recover endangered species, but after three decades of implementation, do these sound like the statistics of a successful law? Of course not, but the defenders of the three-decades-status-quo are just getting warmed up.

To help demonstrate what some have called their "blind faith" in this law, opponents of change may even go so far as to tell you that species with designated critical habitats are more likely to be improving, even though the official position of the Service, in successive administrations, both Democrat and Republican, is that 30 years of critical habitat has done very little—if anything—to help species. On the contrary, it just causes conflict, litigation, and wastes valuable agency resources that could otherwise be spent in the field on species in need.

It could go on and on, but the bottom line is the Endangered Species Act is in desperate need of an update. I would wager that none of my colleagues on this dais could say with a straight face, that almost 34 years ago, when Congress passed its first attempt at a species recovery law, we got it EXACTLY right. Congress gets NOTHING exactly right.

The ESA must be updated to incorporate 30 years of lessons learned. It must be modernized for the 21st century to provide flexibility for innovation to achieve results. We must change the Act's chief unintended consequences of conflict and litigation into real cooperative conservation.

The ESA's regulatory Iron Curtain has prevented this from happening. It has hurt species recovery by leading to the trend we all know as "shoot, shovel and shut up." And it has hurt families and ranchers by taking away their property unnecessarily.

In my thirteen years of experience in Congress with the ESA, it is here that the opposing line-in-the-sand has always been drawn. Everyone here today wants this law to work to conserve and recover endangered species, but not everyone wants to help the private property owner do it. Perhaps it is simply an ideological difference.

But I submit to you that if we do not enlist the property owner, we will never increase the ESA's meager results for species recovery. Because 90% of all endangered species in America have habitat on private land, we can never reasonably expect to achieve success if we do not make the landowner an ally of the species and a partner of the federal government.

In this regard, protecting the private property rights of the American landowner is not only what is right constitutionally, it is the KEY to increasing our rates of species recovery.

The bipartisan Threatened and Endangered Species Recovery Act—or TESRA—will do just this. It begins to solve the long-outstanding problems of Endangered Species Act by (1) focusing on species recovery by creating recovery teams and requiring recovery plans by certain dates (2) increasing openness and accountability (3) strengthening scientific standards (4) creating bigger roles for state and local governments (5) protecting and incentivizing private property owners and (6) eliminating dysfunctional critical habitat designations that cause conflict without benefit.

So, as we move forward in this process, I ask the committee to rise above partisanship and hyperbole, as the sponsors of this legislation have, and engage in honest debate. When you hear the tired and inane rhetoric of "gut," "rollback," and "eviscerate," take a step back, look at the official Fish and Wildlife Service data, think of all the conflict, and ask yourself, what could we possibly have to rollback? It's time to move forward, update this law and bring it into the 21st century.

Among the large number of property rights advocates affected by the ESA are the Gun Owners of America. In this letter to the sponsor of Congressman Pombo's bill reforming the ESA, the organization expresses its support on a number of grounds, e.g. its failure to "live up to our intrinsic values as Americans," the economic hardship it imposes on landowners, its failure to achieve its basic goal of protecting rare plants and animals, its undermining of public works projects, and its affront to the 5th Amendment to the Constitution. But it introduces to the debate another quarrel with ESA, viz. that it compromises national security.

1.2. "Letter to Rep. Richard Pombo Re: 'Endangered Species Act' Reauthorization," from the Gun Owners of America

June 16, 2005

Dear Chairman Pombo:

On February 10, you called for a new approach to species conservation.

Pointing out that only one percent of the plants and animals put on the endangered species list over the past thirty years has actually recovered, you said the ESA has failed to live up to "our intrinsic values as Americans." *We agree.*

Since its enactment in 1973, the ESA has penalized landowners for their stewardship of their property. Farmers, ranchers, tree farmers, homeowners and other landowners who harbor endangered species on their property or merely have wildlife habitat are subjected to severe land-use restrictions that often lead to economic ruin. In much of rural America the ESA has turned landowners and endangered species into mortal enemies. To keep their property from falling under the ESA's land-use controls, landowners have to preemptively sterilize their land, making it inhospitable to the species the ESA is supposed to protect. Such are the perverse incentives of this dysfunctional law.

Indeed, rare plants and animals are at greater risk today than they were before the ESA became law.

In states as diverse as North Carolina, Texas, Colorado and California, the ESA has brought much-needed public works projects to a standstill. Hundreds of millions of taxpayer dollars have been diverted to cover the cost of the ESA—often on the basis of the most dubious of scientific data. Once a species has been added to the endangered species list, it can stay there for decades because there is little incentive to recover species or remove them from the endangered list. As long as species remain on the list, greens and bureaucrats can maintain cost-free land-use control. Listing has become an end in itself.

There are some who say the ESA needs to be "strengthened." In truth, the ESA is arguably the most powerful statute on the books. It has opened the floodgates to regulatory takings of private property for which landowners receive no compensation. As such, the ESA is a direct affront to the US Constitution's Fifth Amendment, which clearly states: "Nor shall private property be taken for public use without just compensation."

Those who don't understand what's wrong with the ESA—its almost unchecked power to coerce law-abiding citizens, regardless of the consequences—will never know how to fix the law.

Fixing the ESA is absolutely critical—not just for species, property owners and our nation's economy—but for our nation's security.

The ESA and other command-and-control approaches have undermined the nation's security in an era when we can least afford it. In recent years, "critical habitat" designations have been extended to military installations around the country where they come into direct conflict with the armed forces' ability to train soldiers for combat. Fully 72 percent of the Army's base at Fort Lewis, Washington is critical habitat for the Northern Spotted Owl, even though not a single one of these birds currently resides on the installation.

Camp Pendleton Marine base in California has endangered species on its beaches, in riparian areas, and even on brushy dry land leaving little land available for maneuvers.

What's more, our efforts to secure our borders from illegal entry including entry by members of Al Qaeda have been seriously compromised in the name of species protection.

We remind you that in 1996 Congress appropriated money for Operation Gatekeeper, a Border Patrol initiative to equip fences with state-of-the-art lights, sensors and surveillance equipment along a 14-mile stretch of the US/Mexico Border. After nearly nine years, the project still hasn't been completed because government wildlife officials claim that the final four miles of the fences would disturb seven individual birds—two vireos, two flycatchers and three gnatcatchers.

The ESA and other regulatory schemes are failing the public they are supposed to serve, and failed the wildlife they are supposed to protect.

We can do better, and we can begin by supporting real reform of the ESA.

A new ESA should be rooted in the principles on which this country was founded, and should be commensurate with the creative, innovative talents of our people. At a minimum, an ESA for the 21st century should include:

Compensating landowners for any taking of their property or loss of use of their property resulting from the ESA.

Ending the perverse incentives of the current ESA that turn people against wildlife and replacing them with incentive-based approaches.

Requiring the government to develop a recovery plan, subject to public comment, before a species is added to the endangered species list, and when the recovery goals are met, mandating the removal of the species from the list.

Ensuring that decisions regarding listing and recovery of endangered and threatened species be based on sound, transparent science that is subject to public comment and is subject to doubleblind peer review.

As noted earlier, efforts to fix the ESA will fail miserably without a clear understanding of the reasons why it doesn't work.

As you begin your important work, we urge you to keep in mind that you cannot fix an already poisonous law by increasing its dosage.

Among the stakeholders in the debate over the Endangered Species Act are state and local governments, especially in the West, where most of the habitats of listed species are located. While the following testimony of former Governor Racicot of Montana is to a version of an ESA reform bill considered in 2000, it well represents generally the concerns of States and the problems posed by the Act to their development plans. It also sets forth the Western Governors Association's recommendations for assuaging those concerns, chief among which are a greater role for the states in implementing the act, increased funding, more rigorous listing and delisting processes, and more economic incentives.

1.3. "Testimony of Marc Racicot, Governor of Montana, on behalf of The Western Governors Association Before the House Resources Committee on HR 3160, Common Sense Protection of the 'Endangered Species Act' "

March 1, 2000

Mr. Chairman, Representative Miller, Members of the Committee. My name is Marc Racicot. I am Governor of the State of Montana and am here representing the Western Governors' Association. I appreciate the opportunity to share with you the Governors' perspectives on the Endangered Species Act (ESA).

Comprehensive reauthorization of the Endangered Species Act (ESA) in this Congress is the highest legislative priority of the Western Governors. We appreciate the Committee's efforts to fulfill this goal.

Our states and communities must deal with the effects of proposals to list species and management decisions made under the ESA on literally a daily basis. Recent salmon, steelhead, and bull trout listings affect nearly every watershed in the Pacific Northwest from tidewater areas to head-water streams in Montana. The prairie dog, which the Service has said is warranted but precluded for listing ranges over 11 western states. A listing decision on the lynx is scheduled for March and reaches from Portland, Oregon to Portland, Maine.

Unfortunately, listing under the act places a cloud of uncertainty over nearly every economic and social activity where the species may occur. As a result, our states, counties and local governments must consult with the US Fish and Wildlife Service and the National Marine Fisheries Service to identify and develop best management practices for activities ranging from storm water discharges, to road design, to myriad land uses.

As equally unfortunate are the dynamics of present ESA impacts which stifle cooperative agreements and innovative ways to foster healthy popula-tions. For instance, there are an inadequate number of effective federal-state partnerships which can lead to protective (4d)-rules. This lack of partnership reflects a lack of understanding of what should be understood as effective state and local government practices.

At the same time our farm and ranching communities are trying to learn what practices will comport with the protective (4d)-regulation for species listed as threatened, while our states and communities are coming together and marshaling their resources to reverse the declines in these species. Yet the two Services are not willing or have too few personnel to work with states and private landowners to incorporate creative solutions to meet the requirements of the ESA.

Similarly, Montana has encountered delays with our construction projects under the new highway act. The US Fish and Wildlife Service does has not have the personnel to conduct the Section 7 consultations that are necessary before bridges and roads can be constructed in affected watersheds.

Rural communities and federal and state resource and land management agencies are reeling from the successive listing petitions that have been and are being prepared for each of the species that share the large landscapes of the West—like our prairies and sagebrush steppes, where prairie dogs and grouse are keystone species.

Under the current approach, successive petitions and settlement of legal challenges divert resources and impose deadlines that short-circuit state conservation efforts before they can be completed. This process, quite frankly, frightens away stakeholders who are interested in conserving the species. Yet, in nearly every case, these species spend the majority of their time on private lands. The decline of these species cannot be reversed unless states and private landowners are made partners in achieving the goals of the Act.

These problems are compounded by the fact that landowners are not given the regulatory assurances and financial and technical assistance that they need to actively manage their lands for the benefit of declining species. Even where states have brought stakeholders together to address the threats to a species in conservation agreements, court decisions, which second guess a Secretary's approval of such plans, have set such agreements aside.

In short, our states need immediate, comprehensive improvements in the way the Endangered Species Act is implemented and funded. The intent of the Act remains a laudable goal. Yet the tools within the Act have become outdated and are incomplete.

Governors recognize that the Act can only be reauthorized through legislation developed in a consensus fashion that results in broad bipartisan support.

The governors realize this is no easy task. We started a similar debate in the early 1990s. As a group we had never experienced a more acrimonious debate—so acrimonious in fact that we had to initially back off our attempt. However, with the leadership of Montana's then-Governor Stan Stephens on one side of the debate and Idaho's then-Governor Cecil

Andrus on the other, the Governors became convinced that the only way the Endangered Species Act could be improved was through a consensus process.

Our staff worked with senior representatives of the Fish and Wildlife Service and the National Marine Fisheries Service to improve the Act by drawing on the mutual experience we have gained since 1973 in implementing the Act. That leadership and that consensus resulted in an outstanding proposal which would strengthen the role of the states, streamline the Act, and provide increased certainty and assistance for landowners and water users while at the same time enhancing its conservation objectives.

The consensus has since been endorsed by the Western Governors, the National Governors Association and the 50 state fish and wildlife agencies through their International Association of Fish and Wildlife Agencies. It was forwarded to you first in the form of legislative principles in 1993 and then in legislative language in 1995 and 1997, and most recently in November 1999 when I met with your committee staff.

· · ·

The number and geographic range of listings continues to grow in the West, encompassing major metropolitan areas, public lands, and private forest and farmlands, while the Act remains underfunded and without the tools necessary to enable private landowners and states to be partners in achieving the goals of the Act. Our states desperately need the Act to be reauthorized.

States are vitally interested in maintaining viable programs for the conservation of fish and wildlife that are largely under our jurisdiction. We are committed to success and expect to be held accountable, but only if we are given the proper tools and adequate resources to do the job. Under the existing Act, listing means these species largely become a federal responsibility.

We urge you to work through consensus to give us the tools to help us achieve conservation success in cooperation with our private landowners that builds on their stewardship ethic for these resources.

· · ·

The Society of American Foresters and the American Farm Bureau Federation represent industries whose activities are organically related to the land, and both organizations feel that the expertise of their clients would profitably advance the goals of the Endangered Species Act. Both recommend cooperative initiatives with landowners. The foresters would require peer review of listings to "ensure that high quality scientific data are used;" an improved recovery plan process; and incentives to private landowners. Its position paper comprehensively analyzes what it considers needed refinements to the act and merits extensive reproduction here. The farming community would have Congress, in addition, remove inhibitions on agricultural practices.

1.4. "Protecting Endangered Species on Private Land," Position Paper of the Society of American Foresters

Position

The Society of American Foresters (SAF) recognizes that biological diversity is a function of healthy, productive forests and believes that consistent with landowner objectives, forests should be managed to conserve and enhance biological diversity. . . . The Endangered Species Act of 1973 (ESA) is a regulatory approach to protect listed species and considers habitat protection an integral part of the effort. . . . Under ESA, species of plants and animals may be listed as either "endangered" or "threatened" according to assessments of the risk of their extinction. The SAF endorses ESA's goals and purposes because the conservation of these species and the habitats or ecosystems upon which they depend is important to society and the profession of forestry. . . . Professional foresters can contribute their knowledge, training, and experience to managing landscapes for the conservation of biological diversity. . . . The SAF agrees with a National Wildlife Federation position . . .: ESA can and should balance the needs of people with the urgent treatment of imperiled species. Furthermore, significant changes in the ESA, rather than bureaucratic discretion, are required to assure that balance is achieved in practice. . . .

The SAF recommends that Congress, when considering whether to reauthorize and amend the ESA, should consider changes that would:

1) clarify habitat protection on non-federal lands by reconsidering the statutory intent of "critical habitat" protection as it affects non-federal lands, and

2) require peer review of listings to ensure that high quality scientific data are used to identify:

    a) species needing protection, and
    b) essential "survival habitat" for those species (NRC 1995);

3) improve the recovery plan process by including:

    a) identification of habitat essential for recovery, with analysis of economic and other impacts as the current law requires, and
    b) involvement of non-federal landowners in plan development if their land is identified as essential for species recovery; and

4) provide incentives to encourage private landowners to protect habitat.

Issue

Biodiversity protection and ESA conservation efforts raise many economic, political, and institutional issues that will not soon fade. . . . The SAF has chosen to focus on the protection of habitat on non-federal lands. This issue directly affects many SAF members and their clients, and is something the forestry profession can meaningfully contribute to. It also raises a host of related problems that could be improved by redesigning the ESA by clarifying how habitat essential for species conservation is to be protected.

One of the ESA's stated purposes is to "provide a means whereby the ecosystems upon which endangered species and threatened species may be conserved." The means to this end is the listing of individual species and designation of "critical habitat" essential for their conservation. . . .

In 1994, 90% of protected species had some portion of their habitat on private land and 37% of them were entirely dependent on private land. . . . However, the ESA does not identify a specific means for protecting habitat or ecosystems on non-federal lands. To fill the policy gap, the U.S. Fish and Wildlife Service (FWS) used the regulatory powers granted by the ESA. . . . ESA section 9 prohibits all persons from any action causing "take" of a protected species. ESA defines "take" to include "harm." The FWS regulations define "harm" broadly to include "significant habitat modification." In effect, habitat is fully protected wherever a species happens to be, whether or not critical habitat has been designated. This regulatory approach has proven to be problematic.

Critical habitat designation requires drawing lines on a map and performing economic analysis. . . . ESA requires the designation of "critical habitat" essential for species conservation at the time species are listed. . . . However, the FWS often does not designate critical habitat in part because it regards designation as a low priority activity providing only a marginal increment of protection. . . . As discussed below, critical habitat also vexes private landowners and the courts.

The effect of critical habitat designation on private landowners is uncertain. . . . Irrespective of actual regulatory impacts, many people perceive that private property within designated critical habitat areas is off limits, potentially lowering property values. . . . Some landowners fear that the presence of an ESA-listed species or the designation of critical habitat on their land will result in restrictions of current or future activities on their land and subsequent loss of all or some of their property value. . . . There also is concern that designation of critical habitat could render them susceptible to third-party lawsuits. These perceptions are at least as important as reality. . . .

Different appellate courts have arrived at different interpretations of what Congress intended with regards to critical habitat. . . . A series of lawsuits by citizen conservation groups has recently forced the FWS to spend much of their listing budget on court-ordered critical habitat designations. The Supreme Court ruled in Sweet Home (1995) that the FWS had devised a reasonable interpretation of "harm" and left the door open as to what "significant habitat modification" might mean. . . .

A major ESA policy issue is whether to incorporate further protection for property owners and reduce regulatory impacts or whether to increase the protection afforded listed species. . . . The broad reach of ESA habitat protection through the section 9 taking prohibition on habitat-altering activities on private lands raises the Fifth Amendment constitutional takings issue. . . . It often imposes the costs of protection on a few for the benefit of the many. If the public is serious about protecting species, we must commit adequate resources to underwrite the true costs of species conservation and spread those costs fairly and evenly among those receiving the benefits—the American public. . . .

Recommendations

ESA is designed to protect species. We agree with this intent, however, through time as it has been implemented, there have been numerous implementation problems that have interfered and have possibly been counterproductive in meeting these goals. It is with this experience in mind that we propose the following recommendations as top priorities in revising the ESA. The SAF believes the ESA should be amended legislatively, rather than through administrative regulations, although changes in the administration of the ESA could improve its conservation effectiveness and provide relief to private landowners.

1) Clarify Habitat Protection Mandates and Regulations

The SAF urges Congress to do what two biologists recommended more than a decade ago: "exorcize the ambiguity of critical habitat". . . . Bridging this policy gap is a necessary first step in any attempt to make the ESA more effective at protecting habitat for species conservation on non-federal lands. A bill in the 106th Congress proposed amendments to the critical habitat requirements of the ESA, but was inadequate. It proposed moving designation from the listing process to the recovery process, but did not attempt to clarify the uncertain effect that critical habitat designation has on non-federal landowners. Some felt strongly that some designation should occur at the time of listing (Moore et al. 2000) and the bill did not pass.

A revised ESA should:

- Reconsider the need for designating "critical habitat" in the listing process. SAF advocates that this section of the ESA be given less priority in any revision of the Act. However, SAF recommends that agencies, at a minimum, identify what is known about habitat relationships and essential habitats in the preamble of proposed and final rules, including habitat areas and conditions necessary for the continued existence of the species. This information could then be used formally during the recovery planning process to identify "survival" or critical habitat and would provide a compilation of known data that would allow landowners and agencies to focus conservation efforts.

2) Require Peer Review of Proposals to List Species and Identify "Survival Habitat"

The identification of species that are "listed" as being protected by the ESA should continue, as it has since 1982, to be based solely upon the best scientific and commercial data available. But it should also be tempered by a judgment of the adequacy of that data. Ordinary citizens have demonstrated an ability to filter through scientific information, even when it contains contradictions, and come up with reasonable findings. . . . But there must be some assurance that the best data are of high quality.

Some biologists have not supported peer review in ESA listings. . . . However, if peer review is not part of the listing process it is otherwise difficult to verify the adequacy of scientific data. The extra delay and expense of peer review likely will be more than offset by the increase in public confidence and trust that federal agency biologists are indeed making decisions with adequate data. Although the FWS has a policy to include peer review, it is sometimes not done, as in the case of the Alameda whip snake.

To achieve peer review effectively, each proposal to list a species should be referred to an independent Select Biological Committee (SBC), comprised of federal and state government, university, and private sector scientists who are not involved with federal agency listing activities, prior to notification of a listing in the Federal Register. These scientists should have applicable knowledge or information on the species, its habitat, or the quality of data used in the listing process. The SBC would report its opinion on listing advisability to the Secretary. If the Secretary's subsequent decision to list is inconsistent with the SBC finding, the Secretary should disclose the inconsistency, and explain to the public the reasons for proceeding with the listing.

The designation of critical habitat is also currently required at the time of listing. However, critical habitat designation should include analysis of economic and other impacts of such designations. Thus, it is unreasonable to expect biologists to make timely listing decisions given this analytical burden. As described in recommendation 1) above, the SAF suggests that in the preamble of proposed and final listing rules, the regulatory agencies identify what is known about habitat relationships and essential habitats. Because this information will likely be used to form the core area of habitat essential for recovery, it would be important for effective habitat protection to base identification of habitat essential for survival on the best available data of the highest quality, as confirmed by an independent SBC review. Again, the extra expense and delay of peer review would likely be offset by increased public trust when essential habitat boundaries are delineated.

3) Improve the Recovery Plan Process

Recovery involves a mix of biology in setting species population goals and in land-use planning for altering practices that adversely modify habitat essential for species. The SAF believes that forest management is an integral part of recovery for many plant and animal species. Forest management techniques can be applied by properly trained professionals to aid in species recovery and produce other forest benefits.

Federal agencies have a responsibility to support the development and implementation of recovery plans and to work towards recovery of listed species. A key to recovery, and ultimately delisting, is mitigating the factors affecting the continued existence of listed species. In many cases, that will mean modifying land-use practices that affect habitat, i.e., the ecosystem upon which the species depends. Biologists have suggested that non-biological factors, including social, economic, and political considerations, also be explicitly identified in recovery plans in order to determine which factors contribute to species decline and recovery (Scott et al. 1995). When population goals have been met and factors affecting the continued existence of a species have been mitigated to the satisfaction of the FWS, the species is recovered and delisting can proceed.

A revised ESA should specify that recovery plans address the biological feasibility and consequences, economic efficiency, social acceptability, and operational and administrative practicality of actions aimed at the recovery of listed species. A committee of biologists has noted among its criticisms of ESA implementation that recovery plan delays produced uncertainty, thus increasing disruption of human activities. The committee suggested risk assessments, a habitat-based approach to recovery, guidelines identifying activities consistent with recovery objectives, and criteria developed by recovery working groups. . . . Biologists have recognized that public involvement is a possible key to successful recovery planning. . . . An economist has suggested that recovery plans use an interdisciplinary approach and require public participation in their development. . . . The ESA should require the federal government to seek more participation from state agencies, local authorities, and private landowners, who may often be sources of extensive information on candidate and listed species as well as instrumental in protecting habitat essential for recovery.

. . .

4) Provide Incentives to Encourage Private Landowners to Protect Habitat

Private lands play an important role in the protection and recovery of most protected species. . . . Along with certain rights, as defined in law, private land ownership carries a stewardship responsibility. When habitat essential for species conservation occurs on private lands, the agency responsible for recovery should work cooperatively with private landowners in assessing species recovery needs. This should begin by involving affected landowners in the development of recovery plans. Failure to include human dimensions in recovery planning will lead to a failure to recover species. . . .

Many private landowners are willing to protect and manage their land for the benefit of endangered species. However, the current ESA provides few incentives to do so. Public opinion supports payment of lost income to landowners prevented from developing their property because of endangered species laws. . . . A revised ESA should encourage stewardship through incentive programs designed for various land-use and management activities. These could include easements, tax incentives, cost-sharing grants, and accelerated technical assistance.

A revised ESA, and the implementation of its principles, should recognize the following:

- SAF supports the use of Habitat Conservation Plans, and codifying into the ESA the "no surprises" policy and safe harbor agreements whereby landowners who enter into agreements with the federal government to provide habitat for species on their land at the time of the agreement are not responsible for additional responsibilities for those species. However, these provisions may not be enough. . . .
- Species recovery is a public responsibility. If private lands are essential to species recovery, they should be identified as such and protection efforts concentrated there. However, private landowners who forego management options on their lands in order to protect habitat identified as essential should receive compensation in some form.
- It is a federal responsibility to ensure landowner compliance with the ESA. If a landowner is thought to be in violation of the Act where essential habitat has been identified, citizen suit provisions under section 11(g) of the ESA should be limited to actions against the appropriate federal agencies that have identified the essential habitat. This should motivate federal agencies to include affected landowners

in recovery plan development and to provide incentives for landowner cooperation.

1.5. "'Endangered Species Act' Improvement," Policy Position of the American Farm Bureau Federation

Issue

How can the current Endangered Species Act (ESA) be changed to be less onerous to farmers and ranchers while providing them with more incentives to protect endangered species?

Background

The Endangered Species Act was signed into law in 1973. Its original purpose was to protect such species as the bald eagle and the manatee. Subsequent reauthorizations and legal decisions have expanded the scope of the act to the point that more than 1,260 species are protected under federal law. Only 17 species have been delisted because they have "recovered."

Farmers and ranchers face fines and imprisonment for even the most basic farm practices if federal regulators believe such actions disturb endangered species. While landowners receive payment if government takes land for schools or highways, they receive nothing if they cannot use their land because of listed species.

There have been numerous attempts to reform the ESA in the last few years. Many of these proposals sought to treat landowners, particularly small landowners, in a more fair and equitable fashion. In addition to proposed legislative reforms, Farm Bureau has achieved certain improvements through the regulatory process, including the successful campaign last year to blend the EPA pesticide registration process with the Fish & Wildlife Service consultation process through the promulgation of counterpart regulations.

H.R. 3824, the Threatened and Endangered Species Recovery Act, was introduced in the House on Sept. 19, 2005, and passed the House on Sept. 29, 2005, by a vote of 229–193. The bill encourages cooperative conservation by landowners, eliminates the critical habitat process, provides greater participation for landowners in the consultation and recovery planning processes and strengthens science requirements. AFBF strongly supports H.R. 3824.

AFBF Policy: Farm Bureau believes that farmers and ranchers can be at the forefront of the effort to protect endangered species. However, disincentives, such as prohibitions against usual farming practices, must be removed. In their place should be financial incentives and protections for landowners who find endangered species on their property. Farm Bureau supports better science in making ESA decisions.

...

Among the core challenges to the ESA is its alleged violation of the "just compensation" clause of the U.S. Constitution, i.e. that its implementation deprives landowners of their right to use their property as they choose without being compensated for the concomitant loss of value of that land.

The Pacific Legal Foundation, a public interest legal organization "dedicated to limited government, property rights and individual liberty," has argued this position in court, in the context of a specific case, Tulare Lake Basin Storage District v. United States. (Courts do not hear challenges to statutes or public policies, except as they impose harms on specific parties.) In an op-ed on its website, the Foundation's Vice President Dave Stirling makes the case for the invalidation of the ESA on Fifth Amendment grounds.

1.6. "'Endangered Species Act' Finally Meets the Fifth Amendment," Policy Position of the Pacific Legal Foundation

> "nor shall private property be taken for public use, without just compensation."
>
> Fifth Amendment of the Constitution

Last December, the Bush administration quietly settled a landmark lawsuit involving a federal trial court judgment that the government's enforcement of the Endangered Species Act had violated the constitutionally-protected property rights of farmers in California's Central Valley. The judge had ordered the government to pay $26 million in damages, including interest, for the undelivered water—under the settlement, the government agreed to pay $16.7 million. Even though settlement of a trial court judgment is not precedent-setting (only appellate court decisions establish precedent), we now have, for the first time since ESA became law, a court ruling that government's ESA enforcement triggers the Fifth Amendment's "just compensation" provision.

In the 31 years since the Endangered Species Act became law, owners denied use of their property through its enforcement have filed numerous lawsuits charging the government with taking private property for public use (*i.e.*, species protection) and seeking "just compensation" under the Fifth Amendment. Their claims seem clearly to be supported by the Act itself. Congress declared in its "findings" incorporated into the ESA—that endangered or threatened species of fish, wildlife, and plants are of aesthetic, ecological, educational, historical, recreational, and scientific value to the Nation and its people." Yet, despite this unambiguous statement of ESA's purpose as serving a "public use," no federal agency and no federal court—until now—has ever recognized ESA enforcement as serving a public use, or that the regulation of private property under ESA is a "taking" under the Fifth Amendment, or that the government should pay damaged property owners "just compensation."

At the heart of this case (*Tulare Lake Basin Water Storage District v. United States*) is the federal government's Central Valley Water Project and California's State Water Project—the natural and man-made systems of dams, reservoirs, pumping stations, and aqueducts that transport water from Northern California through the Central Valley to Southern California. For nearly 50 years, the federal and state water projects have contracted with locally-created water districts in the agriculture-based Central Valley to distribute the water to hundreds of farmers to irrigate their crops. Under these contracts, the water districts collect the farmers' payments for the water they use and forward the payments on to the federal and state governments.

During drought conditions in 1992, the National Marine Fisheries Service determined that continued distribution of water from the federal and state water projects to water districts and Central Valley farmers for irrigation was threatening the survival of the winter-run chinook salmon and the delta smelt. Based on that determination and the established presumption that ESA was to be enforced "whatever the cost," the federal and state water projects, for the next three years, halved the annual water allocation to the districts and farmers, and doubled the annual charge the districts and farmers paid for the water.

The water users filed suit against the federal government alleging that the reduction of water was a "taking" of private property under the Fifth Amendment that entitled them to compensation for their losses caused when the water was not delivered. The court ruling that the federal government had taken the water districts' and farmers' property stated:

> The Fifth Amendment to the United States Constitution concludes with the phrase: "nor shall private property be taken for public use, without just compensation." The purpose of that clause is [quoting a US Supreme Court decision] "to bar Government from forcing some people alone to bear public burdens which, in all fairness and justice, should be borne by the public as a whole." . . . The federal government is certainly free to preserve the fish; it must simply pay for the water it takes to do so.

In the debate over ESA between the defenders of private property rights and those who advance the dominant power of government, the champions of individual rights argue that even though Congress preserved fish, wildlife, and plant species for everyone's benefit, *i.e.*, "for public use," ESA enforcement leaves individual property owners with species-preservation losses uncompensated, forcing them to pay disproportionately for a program benefitting everyone. Under the Fifth Amendment, they say, public tax revenues should compensate them for their losses.

Although this argument may seem straightforwardly persuasive, even uncontroversial, it runs directly against the entire history of ESA enforcement. That is what makes the trial court ruling and the Bush administration's settlement so important.

Congress's enactment of the Endangered Species Act in 1973 authorized "the use of all methods and procedures which are necessary" to restore and preserve endangered or threatened species. The first Supreme Court decision to consider ESA—*Tennessee Valley Authority v. Hill* (1979)—held that Congress designed the act to "halt and reverse the trend toward species extinction, whatever the cost" (author's emphasis). From that time on, ESA has been enforced by the US Fish and Wildlife Service and the National Marine Fisheries Service, and interpreted by federal courts, as the nation's most dominant and least assailable federal statute. (While courts have ruled even parts of the 9/11 Patriot Act unconstitutional, they have fully upheld and consistently enforced the provisions of the ESA for more than 30 years.)

Under ESA, when federal enforcement agencies "list" a species as endangered or threatened, or designate land as "critical habitat" for a species, an affected property owner whose activity deliberately or accidentally harms the species or its habitat is subject to civil or criminal penalties, including heavy fines and even imprisonment. Furthermore, neither Fish and Wildlife nor Marine Fisheries will grant property owners permits to improve or modify land designated as habitat without imposing burdensome conditions and costly mitigation procedures. Because of these heavy burdens hanging over property owners, California's 200 ESA-protected species of fish, wildlife, and plants (second only to Hawaii's 300 protected species) have effectively rendered millions of acres of privately-owned land largely unusable by the owners.

The environmental activists, government environmental enforcement bureaucrats, and elected officials who drive the "species-first, people-last" agenda, have been largely successful in court for more than 30 years in keeping ESA enforcement out from under Fifth Amendment protections of individual rights. It was no surprise that they opposed the Bush Administration's *Tulare Lake Basin* settlement, urging instead that the Administration appeal the court's judgment. Even Senator Diane Feinstein expressed concern that a precedent requiring the government to pay property owners for losses they suffered due to government-imposed environmental regulation "would vastly increase public expenditures."

Their real concern is that neither government funds nor taxpayer patience exist in sufficient supply to pay private property owners every time the federal government "takes" property under the ESA. They fear the government will have to moderate, *i.e.* balance, its regulatory enforcement approach so that people's lives, livelihoods, and property rights receive as much consideration as the species.

Thomas Jefferson foresaw the coming of laws like the ESA when he warned that "the natural progress of things is for liberty to yield and government to gain ground." With that in mind, the framers of the Constitution and Bill of Rights strove mightily to give "We the People of the United States" lasting protection from government domination. More than 200 years later, this "natural progress" of government to take power from the people has proven to be a relentless aggressor, justifying Jefferson's warning and the Founding Fathers' efforts to mitigate what James Madison called "the abridgement of the freedom of the people by gradual and silent encroachments of those in power."

It is difficult to say whether the Bush Administration settled in *Tulare Lake Basin* to avoid the binding precedent an appeal might have brought or because the Administration agreed with the court's ruling. But whatever the reason, new ground has been broken, and the federal government's heavy-handed enforcement of the ESA may become more "people-friendly."

Even before Rep. Pombo formally introduced his reform bill, Earthjustice, an environmental/legal advocacy group attacked it, characterizing it as a measure that favors developers and lobbyists at the expense of the wildlife it seeks to protect. It concludes by providing its own interpretation of the data relative to species protection.

1.7. "The Pombo Endangered Species Extinction Bill— He Wants to Pave Habitat to Put Up a Parking Lot," Earthjustice

A View from the Hill: The Pombo Endangered Species Extinction Bill— He Wants to Pave Habitat to Put Up a Parking Lot

By October 2015, the Endangered Species Act as we know it could cease to exist—that is, if House Resources Committee Chairman Richard Pombo (R-CA) has his way. A leaked copy of legislation he helped to draft specifies that the act would "cease to have any force and effect," and all "permits, licenses, and other authorizations" created under the act would "terminate and not be enforceable."

For more than 30 years, the Endangered Species Act has worked to save the rarest members of America's wildlife heritage, including helping to rescue the bald eagle from extinction. Yet in spite of polls that show that nearly 90 percent of Americans support the act, rewriting the Endangered Species Act is a "top priority" for the Resources Committee, according to Chairman Pombo.

Last year, Rep. Pombo failed in his attempt to pass legislation that would have virtually eliminated protections for endangered species habitat, as well as politicized and weakened the science that underlies these protections. This year, it looks as if he may be going for an even bigger prize: reducing the effectiveness of the law in nearly all of its aspects, including habitat protections and science, potentially erasing the law itself, and eradicating within a decade all existing protections for threatened and endangered species.

So far, this year's bill has not officially been made public. But a leaked copy of the June 17, 2005 "staff-discussion" version of the legislation shows that Rep. Pombo's goal is to make the act more friendly to the developers and lobbyists who have funded his recent campaigns, and considerably less friendly to the wildlife that this landmark law is intended to protect.

The draft Pombo bill attempts to:

- Eliminate the very goal of the Endangered Species Act: that federal agencies work toward the recovery of species—not just prevent their extinction;
- Limit the protection of species' habitat to those areas needed to provide survival of the species, excluding areas needed to aid recovery;
- Bar habitat protection on nearly all federal, state, and tribal lands covered by "species-management" plans, even where those plans provide no benefit to endangered species;
- Bar most protections for species listed merely as threatened;
- Prevent new listings of species until the species are nearly extinct throughout their entire range. Not even the bald eagle could have been listed under this requirement;
- Exempt federal agencies from protecting endangered species in other nations;
- Politicize science by allowing the Secretary of the Interior to overturn decisions made by federal biologists, and by redefining what types of scientific information can be used in making decisions about protecting species; and
- Eliminate a vital check and balance provided by the federal wildlife agencies on federal projects and activities that may jeopardize the continued existence of a listed species or harm its critical habitat.

The bill also seeks to limit the types of persons that can appeal certain agency decisions. This could, in turn, limit the ability of individuals and organizations interested in the welfare of the species to appeal and legally challenge decisions that could harm species or their habitat.

If Pombo's version of the law had been enacted in 1973 in place of the Endangered Species Act, many of the species that were hanging on by a thread three decades ago—including wolves, bald eagles, grizzly bears, manatees, and whooping cranes—might already be gone from the lower-48.

Special interests enjoyed early access to Rep. Pombo's draft bill. At a June hearing of the Committee's Water and Power subcommittee, Daniel G. Nelson, executive director of the San Luis & Delta-Mendota Water Authority in California—a powerful representative of the water treatment industry—testified that he had already reviewed a draft of the legislation, and applauded it.

Nelson also spoke highly of a bill introduced in March by Representative Dennis Cardoza (D-CA) that seeks to virtually eliminate protections for critical habitat, defined by the Endangered Species Act as the areas necessary for the recovery of endangered plants and animals. The bill, with the misleading name "The Critical Habitat Enhancement Act" (H.R. 1299), would create a series of loopholes and unattainable standards that attempt to destroy existing protections for critical habitat and endangered wildlife.

So who are these bills really designed to benefit? There's a clue in the fact that more than 800 developers took time out from the National Association of Home Builders' board meeting in Washington DC in April to lobby in favor of H.R. 1299 on Capitol Hill. According to a release from NAHB, one of the association's top priorities is to ask members of Congress "to support H.R. 1299."

A recent fundraising event held by Representatives Cardoza and Pombo provides more evidence. On March 29, the two congressmen used the Cardoza critical habitat bill to help raise money from ranchers and developers at an unusual joint fundraiser. As reported in the Stockton, CA, _Record_, "The lawmakers split the take from a $1,000-a-plate campaign luncheon at the Lodi ranch of developer Fritz Grupe."

Taken together, these events support what we've been saying all along: that developers, and the politicians they give money to, are actively working to weaken protections for endangered species and the places they call home.

Species with designated critical habitat are twice as likely to be recovering as those without it. Yet the Cardoza bill (which stalled in the U.S. House last year) seeks to eliminate critical habitat designations except where economically "practicable," and attempts to substitute a wide range of programs that frequently provide less protection to a species than designated critical habitat does.

A new study by conservation biologists, reported in the June issue of the scientific journal _Natural History_, indicates that the longer a jeopardized species has been protected under the Endangered Species Act, the more likely it is to have increased its numbers. In addition, species with protected critical habitat are more likely to be showing improvements than those without designated critical habitat.

The success of the Endangered Species Act is undeniable. *Natural History* (June, 2005) reported that just 22 of the 1,370 species listed since 1964 have gone extinct. **That's a 98.4% success rate!** Without the Endangered Species Act, 227 species would likely have been lost forever, the biologists found.

Weakening the Endangered Species Act would certainly result in the irretrievable loss of more species. Developers, and the politicians who take their money, must not be allowed to squander America's wildlife heritage. Once a species is lost, it is lost forever.

In this letter delivered to the Senate in January 2006, more than 5,700 biologists make a compelling statement of the importance of science and scientific principles to species conservation. Specifically, the letter affirms the effectiveness of the law in sustaining species since its enactment; decries the reform bill's transfer of the authority to decide the best available science from scientists to political appointees in the Department of Interior and its requirement that decisions be based on empirical data rather than other scientific techniques like modeling, population surveys, and taxonomic and genetic studies; and laments the bill's replacement of the "critical habitat requirement" with an identification of certain areas of special value.

1.8. "A Letter from Biologists to the United States Senate Concerning Science in the Endangered Species Act"

We are writing as biologists with expertise in a variety of scientific disciplines that concern biological diversity and the loss of species. With the Senate considering policies that could have long-lasting impacts on this nation's species diversity, we ask that you take into account scientific principles that are crucial to species conservation. Biological diversity provides food, fiber, medicines, clean water, and myriad other ecosystem products and services on which we depend every day. If we look only at well-studied species groups, nearly one-third of native species in the United States are at risk of disappearing. Extinction is truly irreversible— once gone, individual species and all of the services that they provide us cannot be brought back.

On December 8, 1973, President Richard Nixon signed the Endangered Species Act ("ESA") with the goal of conserving endangered and threatened species and the ecosystems on which they depend. For species that have been listed and provided protection under the ESA, much of that purpose has been achieved. According to an article in the September 30, 2005, edition of *Science*, less than one percent of listed species have gone extinct since 1973, while 10 percent of candidate species still waiting to be listed have suffered that fate. In addition to the hundreds of species that the Act has protected from extinction, listing has contributed to population increases or the stabilization of populations for at least 35 percent of listed species, and perhaps significantly more, as well as the recovery of such signature species as the peregrine falcon. While complete recovery has been realized for just two percent of species listed, given the precarious state of most species when listed, this represents significant progress.

One of the great strengths of the Endangered Species Act is its foundation in sound scientific principles and its reliance on the best available science. Unfortunately, recent legislative proposals would critically weaken this foundation. For species conservation to continue, it is imperative both that the scientific principles embodied in the Act are maintained, and that the Act is strengthened, fully implemented, and adequately funded.

Listing

Objective scientific information and methods should be used in listing species, subspecies, and distinct population segments as endangered or threatened under the Act. While non-scientific factors may appropriately be considered at points later in the process of protecting species, their use in listing decisions is inconsistent with biologically defensible principles. Due to the fragile state of many of those species that require the Act's protections, the listing process needs to proceed as promptly as possible; otherwise, species will go extinct while waiting to be listed.

Habitat

Habitat provides the unique food, shelter, and other complex requirements that each species needs for its survival; habitat loss and degradation are the principal reasons for the decline of most species at risk. Habitat protection is essential if species are to be conserved and the goals of the ESA are to be met. The relationship between species, their habitats, and the threats they face can be exceedingly complex. Therefore, the chances of species recovery are maximized when habitat protection is based on sound scientific principles, and when the determinations of the biological needs of at-risk species are scientifically well informed.

The obligation for federal agencies to consult with the appropriate wildlife agency and its biologists when federal actions could affect habitat for listed species is an indispensable provision in the ESA. It provides the means for science to inform decisions about the habitat-dependent survival and recovery of species at-risk. The designation of critical habitat places further obligations on the Federal government to, among other things, protect the habitat essential to species recovery. It is far more effective, far easier, and far less expensive to protect functioning natural habitats than it is to recreate them once they are gone.

Scientific Tools

The current Endangered Species Act standard of "best available science" has worked well and has been flexible enough over time to accommodate evolving scientific information and practice. Failure to keep the ESA open to the use of scientific information from the best available research and monitoring, and to rely on impartial scientific experts, will contribute to delays in species recovery and to species declines and extinctions. Critical scientific information should not only include current empirical data, but also, for example, historic habitat and population information, population surveys, habitat and population modeling, and taxonomic and genetic studies. Use of scientific knowledge should not be hampered by administrative requirements that overburden or slow the Act's implementation, or by limiting consideration of certain types of scientific information.

Recovery Plans

Recovery plans must be science-based documents that are developed with the input of scientists and are responsive to new information. Recovery plans must be based on the best possible information about the specific biology of each species, must identify threats to each species and address what is needed to mitigate those threats, and must predict how species are likely to respond to mitigation measures that may be adopted. To be most effective, recovery plans need to incorporate scientific principles of adaptive management, so they can be updated as new information on species and their habitats becomes available. Changes to the ESA that would delay completion of recovery plans, or provide for inflexible recovery goals that cannot be informed by new or additional scientific knowledge, should be avoided.

Scientific Advances and New Issues

The scientific community has contributed significant new information on imperiled species, their uses of habitats, and threats to those resources since the ESA was first passed into law. Serious, new, and as yet insufficiently addressed issues, such as global warming and invasive species, have emerged as primary environmental concerns that affect the fate of our native species diversity. We urge Congress to initiate thorough studies to consider the foremost problems that drive species toward extinction.

Losing species means losing the potential to solve some of humanity's most intractable problems, including hunger and disease. The Endangered Species Act is more than just a law—it is the ultimate safety net in our life support system. As Earth has changed and as science has progressed since the Endangered Species Act was authorized in 1973, the ESA has served our nation well, largely because of its flexibility and its solid foundation in science. It is crucial to maintain these fundamental principles. The challenges of effective implementation of the Act should not be interpreted to require substantive rewriting of this valuable, well-functioning piece of legislation. . . .

In recent years, religious groups have participated more actively in political affairs, especially with regard to policies that threaten "God's creation"—global climate change, mountaintop removal, and, here, the protection of endangered species. The following documents prepared by the Evangelical Environmental Network and the Coalition on the Environment and Jewish Life respectively represent such efforts. Noah's Alliance, part of the Coalition, called the ESA a modern day Noah's ark.

1.9. "The Academy of Evangelical Scientists and Ethicists on the Critical Importance of Conserving Endangered Species"

We are scientists and scholars in the scientific and ethical professional community who also are evangelical Christians. We come from diverse denominational and independent church traditions across the full evangelical spectrum—from Anabaptist to Baptist, Pentecostal to Presbyterian, Anglican to Lutheran, Methodist to Reformed. It is our privilege to engage in science and scholarship as our vocation, helping us and others understand, and care for, God's creation worldwide. We are committed scholars both of creation and the Scriptures, and are dedicated to applying what we learn to living rightly on earth.

As evangelical scientists and ethicists we are in accord—based upon scientific knowledge of the workings of God's creation and upon biblical and religious beliefs—on the critical importance and human responsibility to care for the earth's climate system, earth's abundant life and variety, the great lineages of earth's living creatures, and the vitality of ecosystems for the well-being and community of all life.

The beauty, joy, and health of human life on earth depend deeply upon the wide variety and great richness of plant and animal life God has provided. This abundant life brings immense and continuous praise to God (Psalm 148), leaving all people without excuse about knowing God's divinity and everlasting power (Romans 120). Beholding God's creatures and the whole creation supports our spiritual well-being, while living in a world that sustains creation's marvelous variety protects our physical welfare.

However, as evangelical Christians and scientists in our time, we see a most profound threat to the integrity of God's creation in the destruction of endangered species and their God-given habitats. Among scriptural teachings, we believe the biblical story of Noah is a primary one. The story of Noah teaches us the meaning of faithfulness to God's commands, the overarching importance of maintaining the lineages of God's creatures, the vital necessity and stewardly duty to conserve endangered species and their habitats, and God's faithfulness in preserving faithful stewards of God's creation.

Noah was the first human being entrusted with endangered species. Noah was faithful to God's call to preserve the creatures together with his faithful human family—and followed through by returning the creatures he saved to a flourishing earth and diverse habitats that allowed them once again to be fruitful and multiply through succeeding generations (Genesis 8:17). Endangered species were saved by Noah at great cost of time, materials, and reputation. God cleansed the earth of the unfaithful and disobedient and yet did not leave things uncertain for faithful Noah, nor for the ongoing lineages of people and living creatures that were saved, by repeatedly making an everlasting covenant with all life on earth (Genesis 8–9). As a consequence of Noah's faithfulness, people and God's creatures, and the vital ecosystems upon which they depend, flourished on the earth (Genesis 1:22). The privilege and responsibility of human beings to be good stewards of creation was refreshed and renewed (Psalm 8). We believe from our deepest knowledge and convictions that we have the marvelous privilege and responsibility to follow the example of Noah, even as we also follow Jesus Christ—the Maker, Sustainer, and Reconciler of all things, including God's other creatures (Colossians 1:15–20).

Among the great and effective models of conserving endangered species is the U.S. Endangered Species Act of 1973 that passed the Senate on December 19 by voice vote and the House of Representatives on December 20 by a vote of 355 to 4, and was subsequently signed into law by President Nixon. It recognizes that providing for living creatures requires protection of their homes and habitats and engages the U.S. Fish and Wildlife Service to apply the most rigorous science to develop common sense solutions to prevent the extinction of endangered fish, plants, and wildlife. The Act is preventing extinctions, helping species stabilize, and starting species toward recovery. This "emergency room" for endangered and very fragile species is preserving God's creation, despite chronic shortfalls in sufficient funding.

The Endangered Species Act's requirement for common sense solutions based upon application of scientific and ethical understanding is right and necessary. As in the act of Noah, it serves as a safety net for plants and animals that are on the brink of extinction. Beyond simply rescuing species, the Endangered Species Act provides the context for predicting what species might become endangered in the future and thereby encourages voluntary actions of responsible stewardship, both private and public, by groups and individuals to take corrective measures that make it unnecessary to declare species endangered. It also provides a system of checks and balances by requiring federal agencies whose projects could impact endangered species to consult with wildlife biologist experts. The Act safeguards the habitats within which endangered species can regain a foothold on life and ultimately flourish. And it has been viewed as an important model by the rest of the world.

While we owe it to our children and grandchildren to be good stewards of creation, leaving them a legacy of protecting endangered species and their habitats, we also owe this to our Creator through whom and by whom these creatures have been created and are sustained. We count it a privilege to be good and faithful stewards of creation and to image in our lives and landscapes God's care for us and all creation. For us, stewardship also requires witness and includes raising our voices against attempts to weaken public policies that protect the common good, such as the US Endangered Species Act.

The Academy is concerned about efforts to erode provisions of the Endangered Species Act of 1973 that have helped prevent the extinction of many species, including the American Bald Eagle. Weakening of the Endangered Species Act does not serve the common good and undermines our efforts to be faithful stewards. As a society, we must not presume authority to achieve self-interest at the expense of God's creatures and God's creation. Turning away from care for God's creation and the common good in order to promote self-interest shifts seeking the kingdom of God out of its appropriate and necessary first place.

In addition, the Academy is concerned about deceptive statements that couch weakening of the Endangered Species Act in words that mislead people into thinking that actions to weaken the Act are "reforms," "modernizations," "enhancements," and so on. An example is legislation voted on in 2004 that would have significantly hampered the full use of science in informing ESA decisions. Because of this, the bill was publicly opposed by hundreds of scientists and groups like the Ecological Society of America; yet this anti-science legislation was termed by its authors the "Sound Science for Endangered Species Act Planning Act" (H.R. 1662). It is dishonest to dress damaging of the Endangered Species Act in terms that suggest its improvement. We believe such efforts amount to a "wolf in sheep's clothing."

All this means that we, as professional scientists and ethicists, and as believers, find God's creation to be rich and full—created, sustained, and reconciled as beautifully described in Colossians 1:15–20. We know, however, that we have the capacity to destroy ecosystems on a global scale. Our scientific belief in this horrific potential parallels the biblical judgment that the destroyers of the earth themselves will be destroyed (Revelation 11:18), even as we believe that people who truly follow the One who created, sustains, and reconciles all things (Greek: ta panta) are promised everlasting life (John 3:16).

In recognition of the need for people of all faiths to come together to safeguard God's creation, the Academy calls upon other religious communities to address this important and vital need to protect and preserve the lineages of God's living creatures so they will not perish from the earth. We offer our cooperation with other faith traditions in this mutual pursuit. Respectful of our biblical heritage, the Academy particularly invites cooperation with those traditions that take seriously, as we do, the biblical example of Noah as a model for being faithful to God's call to protect endangered species from extinction. Ours is the time for a concert of religious voices to proclaim our privilege and responsibility for not allowing the great lineages of God's living creatures to be broken, for preventing these lineages from becoming but a fading memory for our children and grandchildren, born and unborn.

1.10. "Action Alert: Protect the Endangered Species Act," Coalition on the Environment and Jewish Life

Protect the Endangered Species Act (09/30/2005)

> Behold, I establish My covenant with you, and with your seed after you, and with every living creature that is with you, of the birds, of the cattle, and of every wild animal of the earth with you . . .
>
> Genesis 9:9

Rep. Richard W. Pombo (R-CA) was able to rush his misleadingly-named bill "The Threatened and Endangered Species Reform Act of 2005," through the U.S. House of Representatives on Sep. 29, but by a much narrower margin than observers expected. The bill, which is now awaiting action by the Senate, would make it more difficult for the federal government to protect the critical habitat areas needed for endangered animals and plants to survive. In addition, the legislation would exempt the pesticide industry from the Endangered Species Act's most important provisions. Although the passage of the legislation through the House of Representatives was a setback, at the same time, we were encouraged that some members of Congress, including Democratic Leader Nancy Pelosi (D-CA), Rep. Nick Rahall (D-WV), and Rep. Jay Inslee (D-WA), spoke on the House floor of the religious and moral imperative to protect endangered species.

Now the battle moves to the US Senate, which may consider a bill later this year or early in 2006. We are gearing up to meet with senators and their staffs to make our case for defending the Endangered Species Act. We also plan to mobilize Jewish community leaders, rabbis, congregations, and other Jewish institutions to get involved in the Noah Alliance campaign. Representatives of other faiths are doing their part, too.

Jewish teaching is clear and unequivocal on the topic of species protection.

Torah does not permit a killing that would uproot a species, even if it permitted the killing [of individuals] in that species. Nachmanides (Ramban), Commentary on Deuteronomy 22:6.

Our message to Congress needs to be clear and strong. Please contact your Senators, and ask them to protect the Endangered Species Act. Let them know that, as a constituent and an active member of the Jewish community in their state, this is a priority issue for you and one that you will be following closely.

Remind your Senators that after Noah's flood, God created a covenant not only with human beings, but with all of creation. As stewards of the Earth, we must care for creation and honor that covenant.

Background

For over thirty years, the Endangered Species Act has served as a safety net for the variety of wildlife, fish and plants that are on the brink of extinction. In that time, the Act has saved nearly 99 percent of protected species from extinction—only 9 of the 1,800 plants and animals protected by the Act have been declared extinct. Without the Endangered Species Act, wildlife such as the bald eagle, American alligator, California condor, Florida panther and many other animals that are part of America's natural heritage could have disappeared from the planet years ago. The Endangered Species Act works because it safeguards the places where endangered animals and plants live.

Representative Pombo's bill will weaken the Act by doing the following:

1) Eliminating conservation measures on tens of millions of acres of land around the country, the "critical habitat" of endangered species, and prevent such conservation activities in the future. Analysis of information from the US Fish and Wildlife Service shows a strong correlation between the conservation of critical habitat and the recovery of endangered species. Species with critical habitat are more likely to be increasing in number by a 2:1 ratio.

2)   Repealing established conservation measures that prohibit the killing or injuring of hundreds of threatened species, such as the bald eagle.

3)   Bankrupting public conservation programs by creating a new entitlement that requires the federal government to pay developers, the oil industry and other special interests to keep them from killing or injuring publicly-owned fish and wildlife.

4)   Exempting pesticide companies from one of the Endangered Species Act's most important provisions.

The following summary of S-4087 of 2006, a precursor to pending bill S-700 of 2007, details the financial incentives provided, and recognizes the imperative of bringing private interests into the restoration effort.

1.11. "Partnerships for Conservation: The Endangered Species Recovery Act of 2006"

For more than 30 years, the Endangered Species Act has been the driving force behind protecting America's imperiled plants and animals. Thanks to the Act, animals such as wolves, manatees and bald eagles are on the road to recovery. Regrettably, the Act does not have adequate tools to help aid this progress on private lands. Fortunately, Senator Crapo (R-ID), Senator Lincoln (D-AR) and others have introduced The Endangered Species Recovery Act of 2006 (S-4087), an exciting step forward for endangered species conservation.

Recognizing that partnering with private landowners on wildlife conservation is absolutely critical, The Endangered Species Recovery Act would provide $400 million annually in new tax credits, plus additional deductions and exclusions, for private landowners who take steps to help endangered or threatened species on the properties they own.

Habitat Protection

The bill identifies two types of tax credits for taxpayers who enter into an enforceable agreement to protect the habitat of a qualified species by placing an easement on private land. A perpetual easement provides 100 percent of the difference between the value of the property prior to and following entering into the agreement. A 30-year easement provides 75 percent of the difference.

These agreements must include an approved habitat management plan designed to restore or enhance the habitat or to manage the habitat to reduce threats to the species. The plan must identify management practices, provide a schedule of deadlines, identify the entity that will provide technical assistance and provide for monitoring. Best of all, the legislation requires the plan to be consistent with any recovery plans approved under the ESA.

Habitat Restoration

As with the tax credits for easements, the habitat restoration tax credit is available to taxpayers who enter into an agreement to conduct restoration projects on their land. The bill also provides safeguards to ensure that the habitat restoration credits do not pay for actions required by law or actions that are already being financed by other conservation programs.

These credits also require an approved habitat management plan with all of the safeguards described above. The three types of habitat restoration that can generate tax credits include: 100 percent of the restoration costs to the taxpayer during the taxable year for a permanent agreement, 75 percent of the costs for a 30-year agreement, and 50 percent of the costs for any other timeframe.

Deductions

The bill also provides tax deductions for specific actions recommended in recovery plans approved under the ESA. Under current law, the costs of many actions are already being deducted as ordinary business expenses; the new deduction is not limited to business owners.

For deductions, no agreements or plans are required for the landowner to qualify for these tax benefits. Simply, the costs of any recovery actions taken are deductible, so long as that action is recommended in a recovery plan approved under the Endangered Species Act.

Funding

Beginning in 2007, the bill limits the amount of credits that can be given out to $300 million for perpetual agreements, $60 million for 30-year agreements, and $40 million for agreements under 30 years. If not all of the funds are allocated in a single year, the unused money may be carried over to the subsequent year.

The bill also identifies 11 different criteria to determine the allocation of these funds. These criteria include such things as the likelihood the activities will contribute to recovery and delisting of species, the activities cost-effectiveness, the urgency of the need to protect the species, and the ability to help resolve conflicts between species conservation and economic activities.

Exclusions and Cost-Share Programs

Finally, the bill includes provisions to ensure it does not deter taxpayers from participating in conservation programs including Partners for Fish and Wildlife Program, Landowner Incentive Program, State Wildlife Grants Program, and Private Stewardship Grants Program. Instead, it allows taxpayers to exclude from taxable income any payments received from the federal government under these cost-share programs.

Partnership is the Key

The recovery of many of our most imperiled wildlife species will require the cooperation of the nation's landowners, particularly its farmers, ranchers and forest landowners, yet there are few significant incentives to encourage landowners to do so. The Endangered Species Recovery Act of 2006 recognizes the need for and provides positive incentives for land-owners. This bill acknowledges the significant public contributions of the conservation actions of private landowners, benefiting people and endangered species alike.

Following is a summary of S-700 of 2007, prepared by the non-partisan Congressional Research Service. The full text of the bill can be accessed at http://thomas.loc.gov. The bill may well undergo amendment during its course through the committee review process, but optimism regarding its fate is founded both on the initial support it has received from both supporters and opponents of the ESA as well as the fact that among its 18 co-sponsors are the Chairs of the standing reference committees that will review it.

1.12. "Summary of S-700, the 'Endangered Species Recovery Act of 2007'"

S-700

Title: A bill to amend the Internal Revenue Code to provide a tax credit to individuals who enter into agreements to protect the habitats of endangered and threatened species, and for other purposes.

Sponsor: Sen Crapo, Mike [ID] (introduced 2/28/2007) Cosponsors (18)

Related Bills: H.R.1422

Latest Major Action: 2/28/2007 Referred to Senate committee. Status: Read twice and referred to the Committee on Finance.

SUMMARY AS OF:
2/28/2007—Introduced.
Endangered Species Recovery Act of 2007:

Amends the Internal Revenue Code to allow certain landowners whose
property contains the habitat of an endangered or threatened species and
who enter into a habitat protection agreement a tax credit for costs
relating to habitat protection easements and restoration.
Places limits on the amount of such credit for calendar years 2008, 2009,
2010, 2011, and 2012.
Directs the Comptroller General of the United States to study and report
to Congress on the effectiveness of such credit.
Allows a tax deduction for expenditures related to recovery plans approved
by the Endangered Species Act of 1973.
Excludes from gross income certain payments under: (1) the Partners for
Fish and Wildlife Program authorized by the Partners for Fish and
Wildlife Act; and (2) the Landowner Incentive Program, the State
Wildlife Grants Program, and the Private Stewardship Grants Program
authorized by the Fish and Wildlife Act of 1956.

*The Defenders of Wildlife and the Center of Biological Diversity are the two most
prominent conservation organizations supporting the ESA. Both laud the pending bill
sponsored by Senator Crapo and, with some reservations on the part of the Center,
regard it as a watershed in the decades-long debate on the law. Defenders particularly
note that "partnering with private landowners on wildlife conservation is absolutely
critical."*

1.13. Press Release: Defenders of Wildlife Applaud [sponsors] of S-700

Washington, DC—Defenders of Wildlife hailed the introduction of The
Endangered Species Recovery Act of 2007 as a significant step forward in
protecting threatened and endangered species that reside on private land.
The bill, sponsored by Senators Mike Crapo (R-ID) and Blanche Lincoln
(D-AR), as well as other Senators including Senator Max Baucus (D-MT),
Chairman of the Finance Committee, and Senator Charles Grassley (R-IA),
Ranking Member of the Finance Committee, aims to make private landowners partners in conservation by providing $400 million a year in new
tax credits, plus additional deductions and exclusions, for citizens who
take steps to help endangered or threatened species on the properties
they own.

"Partnering with private landowners on wildlife conservation is absolutely critical," said Defenders of Wildlife president Rodger Schlickeisen.

"This legislation provides key incentives to enlist more landowners in this effort, which benefits people and endangered species alike. Senators Crapo, Lincoln, Baucus and Grassley are to be congratulated for their foresight on this vital issue and we look forward to continuing to work with them to enact this important legislation."

The bill has four major tax incentive components: habitat protection easement credits, habitat restoration tax credits, deductions and market mechanisms. Specifically the bill provides tax credits to landowners who place an easement on their property to further the recovery of threatened or endangered species. The size of the tax credit increases with the duration of the easement, with a permanent easement providing a credit equal to 100 percent of the difference between the value of the property before and after the establishment of the easement.

Moreover, landowners who conduct habitat restoration projects on their land can receive tax credits up to 100 percent of the restoration costs. In addition, those who engage in actions recommended in recovery plans approved under the Endangered Species Act can deduct the cost of the actions they have taken. For those landowners who may not have the funds to undertake conservation measures themselves, or sufficient taxable income to take full advantage of the bill's incentives, the bill contains a provision that allows partnerships to fund the species conservation activities and still receive the tax incentives. "Whether going alone or partnering with other landowners, this bill creates a potential market that should result in more conservation, particularly for farmers and ranchers who may be land-rich but cash-poor," declared Schlickeisen.

"This bill provides essential financial tools to assist landowners in preserving and protecting endangered species on their land," said Schlickeisen. "Most importantly, it backs up the government's commitment to safeguard America's most imperiled wildlife with money that will go directly to efforts to protect vulnerable species. Partnering with private landowners is often the most effective, cost-efficient and results-oriented way to protect our nation's wildlife for future generations."

1.14. Press Release: Center for Biological Diversity Praises S-700

WASHINGTON, DC—The conservation group Center for Biological Diversity praised legislation S-700, introduced by a group of bipartisan senators, which would provide tax credits, tax deductions and income exclusions for various recovery-based actions on behalf of endangered species and their habitats.

"While we must ensure that this new tax program remains publicly accountable and that the administration does not abuse its discretion in picking incentive sites, this proposed legislation has the potential to revolutionize wildlife conservation on private lands and make the Endangered Species Act even more successful. This may be the first tangible sign that a fresh breeze is blowing on Capitol Hill," said Bill Snape, senior counsel with the Center for Biological Diversity.

Since an earlier version of this bill was introduced late in the 109th Congress, a wide variety of conservation, scientific, sportsmen and related groups have worked with Senators Baucus (D-MT), Crapo (R-ID), Collins (R-ME), Lincoln (D-AR), Grassley (R-IA), and Lieberman (I-CT), among others, to further improve the bill. Specifically, conservation groups have sought to ensure that all tax benefits authorized under the bill would be explicitly tied to recovery objectives under the Endangered Species Act, and that the legislation would provide mechanisms to assess the success of the tax incentive program in a transparent fashion.

For the first time ever, financial awards will be available to landowners who actively seek to implement an endangered-species recovery plan. Further, under the bill, the Government Accountability Office will be requested to assess the overall efficacy of the tax-credit program; this will be important for fiscal accountability and should be expanded to the deductions and exclusions under the bill, particularly with regard to assessing global warming's growing impact on domestic conservation measures.

"Although the authors of this bill have not yet ensured that habitat management and protection plans, as well as related final agency funding decisions and monitoring documents, will be unquestionably subject to the Freedom of Information Act—a problem that has arisen under some Farm Bill conservation programs—there is a commitment by some to see such non-controversial language added during the Senate Finance Committee consideration of the bill, which also must pass the House of Representatives," explained Snape. "Barring weakening amendments, and the inclusion of the public's right to government documents, we expect to support this bill."

As indicated in the introductory background section, the Department of Interior, through its Solicitor David Bernhardt, has proposed a new interpretation of the statutory phrase "significant portion of its range" as one criterion for the listing of a species as endangered. His proposal would, in the opinion of environmental groups, represent a substantial restriction of the reach of the ESA. What follows are brief excerpts of Solicitor Bernhardt's legal opinion justifying the proposal, followed by a rebuttal from the Defenders of Wildlife, and, more unusual and more significant, a letter from a group of influential Senators expressing their opposition, followed by their questions to the Department of Interior. Also worthy of note is that the regulatory proposal, if adopted and promulgated, would not require legislative approval.

1.15. "US Department of Interior/Office of the Solicitor, March 16, 2007 Subject: The Meaning of 'In Danger of Extinction Throughout All or a Significant Portion of its Range' "

Since 1973, the Endangered Species Act (ESA) has defined "endangered species" as "any species which is in danger of extinction throughout all or a significant portion of its range." . . . Thirty three years later, questions continue to be raised about the meaning of the phrase "in danger of extinction throughout . . . a significant portion of its range" (SPR phrase/SPR language).

. . . the 2001 decision of the Ninth Circuit Court of Appeals . . . rejected the interpretation of the SPR phrase favored by the Department. . . . The Ninth Circuit interprets the SPR phrase as a "substantive standard" for determining whether a species is an endangered species. Under the court's interpretation, there are two situations in which the Secretary must determine a species to be . . . endangered . . .: 1) where the Secretary finds that the species is in danger of extinction throughout all of its range; or 2) where the Secretary finds that the species is in danger of extinction throughout a significant portion of its range."

Since approximately 2000, the Department, on the other hand, has interpreted the SPR phrase to mean that a species is in danger of extinction throughout a portion of its current range that is "so important to the continued existence of a species that threats to the species in that area can have the effect of threatening the viability of the species as a whole." . . . . Under the Department's interpretation, there is only one situation in which the Secretary must find a species to be an endangered species—when the Secretary finds that it is endanger of extinction in every portion of its range. Instead, if the Secretary can demonstrate that the species faces threats in only a portion of its range so severe as to threaten the viability of the species throughout its range, a determination that a species is an endangered species would be justified. . . .

. . . I conclude that:

1   The SPR phrase is a substantive standard for determining whether a species is an endangered species—whenever the Secretary concludes because of the statutory five-factor analysis that a species is "in danger of extinction throughout . . . a significant portion of its range," it is to be listed and the protections of the ESA applied to the species in that portion of its range where it is specified as an "endangered specis";

2   the word "range" in the SPR phrase refers to the range in which a species currently exists, not to the historical range of the species where it once existed;

3   the Secretary has broad discretion in defining what portion of a range

is "significant," and may consider factors other than simply the size of the range portion in defining what is "significant"; and

4   the Secretary's discretion in defining "significant" is not unlimited; he may not, for example, define "significant" to require that a species is endangered only if the threats faced by a species in a portion of its range are so severe as to threaten the viability of the species as a whole. . . .

Reading the Act to require protection for a species only where it is endangered . . . provides precisely the flexibility that the Nixon Administration sought in 1972 and the Congress provided in 1973.

1.16. "New Bush Administration Policy Limits Endangered Species Listings: Many Species Would No Longer Qualify for ESA Protection" (Defenders of Wildlife)

The Solicitor of the Department of the Interior—the Bush Administration's top lawyer on endangered species issues—released a legal opinion on March 16, 2007, that prescribes how the Administration will decide whether to list species as threatened or endangered under the Endangered Species Act in the future. The decision casts aside thirty years of precedent on how to interpret the phrase "significant portion of [a species'] range" in the ESA and does so in a way that—had it been in effect years ago—would have denied protections for many of the ESA's greatest recovery stories, including the gray wolf, grizzly bear, and bald eagle. The opinion is an attempt to insulate listing decisions from legal challenge—at the expense of saving and recovering America's imperiled wildlife.

Q—What is at Issue in the Solicitor's Opinion?

At issue is the very definition of an "endangerd species" and thus the scope of protections available to imperiled wildlife under the Endangered Species Act. The ESA defines an endangered species as one that is "in danger of extinction throughout all or a significant portion of its range." 16 U.S.C. § 1532(6). The statute does not define the phrase "significant portion of its range," thus it has been left to the Department of the Interior and the courts to interpret.

Q—Why was This Opinion Prepared?

The Bush Administration previously attempted to limit the scope of the ESA by reinterpreting the definition of an endangered species under the Act. Numerous federal courts have now rejected this interpretation.

The Solicitor's opinion is a response to those court decisions and an attempt to refine the Administration's position in light of these losses.

Since 2000, the Bush Administration has argued that in order to list a species as endangered it must be in danger of extinction throughout all of its range. This interpretation conflates two standards into one. As noted above, an endangered species is defined as one that is "in danger of extinction throughout all *or* a significant portion of its range" (emphasis added). Elementary principles of statutory interpretation counsel that when two clauses are joined by the word "or" they are to be viewed as separate standards of distinct meaning. By contrast, the Bush Administration tried to argue in court that the second clause merely says that endangered status is warranted when threats in one area of the species' range are of such a magnitude as to cause a risk of extinction to the whole.

Defenders of Wildlife and other conservation groups have successfully argued in various courts that the definition of endangered species should be given its plain meaning to cover species that are either 1) in danger of extinction everywhere or 2) in danger of extinction in some smaller, but significant, part of its range. The Solicitor's opinion is the result of these repeated losses in federal court, most notably *Defenders of Wildlife v. Norton*, 258 F.3d 1136 (9th Cir. 2001) (flat-tailed horned lizard). The issue has also come up in cases involving the gray wolf, Canada lynx, coastal cutthroat trout, green sturgeon, Queen Charlotte goshawk, and the Florida black bear. In total, seven district courts have adopted or followed the Ninth Circuit's ruling.

Q—What Does the Opinion Do?

The Solicitor's opinion acknowledges the plain language of the statute that a species must be considered endangered under the ESA if it is at risk of extinction generally or within a significant portion of its range. Unfortunately, the opinion then goes on to limit protection for endangered species by defining the word "range" to include only the range in which a species currently exists, not the historic range of the species where it once existed. This portion of the Solicitor's opinion flatly contradicts the Ninth Circuit's ruling and subsequent court decisions requiring the agency to consider historic range. Defenders of Wildlife, 258 F.3d at 1145; see *Northwest Ecosystem Alliance v. U.S. Fish & Wildlife Serv.*, 475 F.3d 1136, 2007 U.S. App. LEXIS 2296, at *35–36 (9th Cir. Feb. 2, 2007); *Tucson Herpetological Soc'y v. Norton*, No. CV-04-0075-PHX-NVW, sip op. At 9 (D. Ariz. Aug 30, 2005).

Additionally, the opinion grants the Secretary of the Interior considerable discretion in deciding what portion of the range is "significant." For example, the Secretary may consider factors other than just the size of the range portion in determining what is significant. The opinion explicitly rejects the Administration's prior position that a species is only endangered if the threats faced in a portion of the range could lead to the extinction of the species as a whole. Thus, the Secretary cannot interpret the phrase "significant portion" of the range to be coterminous with a global threat to the species.

Q—How Does the Opinion Harm Species?

The Solicitor's opinion undermines endangered species protection in two important respects:

First, by limiting ESA protection to a species' current range, the opinion rejects the Ninth Circuit's holding that a species can be considered extinct in a significant portion of its range "if there are major geographic areas in which it is no longer viable but once was." *Defenders of Wildlife v. Norton*, 258 F.3d at 1145. By contrast, the Solicitor argues that if a species can no longer be found in an area, then it is extinct in that area, not "in danger of extinction." Accordingly, the Solicitor maintains that since a species can only be "in danger" within its current range, the Secretary must only consider the current range of a species in determining whether it is endangered.

Such a position raises numerous questions about the Department of the Interior's obligation to recover a species throughout its historic range. It also calls into question whether the Department ever need restore or reintroduce a species to areas where it no longer exists.

Restoration of wolves in the Northern Rockies, for example, might not have occurred under this policy. When wolves were reintroduced to Yellowstone National Park and Idaho, they could be found only in Canada, Alaska, and Minnesota. The rest of the United States would not have been considered "current range" for the wolf; thus the species would not have qualified as endangered, despite its extirpation from most of the lower 48 states. Under this standard, grizzly bears, bald eagles, and many other species that are abundant in some areas but no longer found in large portions of their historic range might not warrant listing irrespective of the scientific basis for doing so. Looking forward, the policy could even require that the Secretary of the Interior delist species in the portions of their range that are no longer occupied—a move that could compromise the recovery of many more listed species.

Second, the opinion appears to permit the Secretary to list and delist species by state boundaries—a significant reversal of longstanding policy. In reviewing the ESA's legislative history, the opinion states that "[s]ome of the floor debate and hearing testimony strongly suggest the Secretary has the discretion to divide the range of a species along political boundaries and declare it endangered only in states where the state authorities are not providing adequate protection of species." It further states that "For example, the Secretary might examine the American alligator as a species, determine that Florida is a significant portion of the American alligator's range, and conclude that American alligators in Florida are in danger of extinction, even though alligators elsewhere are not."

Such an interpretation raises particularly grave concerns in the Northern Rockies where the states of Wyoming and Idaho are urging the Department of the Interior to delist gray wolves and permit greater state management of the species. Both states are hostile to wolves and have expressed intentions to dramatically cull wolf populations as soon as federal protections are listed. Delisting wolves on a state-by-state basis could lead to patchwork protections that would undermine region-wide efforts to recover wolves in the Northern Rockies and restore them to appropriate habitats throughout the Northwest.

Q—Can the Opinion be Challenged?

Not directly. The opinion is intended as a legal guide for future actions. As the policy is implemented in listing decisions and any formal rulemaking, however, those decisions and the validity of the Solicitor's opinion on which they are based can and likely will be challenged in federal court.

The following letter to Interior Secretary Kempthorne from five U.S. Senators expresses their deep concern about the proposed changes to the rules implementing the Endangered Species Act. These prospective changes were defended by the Department's Solicitor David Bernhardt in the document reproduced above. The Senators follow their concerns with a series of challenging questions, foreshadowing a perhaps long and testy battle if the rules are formally proposed. Such involvement of members of Congress at this stage of the rule-making process is by and large unprecedented.

1.17. "Letter from US Senators to Secretary of the Interior Dirk Kempthorne on Proposed Changes to Rules Governing the Administration of the Endangered Species Act," April 25, 2007

Dear Secretary Kempthorne:

We are writing to express concern over the changes that you reportedly are considering making to the Fish and Wildlife Service rules that implement the Endangered Species Act.

We have seen reports of a document reflecting extensive, draft revisions to a subchapter of the Wildlife and Fisheries title of the Code of Federal Regulations. Additional documents that have surfaced recently suggest that major rule revisions remain under active consideration.

Together, the documents that have come to light describe regulatory changes that would loosen existing wildlife protection requirements while also narrowing their applicability. We find the draft revisions troubling for at least three reasons.

First, we believe that the changes put into place by the rule revisions would reduce dramatically the current scope and positive impact of the Endangered Species Act. Indeed, if the draft revisions had been in place thirty years ago, it is hard to imagine that we ever could have achieved the successes—with bald eagles, grizzly bears, sea turtles, sea otters, and many other species—of which we now are deservedly proud.

Second, many of the changes under consideration would reverse settled understanding and policies, of which Congress long has been aware, and which Congress has chosen to leave undisturbed. We are concerned about any attempt to overhaul the Endangered Species Act program administratively, without the involvement of Congress.

Finally, the draft revisions create the impression that the Department's leadership is focusing on reducing the scope and weakening the substance of the federal government's wildlife protection laws. We hope that is not the case, because we believe there are, immediately at hand, much less controversial and much more constructive initiatives to which you could devote your attention with broad support in Congress and the American public in order to achieve the Endangered Species Act's overarching goal of recovery. In particular, we believe you could advance wildlife protection, while at the same time alleviating controversies that have arisen in the pursuit of that goal, by requesting increased funding for recovery-related activities, by expanding (rather than eliminating) incentive programs like the Private Stewardship Grants program and the Landowner Incentives Program, and by actively supporting the Endangered Species Recovery Act of 2007.

We request that you respond to the enclosed questions and information requests. Please take no longer than one month to respond in full, and please do not move any closer to promulgating any revisions until you have answered our questions.

We look forward to working with you to resolve our concerns, and we thank you in advance for your responses to our questions.

Sincerely,

Joe Liberman, Barbara Boxer, Frank R. Lautenberg, Bernard Sanders, and Benjamin Cardin

Questions

1   How would these rule revisions, and any other new rule makings or policies you are considering, specifically promote species conservation and recovery?

2   The draft rule revisions would remove the term "recovery" from many places in the regulations and re-define the term "conservation" so that

it no longer would be synonymous with "recovery." How would these changes improve recovery of species under the Endangered Species Act (ESA)?

3 The draft rule revisions would define for the first time terms within the definitions of "endangered species" and "threatened species," such as "in danger of extinction," "significant portions of its range," and "foreseeable future." What effect would these changes have in the future on the likelihood of a species being listed, the number of species listed, and the status of a species (number of remaining individuals) at the time of listing?

4 What effect would the draft rule revision requiring concurrence of the Governor prior to establishment of non-essential experimental populations have on the likelihood that such experimental populations will be established in the future?

5 What effect would the draft rule revisions have on the likelihood that a given federal agency action would be the subject of section 7 consultation with the Fish and Wildlife Service?

6 How would the attempt to base jeopardy analysis on a comparison of "with" and "without" project conditions contribute to species conservation and recovery? How would this change conform to the requirements of the ESA, in light of the recent Ninth Circuit ruling, which rejected that approach as an "analytical slight of hand," stating "ESA compliance is not optional?" *National Wildlife Federation v. Idaho* (9th Cir. Apr. 9, 2007) (Slip. Op.)

7 How would the change allowing agencies to make their own effects determinations contribute to species conservation and recovery? How is it consistent with the recent decision determining that the ESA "reinforces the notion that a section 7(a)(2) determination is not to be unilaterally made?" *Washington Toxics Coalition v. U.S. Dept. of the Interior*, 457 F.Supp.2d-1158, 1179 (W.D. Wash. 2006).

8 How does the move to limit the ESA's applicability to only a narrow subset of federal agency activities contribute to species conservation and recovery? How would it follow legal precedent finding that because the ESA applies to "any" action "authorized, funded, or carried out" by a federal agency, "we take the regulation as a gloss on what the statutory limitation means and interpret the term 'discretionary' accordingly." *Defenders of Wildlife v. EPA*, 420 F.3d 946, 967 (9th Cir. 2005).

9 Who wrote and/or participated in drafting these proposed regulations within your Department? Did other federal agencies (e.g., Department of Commerce and NOA Fisheries) participate in the drafting, and if so, how?

10 What has Deputy Assistant Secretary Julie MacDonald's involvement been in these draft rule revisions?

11 It appears that many of these regulations were drafted or considered before your "listening tour" on the ESA last year. Will the listening tour inform your administrative and regulatory oversight of the ESA? Will the results of the listening tour be made public before any draft regulations are proposed? What timing do you anticipate for these actions?

12 Is the Department considering issuing any new policy positions under the ESA? Do you anticipate further Interior Solicitor's opinions, such as the recent one that would weaken the statutory requirement to list species threatened or endangered in a "significant portion of its range?"

13 Which industry and/or commercial groups or entities have given opinions, input, or information regarding these draft rule revisions?

14 Which environmental, conservation, scientific, religious, and/or citizen groups have given opinions, input, or information regarding these draft rule revisions?

15 How would these draft rule revisions, and any other draft regulations or policies you are considering, take into account the present and growing threat of global warming and climate change to imperiled and/or listed species?

QUESTIONS FOR CONSIDERATION

1   The debate over the success, or lack thereof, of the ESA hinges on the criteria upon which that evaluation is made. What criteria do those who have sought major reform apply to support their case, and what criteria do the scientific and environmental communities use to justify their position? Is this another example of Tim Hammonds' wry observation that "The public has become used to conflicting opinion . . . Many have come to feel that for every Ph.D. there is an equal and opposite Ph.D."?

2   While S-700 has the support of a wide range of interests, many of whom have called for major reform, if not outright repeal, of the ESA, it proposes an exclusively financial fix. What shortcomings of the ESA that opponents have perennially pointed to are not addressed by the pending legislation? Do you think that those who sought more comprehensive reform will come back to them after they "get their money"? Or will conscripting state and local governments and private landowners into the conservation effort insulate the Act from opposition for years to come?

3   If S-700 is enacted and leads to significant improvement of the endangered species protection effort, can it serve as a template for the solution of other environmental and conservation problems? Are we entering a new era in environmental protection wherein a partnership between the private and public sectors promises more success in dealing with increasingly complex issues?

4   Does it diminish ESA's cause that its opposition seems to have evaporated when financial incentives and compensation were put on the table? Or is it true that this measure will not end the controversy at all, but merely be the first of a number of concessions that the environmental and scientific communities will have to make? As of this writing, a draft proposal for an extensive *regulatory* fix was being circulated. It is not at all uncommon for advocates of policies that can't be accomplished legislatively turn to the more clandestine and pliant regulatory arena. This draft proposal, in fact, responds directly to many of the recommendations for ESA reform embodied in some of the above position papers.

5   In what ways is the debate over the ESA unique, and in what ways is it a paradigm of many, if not most, environmental issues?

Chapter 2

Alternate Energy/Biofuels

Primary Documents

Biofuels

2.1. "Statement of American Petroleum Institute President and CEO Red Cavaney before the Senate Energy and National Resources Committee," April 12, 2007

2.2. "Ethanol Facts: Food vs. Fuel," Fact Sheet, Renewable Fuels Association

2.3. "Letter from Cal Dooley, President and Chief Executive Officer, Grocery Manufacturers Association," to House and Senate Chairs on the RFS Legislation, December 5, 2007

2.4. "Setting the Record Straight on Ethanol," Position Paper of Nathan Glasgow and Lena Hansen, Rocky Mountain Institute

2.5. "The Coming Biofuels Disaster," Joe Brewer, Truthout.org, Guest Column

2.6. "The Great Biofuel Fraud," F. William Engdahl, *Asia Times*

2.7. "Biofuels: Myths of the Agro-Fuels Transition," Eric Holt-Gimenez, Food First

2.8. "Biofuels: Promise or Peril?" David Moberg, *In These Times*

2.9. "Ethanol Demand Outgrows Corn," Eric Kelderman, "Stateline.org"

2.10. "Biofuel Backfire," Frank O'Donnell, "Tom Paine.com," October 26, 2007

2.11. "Dumb, Greedy, and Ugly," William A. Niskanen, The Cato Institute

2.12. "Biofuels, Food, or Wildlife? The Massive Land Costs of US Ethanol," Dennis Avery, Competitive Enterprise Institute, September 21, 2006

2.13. "Green Fuel's Dirty Secret," Sasha Lilley, CorpWatch, June 1, 2006.

2.14. "Ethanol is the Agricultural Equivalent of Holy Water," Robert Bryce, *The Washington Spectator*

BACKGROUND

When Congress passed the Energy Independence and Security Act of 2007 in December of 2007, most of the media attention was devoted to the new mandate that future automobiles meet increased fuel efficiency standards. But another mandate in that same measure and one that seeks to achieve the same goals —reduction of both gasoline consumption and greenhouse gas emissions—is more far-reaching in significance and impact, though it will also be more challenging to implement. By setting the nation on a course to increase production of biofuels to 36 billion gallons by 2022, 16 billion of which to be derived from corn, Congress has reshaped national and world agriculture, and put increased pressure on food prices and the environment.

On the surface, biofuels offer much of what the nation needs and wants—a source of energy that is renewable, clean, natural, and, perhaps most attractive of all, homegrown. It has the potential to reduce our dependence on oil imports from politically unstable countries, jumpstart our struggling rural economies, and begin to address the adverse consequences of global warming. If those goals can in fact be realized, the new policy could be among the most important energy policy initiatives in our history. But all of those claims have their critics, and each of the benefits has its potential qualifier. All of which has given way to a lively debate among a broad array of interest groups and social observers.

The most common biofuel, ethanol, which is made from corn, has been produced for years, while others are just being developed. Corn has been the US's most heavily subsidized crop for decades, and it has gained even more prominence from the most recent food bill provisions promoting it. It has also played a role in replacing MTBE, an oxygenate that was found to be a suspect carcinogen, in gasoline formulations utilized to meet Clean Air Act standards. But the quantum leap in corn-based biofuel production mandated in the new bill would have significant consequences. While the science on the energy tradeoffs it would involve is not unanimous, as some of the documents below suggest, the prevailing opinion is that ethanol will require the expenditure of almost as much energy as it would yield, when all factors related to its cultivation and transportation are taken into account. Further, the dramatic increase in corn prices, along with those of other commodities, generated by the increased demand are occasioning the conversion of other cropland to corn, altering the diversity of agricultural production. Increased corn prices are correspondingly increasing the cost of livestock feed and, thus, the price of meat, as well as the whole range of processed food of which corn derivatives are a major component. And these financial effects are by no means limited to the United States. A substantial percentage of our commodity exports go most proximately to Mexico, and to a number of countries around the world. The costs of commodity crops are of concern to the United Nations as well as to Washington, DC.

While the appropriation of arable land to the cultivation of corn at the expense of specialty crops is problematic, advocates of biofuel production note that more marginal lands, not as suitable for traditional agriculture, are utilized to grow "cellulosic" materials (e.g. straw, switch grass, wheat stalks, wood chips, and any of a variety of other woody biomass wastes), a source of biofuels with substantially less adverse environmental impact (though, again, such lands do have ecological value). In fact, the new law requires that 16 billion gallons of the target total be supplied from these otherwise relatively useless materials. The technology for producing biofuels from cellulosic materials, however, is not yet fully developed. It's one of the many challenges that the industry will have to overcome.

The new biofuel mandate will also impact the automobile industry. Auto manufacturers will have to supply a greater number of flex-fuel vehicles that can utilize biofuel/gasoline blends, a challenge maximized by the need for biofuel producers to develop pipelines to carry their product from its rural origins to more populated areas. Service stations currently offering ethanol fuels are extremely limited in number and confined largely to the Midwest, where the source crops are cultivated.

Beyond this host of practical problems hovers the overarching ethical question: is it appropriate to trade "food for fuel," as so many of biofuels' opponents characterize it? Adherents claim that this is a false choice, but there is little doubt that the effects of the massive effort to replace a major percentage of gasoline with renewable fuels will reach throughout our country and beyond. Hardly anyone will be unaffected, here or abroad. All of this explains why the policy, so popular in Congress, has attracted such a diverse, and unorthodox, mix of interest group participants.

If the documents reproduced below are disproportionately unfavorable to the new national mandate, it is because the goals and promised benefits of the program are unambiguously desirable and need no defense, while its potential problems and unintended consequences are more complex and far-reaching.

DOCUMENTS

The American Petroleum Institute represents the oil and natural gas industry, and its supportive service companies.

2.1. "Statement of American Petroleum Institute President and CEO Red Cavaney before the Senate Energy and National Resources Committee," April 12, 2007

. . . For centuries, energy and food have been the engines that have given rise to mankind's ascendancy from poverty, particularly in the developing world. To give a family food, warmth, mobility, and a job is to progress toward a more stable world and to nurture an improving standard of living for every man, woman and child.

The International Energy Agency forecasts that world-wide energy demand will increase by 50 percent between now and 2030. For those of us steeped in the energy business for well over a century, one stark conclusion flowing from this forecast stands out—our world, and our nation, will need all commercially viable energy sources for decades into the future, including both fossil and alternative energy sources.

Our companies have long been pioneers in developing alternatives and expanding our utilization of existing sources of energy. From 2000 to 2005, the US oil and natural gas industry invested an estimated $98 billion in emerging energy technologies, including renewables, frontier hydrocarbons such as shale, tar sands, and gas-to-liquids technology. This represents almost 75 percent of the total $135 billion spent on emerging technologies by all US companies and the federal government. Our companies are actively investing in second generation biofuels research in cellulosic ethanol and biobutanol and weekly we hear of new and exciting approaches to growing and utilizing biomass in the motor fuels markets.

Given this huge global appetite for energy, energy security, not "energy independence," should be our nation's energy framework going forward. Today, the US oil and natural gas industry provides two-thirds of all the energy consumed each year by our nation. However, we import more than 60 percent of our oil in order to meet consumer demand.

The United States must do everything it can to access a diversity of resources around the world. "Energy independence" would be at odds with this objective. For all the talk of the need to wean ourselves from Arabian Gulf oil, the fact is the amount of Arabian Gulf oil imported has been substantially unchanged for years. Our real supply security depends on international trade. Our Arabian Gulf partners provide important supply —but they are only one source, representing less than 20 percent of the whole.

As we take steps to meet the energy needs of future generations, we must focus on three areas: meeting growing demand, improving energy efficiency and environmental performance, and developing new energy technologies.

☐ First, we must continue to meet our nation's growing energy needs through diverse sources of oil and natural gas supplies both here and around the world, while alternative and renewable sources continue their rapid rates of growth;

☐ Second, American industry must continue to increase its energy efficiency and the American public should be encouraged to become more energy efficient; and

☐ Third, we must develop new technologies to find and produce increased oil and natural gas supplies, improve energy efficiency, and develop new economic sources of renewable energy.

The current Renewable Fuels Standard (RFS) has stimulated substantial investments to grow biofuels supplies, particularly ethanol, beyond that required to satisfy the RFS. In addition, research into advanced production methods and alternative fuels is underway. The existing RFS has done its job well in stimulating the ethanol industry. Last year, our industry utilized 25 percent more than the target amount of ethanol established under the RFS. Additionally, nearly 50 percent of all gasoline consumed in the US now includes ethanol.

Thanks to the almost seamless transition of huge amounts of ethanol into our nation's gasoline pool, ethanol is gaining broader consumer acceptance. From our experience, we know that customer acceptance is the single most important factor in the success of a product, especially a transportation fuel. It is ever more essential that we maintain and build the consumer acceptance of ethanol.

In assessing policy options to further increase alternative fuels usage, the following should be considered:

☐ Reliance on market forces is the best way to satisfy our growing fuel requirements to ensure reliable supply and deliver the greatest value to consumers. Policies should be performance-based and provide a level playing field for all energy options, including renewable/alternative fuels, without favoring one specific technology over another or creating unsustainable or uneconomic solutions. They should be feedstock neutral;

☐ Government should not over-promise on the potential for renewables to reduce petroleum demand. Overestimates create unrealistic expectations, poor policy and wasted resources;

☐ Government policy should strive to encourage sustainable and competitive second generation technologies;

☐ The most economic and practical use of ethanol is E-10, which should be maximized before considering higher ethanol blends. E-10 requires no modifications to vehicles, no major changes to service station fueling equipment and tankage, and has a lengthy history of successful fuel use by consumers. Consumers will likely be unhappy with the mileage penalty of E-85;

☐ The existing infrastructure/distribution system should continue to grow and be utilized to the extent practicable. The industry was stretched last year in maximizing ethanol integration into the national gasoline pool, due in part to a tight wholesale delivery infrastructure, that is, additional terminals and blending facilities for ethanol, rail cars and rail spurs. The growth in infrastructure must keep pace with consumer demand. Greater cooperative work involving infrastructure among all stakeholders will benefit the consumer;

☐ Wide-spread use of E-85, however, would require that the major technological and economic hurdles of cellulosic ethanol conversion first be overcome. Even with breakthroughs in cellulosic ethanol production technology, significant logistical hurdles will need to be addressed. Gathering the feedstock (biomass such as forestry waste and switch grass), processing it, disposing of "waste" products, and delivering ethanol to markets at a cost comparable to gasoline has yet to be demonstrated on a commercial scale;

☐ E-85 use is also constrained by a number of additional factors. Corn-based ethanol is not sustainable at levels that would support widespread use of E-85. Moreover, E-85 requires flexible-fuel vehicles which currently comprise only 3 percent of the existing vehicle fleet. EIA estimates that flexible-fuel vehicle (FFV) penetration of the vehicle fleet will not rise above 10 percent until sometime after 2030. Even in 2030, new owners of FFVs, like many of the current owners, might fill up with E-10 rather than E-85. Moreover, E-85 also requires special service station fueling equipment and storage tanks;

☐ In increasing biofuels usage, the government should address secondary impacts including the impact on food supplies and the environment (e.g., water use and water quality degradation, pesticide use, and increased VOC/NOx emissions). Because of the potential for widespread effects on the environment, regulatory agencies will need to develop metrics for assessing the relative life-cycle impacts and benefits from potential large-scale increases in biofuels use;

☐ Government policy should encourage the utilization of the existing national refinery infrastructure for the co-processing of renewable feedstocks that can result in products with a renewable content that is compatible with the existing fuel distribution infrastructure;

☐ State-by-state ethanol mandates create additional boutique fuels, interfering with the reliable supply of fuels during times of supply disruptions and increasing distribution costs. State-by-state mandates also conflict with the flexibility and efficiencies provided in the Energy Policy Act of 2005 (EPACT05) with respect to where biofuels are supplied and product type. Just last week, for example, an eighth state passed another, different biofuels mandate. One state law allows and encourages the mixing of clear gasoline and ethanol-blended gasoline in the same retail tank. When this occurs, not only are emissions actually increased but the fuel violates federal environmental regulations. Congress recognized the potential problems from the proliferation of boutique fuels in gasoline and eliminated their expansion in the EPACT05. In that same legislation, the Renewable Fuels Standard stresses maximum fuel flexibility;

☐ Another example of restrictive state requirements can be found in the

Southeastern US, where most states currently fail to provide exceptions or modifications to their gasoline standards to accommodate ethanol's impact on fuel volatility. As a result, refiners/marketers face potential non-compliance with state gasoline standards if they blend ethanol with fungible conventional gasoline. Tailoring the base fuel at the refinery to assure compliance by the finished blend would reduce gasoline supplies and increase fuel cost, thereby removing any incentive to blend ethanol;

□ All mandates for increased renewable fuel usage should be accompanied by periodic technology/feasibility reviews that would allow for appropriate adjustments so that energy companies are not penalized due to the economic and technical hurdles that might prevent reaching biofuels usage targets or goals. All mandates for increased renewable fuel usage should also include contingency provisions that suspend requirements for increased biofuels usage in the event of significant supply or distribution disruptions.

While we have made progress over the past year, important questions remain. These must be addressed if we are to build on our joint progress and ultimately realize the full potential for ethanol within our nation's transportation fuels portfolio.

API also offers these specific comments concerning S-987, the proposed Biofuels for Energy Security and Transportation Act of 2007:

1   Restrictions on federal requirements in Energy Policy Act of 2005 (EPACT05) should continue.

- A federal alternative or renewable fuel mandate should not:
  - Have a per-gallon requirement;
  - Require any particular alternative fuel to be used to meet a mandate;
  - Require an alternative fuel to be used in any particular geographic area; and
  - Require an alternative fuel to be made from particular feedstocks or restrict the use of any feedstock or processing scheme.

2   States (and political subdivisions thereof) should be preempted from setting state alternative or renewable fuel mandates.

□ There should be an explicit, complete federal preemption of states from setting standards/controls of any type for alternative fuels.

□ An alternative would be to set out restrictions on the states in lieu of an explicit preemption.

3 EPA should be provided with additional authority to grant temporary waivers during supply emergencies—EPACT05 section 1541(a)

☐ There should be federal (EPA) preemption of existing state fuel and ASTM performance regulations when a waiver is issued during a supply emergency. During Hurricanes Katrina and Rita, EPA waived certain federal fuel requirements promptly to increase fuel supplies. However, in many cases state action was also required and frequently the state responses were not prompt. The result was unnecessary delays in increasing fuel supplies. EPA should be provided with authority to waive both federal and state environmental and product quality (situations where a state adopts its own product quality regulations and situations where states adopt ASTM specifications) fuel requirements during "an event of national significance."

☐ There should be emergency waiver authority for up to 90 days. The 20-day limit for waivers provided in EPACT05 is adequate for most situations but proved inadequate during Hurricanes Katrina and Rita. Thus, the timeframe for waivers should be increased to "up to 90 days" for an event of "national significance" so designated by the President. This increased time will provide much needed flexibility in terms of arranging for additional fuel supplies, particularly longer lead time product imports.

☐ Waiver authority should remain with the EPA Administrator. EPACT05 language should be retained so that the EPA Administrator—not the President—has authority for fuel waivers and preemption of state regulations. To change authority to the President would prevent speedy implementation of waivers, which is what was intended.

☐ Additional adjustments should be made to the emergency waiver language in EPACT 2005. EPA interpretation of the waiver language has caused some confusion and concern regarding supplying waived fuel. Several changes to the waiver language would help to correct these problems.

4 Alternative fuel technology review should be required with report to Congress and adjustment of alternative fuel standard and phase-in schedule.
☐ All mandates for increased renewable fuel usage should be accompanied by periodic technology/feasibility reviews that would allow for appropriate adjustments so that energy companies and consumers are not penalized due to the economic and technical hurdles that might prevent reaching alternative or biofuels usage targets or goals. We recognize that S-987 provides for a National Academy of Sciences review of this type.

In summary, the US oil and natural gas industry continues to make good progress in meeting our nation's growing energy needs and improving environmental performance. Looking ahead, we need to develop all economically viable energy sources including fossil and renewable fuel sources. By relying, to the greatest extent possible, on market forces, understanding consumer impact and preferences, encouraging development of new technologies, and addressing secondary impacts of expanded renewable fuel usage, I am confident that our industry and the nation will meet the energy challenges in the years ahead. . . .

The Renewable Fuels Association is the national trade organization for the US ethanol industry. The document below addresses charges that biofuel production will substantially increase food costs, and debunks the notion that food and biofuel production are in competition with one another. It commits the industry to providing affordable food and renewable energy mutually.

2.2. "Ethanol Facts: Food vs. Fuel," Fact Sheet, Renewable Fuels Association

As the US ethanol industry continues to expand, the amount of corn used for ethanol production is increasing dramatically. Corn use for ethanol more than doubled between 2001 and 2005. Critics question whether corn growers can satisfy demand for both renewable fuels and traditional uses like livestock and poultry feed, food processing and exports, and the contrived food vs. fuel debate has reared its ugly head once again.

Recently, critics and many in the media have charged that the rising price of corn due to growing ethanol demand is the major culprit for moderately rising consumer food prices. Absent from the discussion is the chief reason for increasing food costs: *escalating energy costs*. According to a June 2007 analysis of food, energy and corn prices conducted by John Urbanchuk of LECG, LLC, "rising energy prices had a more significant impact on food prices than did corn." In fact, the report notes rising energy prices have twice the impact on the Consumer Price Index (CPI) for food than does the price of corn.

"Energy costs have a much greater impact on consumer food costs as they impact every single food product on the shelf," said Urbanchuk. "Energy is required to produce, process, package and ship each food item. Conversely, corn prices impact just a small segment of the food market as not all products rely on corn for production. While it may be more sensational to lay the blame for rising food costs on corn prices, the facts don't support that conclusion. By a factor of two-to-one, energy prices are the chief factor determining what American families pay at the grocery store."

According to the study, "Increasing petroleum prices have about twice the impact on consumer food prices as equivalent increases in corn prices. A 33 percent increase in crude oil prices—the equivalent of $1.00 per gallon over current levels of retail gasoline prices—would increase retail food prices measured by the CPI for food by 0.6 to 0.9 percent. An equivalent increase in corn prices—about $1.00 per bushel over current levels —would increase consumer food prices only 0.3 percent."

The report goes on to find, "Corn and energy prices both affect consumer food prices. However, since increases in corn prices are limited to a relatively small portion of the overall CPI for food, an increase in corn prices resulting from higher ethanol demand or a supply disruption such as a major drought is expected to have about half the impact of the same percentage increase in petroleum and energy prices." Corn demand for ethanol has no noticeable impact on retail food prices. A central theme in the "food versus fuel" myth is the false assertion that moderately higher corn prices, spurred by ethanol demand, are leading to higher retail food prices for consumers. Yet the truth is numerous cost factors contribute to retail food prices. According to USDA, labor costs account for 38 cents of every dollar a consumer spends on food. Packaging, transportation, energy, advertising and profits account for 24 cents of the consumer food dollar. In fact, just 19 cents of every consumer dollar can be attributed to the actual cost of food inputs like grains and oilseeds.

Retail food products such as cereals, snack foods, and beverages sweetened with corn sweeteners contain very little corn. Therefore, fluctuations in the price of corn are not often reflected in the retail prices for these items. As an example, a standard box of corn flakes contains approximately 10 ounces of corn, or about 1/90th of a bushel. Even when corn is priced at $4 per bushel, a box of corn flakes contains less than a nickel's worth of corn.

Retail food price data from the Bureau of Labor Statistics further demonstrates that increased demand for corn for ethanol production has not dramatically increased consumer food prices. While the cash price of No. 2 Yellow Corn has increased from $2.18/bushel in April 2006 to $3.36/bushel in April 2007, consider the change in price in the following grocery items:

Item	Qty	April 06 Price	April 07 Price
Milk	1 gal.	$3.12	$3.14
American cheese	1 lb.	$3.81	$3.73
Butter	½ lb.	$1.40	$1.43
Ice cream	½ gal.	$3.62	$3.79
Turkey	2 lbs.	$2.22	$2.16
Chicken breast	2 lbs.	$6.62	$6.74
Eggs	1 dz.	$1.28	$1.62
Pork chops	2 lbs.	$6.34	$6.30
Bacon	2 lbs.	$6.68	$7.00
Ground beef	1 lbs.	$2.74	$2.82
Beef steak	2 lbs.	$10.18	$10.82
Cola, non-diet	2 ltrs.	$1.10	$1.20
Malt beverage	72 ozs.	$5.00	$5.00
Total		$54.11	$55.75

As the above chart demonstrates, the aggregate increase for these food items from April 2006 to April 2007 is just 3%. For perspective, the 25-year average annual food inflation is 2.9%.

Thus, while it is true increased ethanol production is creating a real market-driven price for corn, energy prices, not ethanol, are responsible for much of the increase in the price of food. Further, the ethanol industry is rapidly developing next generation cellulosic ethanol technology that will allow it to meet the growing demand for renewable fuels from wood chips, switch grass and other materials in addition to corn. Ultimately, the market will adjust and all those in the food, fuel and fiber industry will be able to prosper.

Much of the debate has centered on the notion that the US will not be able to produce enough corn to satisfy all markets, creating shortages and intensifying competition that will continuously drive the price of corn higher. However, advancements in seed, farming and ethanol technologies are allowing American farmers to continue feeding the world while helping to fuel our nation.

"There is no conflict between food and fuel—we can produce both," said Ken McCauley, president of the National Corn Growers Association. "Demand for corn is at unprecedented levels, and we fully expect unprecedented levels of supply as well. This spring US corn growers planted the largest crop this country has seen since the 1940s. Given normal weather conditions this summer, we'll produce the largest corn crop in history, and that will allow us to readily satisfy demand for livestock feed, human food processing, exports and fuel ethanol."

Ethanol production does not reduce the amount of food available for human consumption. Ethanol is produced from field corn which is primarily fed to livestock and is indigestible by humans in its raw form. The ethanol production process produces not only fuel but valuable livestock feed products.

Every 56-pound bushel of corn used in the dry mill ethanol process yields 18 pounds of distillers grains, a good source of energy and protein for livestock and poultry. Similarly, a bushel of corn in the wet mill ethanol process creates 13.5 pounds of corn gluten feed and 2.6 pounds of high-protein corn gluten meal, as well as corn oil used in food processing.

Importantly, ethanol production utilizes only the starch portion of the corn kernel, which is abundant and of low value. While the starch is converted to ethanol, the protein, vitamins, minerals and fiber are sold as high-value livestock feed (distillers grains). Protein, which is left intact by the ethanol process, is a highly valued product in world food and feed markets. Aside from preserving the protein, a considerable portion of the corn's original digestible energy is also preserved in the distillers grains.

Distillers grains have an average protein content (28 to 30%) that is typically at least three times higher than that of corn, making it a valuable ingredient in livestock and poultry diets. In 2006/07, more than 12 million metric tons of distillers grains were produced by ethanol biorefineries and fed to livestock and poultry. It is estimated that distillers grains displaced more than 500 million bushels of corn from feed rations last year, allowing that corn to be used in other markets.

It also is important to remember the amount of field corn actually used for human food is just a small fraction of the total corn supply. For example, cereal accounted for just over one percent of total corn use in 2005.

The overwhelming majority of US corn, including exported corn, feeds livestock—not humans. There is a popular misconception that corn is exported from the US to feed those in malnourished countries, and thus ethanol use will diminish exports to these countries. The truth is the majority of corn exports are used to feed livestock in developed countries. Importantly, the US ethanol industry is helping to satisfy foreign demand for high-protein, high-energy feedstuffs by exporting more than 1 million metric tons of distillers grains to countries around the world in 2005.

Corn growers are responding to increased corn demand. Corn growers make their planting decisions based on signals from the marketplace. If demand for corn is high and projected revenue-per-acre is strong relative to other crops, farmers will plant more corn. And they have. US corn growers have produced the three largest corn crops in history in the past three years. In 2004, farmers harvested a record 11.8 billion bushel crop, followed by an 11.1 billion bushel crop in 2005. After all demands were met, the corn industry finished 2005 with nearly 2 billion bushels in surplus—one of the highest levels since the 1980s. Given normal weather conditions and trend yields in 2007, corn producers will harvest a record crop of approximately 13 billion bushels. Data from ProExporter Network suggests that while total corn demand in 2007/08 will be about 900 million bushels higher than in 2006/07, total supply will be about 1.6 billion bushels higher.

At the same time, corn yields have increased by about 3.5 bushels per acre per year since the 1995–1996 crop year. Increased yields, together with improved farming practices, seed technology developments, and increasing ethanol processing efficiency ensure that the American farmer will continue to meet the world's needs for food, feed, fuel and other uses.

Ethanol production from other non-traditional sources continues to grow. An increasing amount of ethanol is produced from non-traditional feedstocks such as waste products from the beverage, food and forestry industries. In the very near future we will also produce ethanol from agricultural residues such as rice straw, sugar cane bagasse and corn stover, municipal solid waste, and energy crops such as switchgrass.

The Grocery Manufacturing Association is the largest association of food and beverage companies in the world. Contravening the RFA, the GMA laments the prospective increase in food prices that would be stimulated by the legislation.

2.3. "Letter from Cal Dooley, President and Chief Executive Officer, Grocery Manufacturers Association," to House and Senate Chairs on the RFS Legislation, December 5, 2007

Dear Representative:

As the largest association of food and beverage companies in the world, the Grocery Manufacturers Association strongly opposes efforts to increase the Renewable Fuels Standard (RFS) in the energy legislation coming to the House floor this week. The legislation would increase the renewable fuels standard (RFS) to 15 billion gallons of ethanol from corn—over twice the current mandate. Using corn for ethanol production is already having an unintended, adverse impact on Americans' pocketbooks, and we believe if such an RFS is adopted the situation will only be exacerbated.

While we support diversifying our nation's energy supplies and addressing the challenge of global warming, the evidence is mounting on the adverse consequences of an over-reliance on corn ethanol—on the cost of food, both domestically and internationally, and on the environment.

- Farmers are growing 93 million acres of corn—up 16 percent from last year—displacing soybeans, wheat, cotton and other crops.
- The United States is already diverting 20 percent of its corn harvest to ethanol production. Increasing the mandate to 15 billion gallons will require about 46 percent of the total US corn crop.
- Despite major increases in corn production, corn prices have nearly doubled to more than $3.50 per bushel. Soybean and wheat prices have also dramatically increased as supplies of those crops have tightened.
- Feed prices have increased, placing new pressures on livestock operators, dairy farmers and food producers.
- US food prices have risen well above the Consumer Price Index. Rising crop prices caused in part by the current RFS have contributed to higher consumer prices for staples such as eggs, dairy and meat.
- The proposed biodiesel mandate, a total of one billion gallons by 2011, would require fully one-third of the current US vegetable oil production. At a time when the food and restaurant industries are endeavoring to replace transfat with healthier oils, this rapid shift in demand will create new impediments to achieving that goal.

While other factors contribute to higher food costs, the fact remains that an ethanol policy using arbitrary mandates to divert corn from food into fuel—and doing so by subsidizing the sector with billions of dollars in taxpayer money—strains the supply for the commodity and increases prices for all users. It's foolish to think otherwise.

We urge you to vote "no" on the energy bill and instead work with all stakeholders impacted by this legislation to create a reasonable and sustainable alternative. The Grocery Manufacturers Association will take this vote into strong consideration as it compiles its 2007 "key votes" record for our industry's 14 million employees. . . .

The Rocky Mountain Institute is a highly regarded non-profit organization that promotes the efficient use of energy and natural resources through business, civil society, and government initiatives. Nathan Glasgow and Lena Hansen, consultants to the Institute's Energy and Resources Services Team, here defend biofuels against charges that they require more energy to produce than they yield and that their value as carbon reducers are modest, though they are speaking of biofuels made from cellulosic materials rather than corn.

2.4. "Setting the Record Straight on Ethanol," Position Paper of Nathan Glasgow and Lena Hansen, Rocky Mountain Institute

Biofuels, and specifically ethanol, have been the subject of a great deal of criticism in recent months by detractors claiming that more energy is required to produce ethanol than is available in the final product, that it is too expensive, and that it produces negligible carbon reductions.

These critiques are simply not accurate. State-of-the-art technologies have been forecasted to produce ethanol that is far more cost-effective and less energy-intensive than gasoline. In this article, we'll tell you why, and why the critics have gotten it wrong.

When we say biofuels, we mean liquid fuels made from biomass, namely biodiesel and ethanol, which can be substituted for diesel fuel or for gasoline, respectively.

The technology used to produce biodiesel is well understood, although biomass feedstocks are limited, do not include woody biomass, and production is fairly expensive. We will instead focus on ethanol, which we believe has significantly greater potential for both the agricultural and forestry sectors.

Ethanol, which can be substituted for or blended with gasoline, has traditionally been produced from either corn or sugarcane feedstocks. In fact, Brazil currently meets more than 25 percent of its gasoline demand with ethanol made from sugarcane. Even gasoline in the United States contains, on average, 2 percent ethanol (used as a substitute for MTBE to oxygenate fuel). American ethanol is almost exclusively made from the kernels of corn. But conventional processes and feedstocks used to make ethanol are not feasible in the United States on a large scale for three reasons: they're not cost-competitive with long-run gasoline prices without subsidies, they compete with food crops for land, and they have only marginally positive energy balances.

However, in addition to starch-based feedstocks, ethanol can be produced from "cellulosic" feedstocks, including biomass wastes, fast-growing hays like switchgrass, and short-rotation woody crops like poplar. These types of crops are expected to have much higher yields compared to starch-based crops (10–15 ton per acre, up from a conventional 5 tons per acre). And while not cost-competitive today, already observed advances in technology leads us to believe that in the next few years, ethanols made from these crops will become cost-competitive, won't compete with food for cropland, and will have a sizeable positive energy balance.

A common complaint about ethanol is that the quantity of feedstocks is limited and land used to grow feedstocks could be put to better use. For cellulosic feedstocks, the situation is quite the contrary. Cellulosic feedstocks are plentiful: for example, agricultural and forestry wastes can be used to create ethanol, with the positive side-effect of reducing the quantity of waste we must dispose of and creating an additional income stream for landowners.

Using waste to produce fuel has the clear benefit of a virtually free feedstock, and because energy is generally expended to create the product, not the waste, this type of ethanol obviously has a positive energy balance.

Not quite as obvious is to what extent dedicated energy crops can be used to produce ethanol. We believe the answer is straightforward. Research by Oak Ridge National Laboratory shows that dedicated energy crops can be grown without competing with food crops because they can be grown in marginal areas unsuited for food crop production, or on about 17 million acres of Conservation Reserve Program land that is currently being withheld from agricultural use, or on forestry land.

Cellulosic crops have additional environmental benefits for several reasons. First, because crops like switchgrass are deep-rooted perennials, growing them actually prevents soil erosion and restores degraded land. For this same reason, cellulosic crops also have significantly lower carbon emissions.

While corn-based ethanol reduces carbon emissions by about 20 percent below gasoline, cellulosic ethanol is predicted to be carbon-neutral, or possibly even net-carbon-negative.

Many times we've been asked: "But doesn't ethanol require more energy to produce than it contains?" The simple answer is no—the majority of scientific studies, especially those in recent years, do not support this concern.

These studies have shown that ethanol has a higher energy content than the fossil energy used in its production. Some studies that contend that ethanol is a net energy loser include (incorrectly) the energy of the sun used to grow a feedstock in ethanol's energy balance, which misses the fundamental point that the sun's energy is free.

Furthermore, because crops like switchgrass are perennials, they are not replanted every year and therefore use significantly less energy. So, according to the US Department of Energy, for every one unit of energy available at the fuel pump, 1.23 units of fossil energy are used to produce gasoline, 0.74 units of fossil energy are used to produce corn-based ethanol, and only 0.2 units of fossil energy are used to produce cellulosic ethanol.

Critics further discount cellulosic ethanol by ignoring the recent advancements of next-generation ethanol conversion technologies. A recent example that has received significant attention is David Pimentel's March 2005 paper in *Natural Resources Research*, which argues that ethanol production from cellulosic feedstocks requires more fossil energy to produce than the energy contained in the final product. However, Pimentel bases his analysis on only one technology used to produce ethanol, ignoring two other developing technologies. His chosen conversion technology, acid hydrolosis, is the least efficient of the three.

A superior option, thermal gasification, converts biomass into a synthesis gas composed of carbon oxides and hydrogen. The gas is then converted into ethanol through either a biological process using microorganisms or by passing it through a reactor with a specific catalyst. Both of these processes show good potential for increased energy yields and reduced costs by using cellulosic feedstocks. This conversion technology is currently being tested in pilot plants in Arkansas and Colorado.

Still better, enzymatic reduction hydrolosis already shows promise in the marketplace. Such firms as Iogen and Novozymes have been developing enzymes, or "smart bugs," that can turn cellulosic biomass into sugars that can then be converted into ethanol.

Historically, the biggest cost component of this technology was the creation of enzymes. Earlier this year, though, in combination with the National Renewable Energy Laboratory, Novozymes announced a 30-fold reduction in the cost of enzyme production in laboratory trials. Expected benefits from this process include low energy requirements, high efficiency, and mild process conditions. A pilot plant exists in Ontario and another is planned in Hawai'i. The first commercial-scale enzymatic reduction hydrolosis plant is scheduled to be built and operational by Iogen within two years, producing ethanol at a targeted cost of $1.30 per gallon.

No matter which of these conversion technologies ultimately wins, it is clear that cost-effective and efficient ethanol production from cellulose is on the horizon—which is good news for the United States, where mobility consumes seven of every ten barrels of oil we use. Our voracious appetite for that oil comes at a cost—we have to buy it, we have to deal with the pollution that comes from using it, and, because most of our oil comes from the Middle East, we have to defend it.

Because mobility consumes the majority of the oil we use, mostly by burning gasoline, it's the first place to look for a solution.

In our recent publication, *Winning the Oil Endgame* (www.oilendgame.com), we argue that the critical first step to reducing our oil consumption is automobile efficiency. But there's no reason to stop there. Using biofuels instead of gasoline to power our cars has the potential to displace 3.7 million barrels per day of crude oil—that's a fifth of our forecasted consumption in 2025, after more efficient use. And our analysis forecasts that, with the technological developments discussed above, this can happen at a cost of $0.75 per gallon of gasoline-equivalent in 2025.

Clearly, monopolizing on the nexus of the agriculture and energy value chains will create huge opportunities for business and huge wins for our country. The critics simply have it wrong.

Joe Brewer and F. William Engdahl are both independent authors/journalists. Their bitter attacks on the policy that was to become national are articulate, comprehensive, and informative.

2.5. "The Coming Biofuels Disaster," Joe Brewer, Truthout.org, Guest Column

Have you ever tried to solve a problem only to discover that you made things worse in the process? This is happening right now with biofuels. We are on the road to disaster because the problem we are trying to solve has been framed inadequately. Harmful impacts from large-scale biofuel production are largely overlooked. And we aren't even addressing the right problem! The truth can be seen when we frame issues in the context of livability.

Solving the Wrong Problem

Policymakers have been grappling with the fact that an excessive amount of carbon dioxide is polluting our atmosphere, disrupting global weather patterns and shifting the world's climate beyond safe boundaries. The solution required by this problem is that we stop increasing greenhouse pollution levels. This can be accomplished by shifting our energy sector in a direction that ultimately reduces the amount of heat-trapping gases that have accumulated since the dawn of the industrial revolution.

On the surface, biofuels present the ideal solution to this problem. We can grow them in large amounts, and the carbon that is released by burning them is equal to the amount they breathe in as they grow. This simple mental accounting is very appealing, but woefully inaccurate for describing what is really going on.

The real problem is that the way we use energy is out of balance with natural processes, driving us away from the equilibrium necessary for our communities to survive. This is evident in the planet's atmosphere where global warming is running rampant; our cities are submerged in toxic gases, and the protective ozone shield is tattered. It is also evident in the biosphere, where we are in the midst of the Earth's sixth mass extinction (the first in the planet's 4.5 billion-year history caused by a single species—humans). Soils in our agricultural plains are lost to wind and water, reducing the land's capacity to produce food. And our water supplies are being diverted, drained and contaminated by toxic run-off. We need to find livable solutions to this problem.

A glance at biofuels in the context of livability shows how woefully inadequate they are for solving it. In truth, they will make things worse. The biofuels hoax, as ecologist Eric Holt-Gimenez calls it, is based on several misunderstandings that arise in the language of the energy debate.

The Biofuel Myth of Renewal

Biofuels are not the clear solution they seem to be. For starters, the word biofuel is problematic. The augmentation of the word fuel with the prefix bio- creates a meaning that uses our experience with biological organisms (namely that they are able to reproduce themselves). This meaning implies biofuels are renewable because the crops used to create them can also be reproduced. But biofuels are not renewable without dramatically changing the ways we grow crops and manufacture/distribute products.

Large-scale agricultural practices deplete soils, contaminate water supplies and are vulnerable to pests and disease when single crops (monocultures) are grown in large fields. The widespread use of pesticides (manufactured using fossil fuels) is also contributing to the cancer epidemic wreaking havoc on our communities. Current agricultural practices also require non-renewable resources and utilize vast distribution networks that are very high in resource demand—including the need for lots of energy.

In some areas, such as Indonesia and Malaysia, entire forests are decimated to grow biofuel crops. The plant-life destroyed in this process releases huge amounts of carbon dioxide as the dead trees and undergrowth decompose, exacerbating the problem they are meant to address.

Biofuels are not renewable! Soils are depleted. Water supplies are depleted. Highways and factories deplete mineral resources. Entire forests are depleted.

This truth is hidden by the blending of the concepts for living organism and fuel in the word biofuel.

The word biofuel tells us that the fuel is natural. Things that are natural are considered to be safer than things that are manufactured. This understanding of natural tells us that biofuels are better than manufactured fuels.

The natural frame leads to two false impressions:

1 Biofuels are presumed to be good for the environment.
2 Biofuels are presumed to be better for us than manufactured fuels.

The first impression is false because of the agricultural production systems we currently use. The second impression is false because biofuels are manufactured in two ways. First, the fuel is produced through an industrial refinement process where ethanol is extracted from plant materials. And second, there is considerable emphasis on genetically engineering plants to be grown as fuel sources. These plants—including corn, palm trees, switch grass and algae—are not natural if they are the product of intentional design by genetic engineering.

One area of genetic research that isn't talked about nearly enough is devoted to increasing plant resistance to pests. With something like switch grass that grows quickly, the prospect of making it resistant to pests is a recipe for a super weed. The last thing we want is an aggressive weed that is immune to natural predators.

We shouldn't call genetically engineered plants biofuels. They are frankenfuels. By tampering with plant DNA, we run the risk of getting further out of balance, possibly introducing new and unexpected harms like invasive species that take over croplands and natural ecosystems.

The precautionary principle, which tells us that possible threats with dire consequences should be avoided, automatically applies when the discussion is about finding livable solutions.

Myth of Transition

The energy debate has explored biofuels as a "transition" to renewable energy. The livability lens already shows us that they are not renewable, but supporters often reply to such criticism by stating biofuels are a step in the right direction. They claim biofuels are better than oil (in the context of the carbon emissions problem) and are a significant step toward a society based entirely on renewable energy.

This is simply not true. We are dependent on oil because the massive infrastructure of our societies is based on the use of fossil fuels. Changing over to a biofuel society involves building a similarly massive infrastructure. An honest account of this option includes this truth.

In order to meet current energy demands, we must grow crops over huge areas, build factories and storage facilities, redesign automobiles to run on biodiesel, and more. We would be entrenched in a biofuel society as much as we are now in a fossil fuel society. Either way, we are still dependent on some kind of fuel.

Feeding Cars or People?

Another kind of transition will happen if we invest significantly in biofuels: We will shift crop yields away from food production. Basic economics tells us that the cost of goods go up when supply decreases. The growing demand for grains to produce fuel has increased the cost of food.

The economic incentive to grow crops for fuels instead of food will drive down food production in the long run, permanently inflating the cost of food. At the same time, less food will be produced. This combination creates a situation where landowners are motivated by profits to grow fuel crops, which will lead to an increase in the number of hungry people in poor countries.

We are starving poor people to feed our cars!

This economic truth does not emerge in the context of carbon dioxide levels. Only by framing the problem in the context of livability does the impact on poor people become apparent.

Bypassing Disaster with Livability

The biofuels debate has been centered on the wrong question. The problem is not simply the amount of carbon dioxide in the atmosphere. If we address the "carbon problem" without recognizing the "livability problem" our solutions will fail. This is the challenge. We have to look at these problems holistically to see the impacts of our choices.

Addressing the climate crisis requires us to do a lot more than change from fossil fuels to plant-based fuels. Global warming is a problem because the way we live is out of sync with nature. The solution is to rethink how we relate to our natural environment. This is where livability is paramount. We need to be thinking about family farms, not factory farms. In the family farm frame, people are interacting with the earth to produce food. The factory farm frame has people interacting with the earth to produce money.

All of the problems with biofuels have been largely overlooked because of the way the situation has been framed. Experts have known about these problems for a long time, but public discourse has been too narrow to recognize them.

When thinking about the essential features of a livable community, we can see that biofuels will not work in their current incarnation. A livable community:

Provides essential resources like potable water and breathable air
Preserves these essential resources for future generations
Provides food security (now and into the future)
Promotes the flourishing of life (including the millions of species we
  co-exist with—and cannot exist without!)

A livable community promotes life. This means it is not destructive. Current emphasis on pesticides and herbicides, for example, are chemical killers that destroy life. By growing diverse crops locally, we don't need nitrogen fertilizer that runs off into rivers and kills life in lakes and oceans. Instead, a livable community's central activities involve growing food in a way that supports many different kinds of plants and animals. This diversity provides a buffer for the community to protect it against changes in climate (where some plants may no longer grow, but others will). In a livable community, energy is generated to serve the needs of people. A variety of ways to generate energy provides another kind of buffer against change. Some sources, such as coal and oil, will be phased out when they threaten the security of people in the community.

It is not even clear whether biofuels can be part of the solution at all. The family farm that supports life is inherently local and small. Introduction of an economic incentive to grow fuel crops will drive local farmers to grow ever larger biofuel crops, resulting in the pattern that is occurring now.

We can solve the "livability problem" by looking for ways to promote life. The carbon dioxide problem will get fixed along the way.

2.6. "The Great Biofuel Fraud," F. William Engdahl, *Asia Times*

That bowl of Kellogg's cornflakes on the breakfast table or the portion of pasta or corn tortillas, cheese or meat on the dinner table is going to rise in price over the coming months as sure as the sun rises in the East. Welcome to the new world food-price shock, conveniently timed to accompany the current world oil-price shock.

Curiously, it's ominously similar in many respects to the early 1970s when prices for oil and food both exploded by several hundred percent in a matter of months. That mid-1970s price explosion led the late US president Richard Nixon to ask his old pal Arthur Burns, then chairman of the Federal Reserve, to find a way to alter the Consumer Price Index (CPI) inflation data to take attention away from the rising prices. The result then was the now-commonplace publication of the absurd "core inflation" CPI numbers—*sans* oil and food.

The late American satirist Mark Twain once quipped, "Buy land: They've stopped making it." Today we can say almost the same about corn, or all grains worldwide. The world is in the early months of the greatest sustained rise in prices for all major grains, including maize, wheat and rice, that we have seen in three decades. Those three crops constitute almost 90% of all grains cultivated in the world. Washington's calculated, absurd plan.

What's driving this extraordinary change? Here things get pretty interesting. The administration of US President George W Bush is making a major public relations push to convince the world it has turned into a "better steward of the environment." The problem is that many have fallen for the hype.

The center of Bush's program, announced in his January State of the Union address, is called "20 in 10," cutting US gasoline use 20% by 2010. The official reason is to "reduce dependency on imported oil," as well as cutting unwanted "greenhouse gas" emissions. That isn't the case, but it makes good PR. Repeat it often enough and maybe most people will believe it. Maybe they won't realize their taxpayer subsidies to grow ethanol corn instead of feed corn are also driving the price of their daily bread through the roof.

The heart of the plan is a huge, taxpayer-subsidized expansion of use of bio-ethanol for transport fuel. The president's plan requires production of 35 billion US gallons (about 133 billion liters) of ethanol a year by 2017. Congress has already mandated with the Energy Policy Act of 2005 that corn ethanol for fuel must rise from 4 billion gallons in 2006 to 7.5 billion in 2012.

To make certain it will happen, farmers and big agribusiness giants like ADM or David Rockefeller get generous taxpayer subsidies to grow corn for fuel instead of food. Currently ethanol producers get a subsidy in the US of 51 cents per gallon (13.5 cents per liter) of ethanol paid to the blender, usually an oil company that blends it with gasoline for sale.

As a result of the beautiful US government subsidies to produce bioethanol fuels and the new legislative mandate, the US refinery industry is investing big-time in building new special ethanol distilleries, similar to oil refineries, except they produce ethanol fuel. The number currently under construction exceeds the total number of oil refineries built in the US over the past 25 years. When they are finished in the next two to three years, the demand for corn and other grain to make ethanol for car fuel will double from present levels.

And not just US bio-ethanol. In March, Bush met with Brazilian President Luiz Inacio Lula da Silva to sign a bilateral "Ethanol Pact" to cooperate in research and development of "next generation" biofuel technologies such as cellulosic ethanol from wood, and joint cooperation in "stimulating" expansion of biofuel use in developing countries, especially in Central America, and creating a biofuel cartel along the lines of the Organization of Petroleum Exporting Countries (OPEC) with rules that allow formation of a Western Hemisphere ethanol market.

In short, the use of farmland worldwide for bio-ethanol and other biofuels—burning the food product rather than using it for human or animal food—is being treated in Washington, Brazil and other major centers, including the European Union, as a major new growth industry.

Phony Green Arguments

Biofuel—gasoline or other fuel produced from refining food products—is being touted as a solution to the controversial global-warming problem. Leaving aside the faked science and the political interests behind the sudden hype about dangers of global warming, biofuels offer no net positive benefits over oil even under the best conditions.

Their advocates claim that present first-generation biofuels save up to 60% of the carbon emission of equivalent petroleum fuels. As well, amid rising oil prices at $75 per barrel for Brent marker grades, governments such as Brazil's are frantic to substitute home-grown biofuels for imported gasoline. In Brazil today, 70% of all cars have "flexi-fuel" engines able to switch from conventional gasoline to 100% biofuel or any mix. Biofuel production has become one of Brazil's major export industries as well.

The green claims for biofuel as a friendly and better fuel than gasoline are at best dubious, if not outright fraudulent. Depending on who runs the tests, ethanol has little if any effect on exhaust-pipe emissions in current car models. It has significant emission, however, of some toxins, including formaldehyde and acetaldehyde, a suspected neurotoxin that has been banned as carcinogenic in California.

Ethanol is not some benign substance as we are led to think from the industry propaganda. It is highly corrosive to pipelines as well as to seals and fuel systems of existing car or other gasoline engines. It requires special new pumps. All that conversion costs money.

But the killer about ethanol is that it holds at least 30% less energy per liter than normal gasoline, translating into a loss in fuel economy of at least 25% over gasoline for an Ethanol E-85% blend.

No advocate of the ethanol boondoggle addresses the huge social cost that is beginning to hit the dining-room tables across the US, Europe and the rest of the world. Food prices are exploding as corn, soybeans and all cereal-grain prices are going through the roof because of the astronomical —US Congress-driven—demand for corn to burn for biofuel.

This year the Massachusetts Institute of Technology issued a report concluding that using corn-based ethanol instead of gasoline would have no impact on greenhouse-gas emissions, and would even expand fossil-fuel use because of increased demand for fertilizer and irrigation to expand acreage of ethanol crops. And according to MIT, "natural-gas consumption is 66% of total corn-ethanol production energy," meaning huge new strains on natural-gas supply, pushing prices of that product higher.

The idea that the world can "grow" out of oil dependency with biofuels is the PR hype being used to sell what is shaping up to be the most dangerous threat to the planet's food supply since the creation of patented genetically manipulated corn and other crops.

US Farms Become Biofuel Factories

The main reason US and world grain prices have been soaring in the past two years, and are now pre-programmed to continue rising at a major pace, is the conversion of US farmland to become de facto biofuel factories. Last year, US farmland devoted to biofuel crops increased by 48%. None of that land was replaced for food-crop cultivation; the tax subsidies make it far too profitable to produce ethanol fuel.

Since 2001, the amount of corn used to produce bio-ethanol in the US has risen 300%. In fact, in 2006 US corn crops for biofuel equaled the tonnage of corn used for export. In 2007 it is estimated it will exceed the corn for export by a hefty amount. The United States is the world's leading corn exporter, most going for animal feed to EU and other countries. The traditional US Department of Agriculture statistics on acreage planted to corn is no longer a useful metric of food prices, as all marginal acreage is going for biofuel growing. The amount available for animal and human feed is actually declining.

Brazil and China are similarly switching from food to biofuels with large swatches of land.

A result of the biofuel revolution in agriculture is that world carryover or reserve stocks of grains have been plunging for six of the past seven years. Carryover reserve stocks of all grains fell at the end of 2006 to 57 days of consumption, the lowest level since 1972. Little wonder that world grain prices rose 100% over the past 12 months. This is just the start.

That decline in grain reserves, the measure of food security in event of drought or harvest failure—an increasingly common event in recent years—is pre-programmed to continue going as far ahead as the eye can see. Assuming a modest world population increase annually of some 70 million over the coming decade, especially in the South Asian sub-continent and Africa, the stagnation or even decline in the tonnages of feed corn or other feed grains, including rice, that is harvested annually as growing amounts of bio-ethanol and other biofuels displaces food grain in fact means we are just getting started on the greatest transformation of global agriculture since the introduction of the agribusiness revolution with fertilizers and mechanized farming after World War II.

The difference is that this revolution is at the expense of food production. That pre-programs exploding global grain prices, increased poverty, and malnutrition. And the effect on gasoline import demand will be minimal.

Professor M A Altieri of the University of California at Berkeley estimates that dedicating all US corn and soybean production to biofuels would only meet 12% of gasoline and 6% of diesel needs. He notes that although one-fifth of last year's US corn harvest went to bio-ethanol, it met a mere 3% of energy needs. But the farmland is converting at a record pace. In 2006 more than 50% of Iowa and South Dakota corn went to ethanol refineries.

Farmers across the US Midwest, desperate for more income after years of depressed corn prices, are abandoning traditional crop rotation to grow exclusively soybeans or corn, with dramatic added impact on soil erosion and needs for added chemical pesticides. In the US some 41% of all herbicides used are already applied to corn. Monsanto and other makers of glyphosate herbicides such as Roundup are clearly smiling on the way to the bank.

Going Global with Biofuels

The Bush-Lula pact is just the start of a growing global rush to plant crops for biofuel. Huge sugarcane, oil-palm and soy plantations for biofuel refining are taking over forests and grasslands in Brazil, Argentina, Colombia, Ecuador and Paraguay. Soy cultivation has already caused the deforestation of 21 million hectares in Brazil and 14 million hectares in Argentina, with no end in sight, as world grain prices continue to rise. Soya is used for bio-diesel fuel.

China, desperate for energy sources, is a major player in biofuel cultivation, reducing food-crop acreage there as well. In the EU, most bio-diesel fuel is produced using rapeseed plants, a popular animal feed. The result? Meat prices around the globe are rising and set to continue rising as far as the eye can see. The EU has a target requiring minimum biofuel content of 10%, a foolish demand that will set aside 18% of EU farmland to cultivate crops to be burned as biofuel.

Big oil is also driving the biofuels bandwagon. Professor David Pimentel of Cornell University and other scientists claim that net energy output from bio-ethanol fuel is less than the fossil-fuel energy used to produce the ethanol. Measuring all energy inputs to produce ethanol, from production of nitrogen fertilizer to energy needed to clean the considerable waste from biofuel refineries, Pimintel's research showed a net energy loss of 22% for biofuels—they use more energy than they produce. That translates into little threat to oil demand and huge profit for clever oil giants that re-profile themselves as "green energy" producers.

So it's little wonder that ExxonMobil, Chevron and BP are all into biofuels. This past May, BP announced the largest ever research-and-development grant to a university, $500 million to the University of

California-Berkeley, to fund BP-dictated R&D into alternative energy, including biofuels. Stanford University's Global Climate and Energy Program got $100 million from ExxonMobil; University of California-Davis got $25 million from Chevron for its Bio-energy Research Group. Princeton University's Carbon Mitigation Initiative takes $15 million from BP.

Lord Browne, the disgraced former chief executive officer of BP, declared last year, "The world needs new technologies to maintain adequate supplies of energy for the future. We believe bioscience can bring immense benefits to the energy sector." The biofuel market is booming like few others today. This all is a paradise for global agribusiness industrial companies.

All this, combined with severe weather problems in China, Australia, Ukraine and large parts of the EU growing areas this harvest season, guarantees that grain prices are set to explode further in coming months and years. Some are gleefully reporting the end of the era of "cheap food." With disappearing food-security reserves and disappearing acreage going to plant corn and grains for food, the biofuel transformation will impact global food prices massively in coming years.

Another Agenda Behind Ethanol?

The dramatic embrace of biofuels by the Bush administration since 2005 has clearly been the global driver for soaring grain and food prices in the past 18 months. The evidence suggests this is no accident of sloppy legislative preparation. The US government has been researching and developing biofuels since the 1970s.

The bio-ethanol architects did their homework, we can be assured. It's increasingly clear that the same people who brought us oil-price inflation are now deliberately creating parallel food-price inflation. We have had a rise in average oil prices of some 300% since the end of 2000 when George W Bush and Dick "Halliburton" Cheney made oil the central preoccupation of US foreign policy.

Last year, as bio-ethanol production first became a major market factor, corn prices rose by some 130% on the Chicago Mercantile Exchange in 14 months. It was more than known when Congress and the Bush administration made their heavy push for bio-ethanol in 2005 that world grain reserves had been declining at alarming levels for several years at a time when global demand, driven especially by growing wealth and increasing meat consumption in China, was rising.

As a result of the diversion of record acreages of US and Brazilian corn and soybeans to biofuel production, food reserves are literally disappearing. Global food security, according to Food and Agriculture Organization data, is at its lowest since 1972. Curiously, that was just the time that Henry Kissinger and the Nixon administration engineered, in cahoots with Cargill and ADM—the major backers of the ethanol scam today—what was called the Great Grain Robbery, sale of huge volumes of US grain to the Soviet Union in exchange for sales of record volumes of Russian oil to the West. Both oil and corn prices rose by 1975 some 300–400% as a result. Just how that worked, I treated in detail in *A Century of War: Anglo-American Oil Politics*.

Today a new element has replaced Soviet grain demand and harvest shortfalls. Biofuel demand, fed by US government subsidies, is literally linking food prices to oil prices. The scale of the subsidized biofuel consumption has exploded so dramatically since the beginning of 2006, when the US Energy Policy Act of 2005 first began to impact crop-planting decisions, that there is emerging a de facto competition between people and cars for the same grains.

Environmental analyst Lester Brown recently noted, "We're looking at competition in the global market between 800 million automobiles and the world's 2 billion poorest people for the same commodity, the same grains. We are now in a new economic era where oil and food are interchangeable commodities because we can convert grain, sugarcane, soybeans—anything—into fuel for cars. In effect the price of oil is beginning to set the price of food."

In the mid-1970s, secretary of state Henry Kissinger, a protegé of the Rockefeller family and of its institutions, stated, "Control the oil and you control entire nations; control the food and you control the people." The same cast of characters who brought the world the Iraq war, and who cry about the "problem of world overpopulation," are now backing conversion of global grain production to burn as fuel at a time of declining global grain reserves. That alone should give pause for thought. As the popular saying goes, "Just because you're paranoid doesn't mean they aren't out to get you."

The Institute for Food and Development Policy (Food First) is dedicated to analyzing the root causes of global hunger, poverty, and ecological degradation, and works to develop solutions jointly with movements for social change.

2.7. "Biofuels: Myths of the Agro-Fuels Transition," Eric Holt-Gimenez, Food First

Biofuels invoke an image of renewable abundance that allows industry, politicians, the World Bank, the UN, and even the Intergovernmental Panel on Climate Change to present fuel from corn, sugarcane, soy and other crops as a smooth transition from peak oil to a renewable fuel economy. Myths of abundance divert attention away from powerful economic interests that benefit from this transition, avoiding discussion of the growing price that citizens of the Global South are beginning to pay to maintain the consumptive, oil-based lifestyle of the North. Biofuels mania obscures the profound consequences of the industrial transformation of our food and fuel systems—the agro-fuels transition.

The Agro-Fuels Boom

Industrialized countries have unleashed an "agro-fuels boom" by mandating ambitious renewable fuel targets. Renewable fuels are to provide 5.75% of Europe's transport fuel by 2010, and 10% by 2020. The US goal is 35 billion gallons a year. These targets far exceed the agricultural capacities of the industrial North. Europe would need to plant 70% of its farmland to fuel. The US's entire corn and soy harvest would need to be processed as ethanol and bio-diesel. Northern countries expect the Global South to meet their fuel needs, and southern governments appear eager to oblige. Indonesia and Malaysia are rapidly cutting down forests to expand oil-palm plantations targeted to supply up to 20% of the EU bio-diesel market. In Brazil—where fuel crops already occupy an area the size of Netherlands, Belgium, Luxembourg and Great Britain combined—the government is planning a five-fold increase in sugarcane acreage with a goal of replacing 10% of the world's gasoline by 2025.

The rapid capitalization and concentration of power within the agro-fuels industry is breathtaking. From 2004 to 2007, venture capital investment in agro-fuels increased eightfold. Private investment is swamping public research institutions, as evidenced by BP's recent award of half a billion dollars to the University of California. In open defiance of national anti-trust laws, giant oil, grain, auto and genetic engineering corporations are forming powerful partnerships: ADM with Monsanto, Chevron and Volkswagen; also BP with DuPont, and Toyota. These corporations are consolidating research, production, processing, and distribution chains of our food and fuel system under one colossal, industrial roof.

Agro-Fuel champions assure us that because fuel crops are renewable, they are environmentally-friendly, can reduce global warming, and will foster rural development. But the tremendous market power of global agro-fuel corporations, coupled with weak political will of governments to regulate their activities, is a recipe for environmental disaster and increasing hunger in the Global South. It's time to examine the myths fueling this agro-fuel boom—before it's too late.

Myth #1: Agro-Fuels are Clean and Green

Because photosynthesis from fuel crops removes greenhouse gases from the atmosphere and can reduce fossil fuel consumption, we are told fuel crops are green. But when the full "life cycle" of agro-fuels is considered—from land clearing to automotive consumption—the moderate emission savings are undone by far greater emissions from deforestation, burning, peat drainage, cultivation, and soil carbon losses. Every ton of palm oil produced results in 33 tons of carbon dioxide emissions—10 times more than petroleum. Tropical forests cleared for sugarcane ethanol emit 50% more greenhouse gasses than the production and use of the same amount of gasoline. Commenting on the global carbon balance, Doug Parr, chief UK scientist at Greenpeace, states flatly, "If even five percent of biofuels are sourced from wiping out existing ancient forests, you've lost all your carbon gain."

There are other environmental problems as well. Industrial agro-fuels require large applications of petroleum-based fertilizers, whose global use—now at 45 million tons/year—has more than doubled the biologically available nitrogen in the world, contributing heavily to the emission of nitrous oxide, a greenhouse gas 300 times more potent than CO^2. In the tropics—where most of the world's agro-fuels will soon be grown—chemical fertilizer has 10–100 times the impact on global warming compared to temperate soil applications. To produce a liter of ethanol takes three to five liters of irrigation water and produces up to 13 liters of waste water. It takes the energy equivalent of 113 liters of natural gas to treat this waste, increasing the likelihood that it will simply be released into the environment to pollute streams, rivers and groundwater. Intensive cultivation of fuel crops also leads to high rates of erosion, particularly in soy production—from 6.5 tons per hectare in the US to up to 12 tons per hectare in Brazil and Argentina.

Myth #2: Agro-Fuels will not Result in Deforestation

Proponents of agro-fuels argue that fuel crops planted on ecologically degraded lands will improve, rather than destroy, the environment. Perhaps the government of Brazil had this in mind when it re-classified some 200 million hectares of dry-tropical forests, grassland, and marshes as "degraded" and apt for cultivation. In reality, these are the bio-diverse ecosystems of the Mata Atlantica, the Cerrado, and the Pantanal, occupied by indigenous people, subsistence farmers, and extensive cattle ranches. The introduction of agro-fuel plantations will simply push these communities to the "agricultural frontier" of the Amazon where deforestation will intensify. Soybeans supply 40% of Brazil's diesel-fuels. NASA has positively correlated their market price with the destruction of the Amazon rainforest—currently at nearly 325,000 hectares a year. Called "The Diesel of Deforestation," palm oil plantations for bio-diesel are the primary cause of forest loss in Indonesia, a country with one of the highest deforestation rates in the world. By 2020, Indonesia's oil-palm plantations will triple in size to 16.5 million hectares—an area the size of England and

Wales combined—resulting in a loss of 98% of forest cover. Neighboring Malaysia, the world's largest producer of palm oil, has already lost 87% of its tropical forests and continues deforesting at a rate of seven percent a year.

Myth #3: Agro-Fuels will bring Rural Development

In the tropics, 100 hectares dedicated to family farming generates 35 jobs. Oil palm and sugarcane provide 10 jobs, eucalyptus two, and soybeans just one half job per 100 hectares, all poorly paid. Until this boom, agro-fuels primarily supplied local markets, and even in the US, most ethanol plants were small and farmer-owned. Big Oil, Big Grain, and Big Genetic engineering are rapidly consolidating control over the entire agro-fuel value chain. These corporations enjoy immense market power. Cargill and ADM control 65% of the global grain trade, Monsanto and Syngenta a quarter of the $60 billion gene-tech industry. This market power allows these companies to extract profits from the most lucrative and low-risk segments of the value chain—inputs, processing and distributing. Growers of fuel crops will be increasingly dependent on this global oligopoly of companies. In the long run, farmers are not likely to receive many benefits. Smallholders will likely be forced off the land. Hundreds of thousands have already been displaced by soybean plantations in the "Republic of Soy," a 50+ million hectare area covering southern Brazil, northern Argentina, Paraguay, and eastern Bolivia.

Myth #4: Agro-Fuels will not Cause Hunger

Hunger, said Amartya Sen, results not from scarcity, but poverty. According to the FAO, there is enough food in the world to supply everyone with a daily 3,200-calorie diet of fresh fruit, nuts, vegetables, dairy and meat. Nonetheless, because they are poor, 824 million people continue to go hungry. In 1996, world leaders promised to halve the proportion of hungry people living in extreme poverty by 2015. Little progress has been made. The world's poorest people already spend 50–80% of their total household income on food. They suffer when high fuel prices push up food prices. Now, because food and fuel crops are competing for land and resources, high food prices may actually push up fuel prices. Both increase the price of land and water. This perverse, inflationary spiral puts food and productive resources out of reach for the poor. The International Food Policy Research Institute warns that the price of basic food staples could increase 20–33% by the year 2010 and 26–135% by the year 2020. Caloric consumption typically declines as price rises by a ratio of 1:2. With every one percent rise in the cost of food, 16 million people are made food insecure. If current trends continue, some 1.2 billion people could be chronically hungry by 2025–600 million more than previously predicted. World food aid will not likely come to the rescue because surpluses will go into our gas tanks. What is urgently needed is massive transfers of food-producing resources to the rural poor; not converting land to fuel production.

Myth #5: Better "Second-generation" Agro-Fuels are Just Around the Corner

Proponents of agro-fuels argue that present agro-fuels made from food crops will soon be replaced with environmentally-friendly crops like fast-growing trees and switchgrass. This myth, wryly referred to as the "bait and switchgrass" shell game, makes food-based fuels socially acceptable.

The agro-fuel transition transforms land use on a massive scale, pitting food production against fuel production for land, water and resources. The issue of which crops are converted to fuel is irrelevant. Wild plants cultivated as fuel crops won't have a smaller "environmental footprint." They will rapidly migrate from hedgerows and woodlots onto arable lands to be intensively cultivated like any other industrial crop, with all the associated environmental externalities.

Industry aims to genetically engineer cellulosic agro-fuel crops that break down easily to liberate sugars, especially fast-growing trees. Trees are perennial and spread pollen farther than food crops. Cellulosic candidates miscanthus, switchgrass, and canary grass, are invasive, virtually assuring massive genetic contamination. Agro-Fuels will serve as the Monsanto/Syngenta genetic Trojan horse, allowing them to fully control both our fuel and food systems.

Cellulosic ethanol, a product that has yet to demonstrate any carbon savings, is unlikely to replace agro-fuel within the next five to eight years—in time to avoid the worst impacts of global warming. Major discoveries in plant physiology are required to permit the economically efficient breakdown of cellulose, hemi-cellulose, and lignin. Industry is either betting on miracles or counting on taxpayer bail-outs. Faith in science is not science. Selective faith in unproven and possibly unattainable second-generation biofuel—rather than working to improve existing solar, wind, or conservation technologies—is a bias in favor of agro-fuel giants.

Corporate Agro-Fuel: A New Industrial Revolution?

The International Energy Agency estimates that over the next 23 years, the world could produce as much as 147 million tons of agro-fuel. This will be accompanied by a lot of carbon, nitrous oxide, erosion, and over 2 billion tons of waste water. Remarkably, this fuel will barely offset the yearly increase in global oil demand, now standing at 136 million tons a year —and will not offset any of the existing demand.

The agro-fuel transition is based on a 200-year relation between agriculture and industry that began with the Industrial Revolution. The invention of the steam engine promised an end to drudgery. As governments privatized common lands, dispossessed peasants supplied cheap farm and factory labor. Cheap oil and petroleum-based fertilizers opened up agriculture itself to industry. Mechanization intensified production, keeping food prices low and industry booming. The second century saw a three-fold global shift to urban living with as many people now living in cities as in the countryside. The massive transfer of wealth from agriculture to industry, the industrialization of agriculture, and the rural-urban shift are all part of the "Agrarian Transition," transforming most of the world's fuel and food systems and establishing non-renewable petroleum as the foundation of today's multi-trillion dollar agri-foods industry.

The pillars of this agri-foods industry are the great grain corporations, including ADM, Cargill and Bunge. They are surrounded by an equally formidable consolidation of agro-chemical, seed, and machinery companies, on the one hand, and food processors, distributors, and supermarket chains, on the other. Together, these industries consume four of every five food dollars. However, profits have stalled for some time.

Government-subsidies and mandated targets for agro-fuels are the perfect answer to this slump in agribusiness profits, growing as oil shrinks, and concentrating market power in the hands of the most powerful players in the food and fuel industries. Like the original Agrarian Transition, the Corporate Agro-Fuels Transition will "enclose the commons" by industrializing the remaining forests and prairies of the world. It will drive the planet's remaining smallholders, family farmers, and indigenous peoples to the cities. This government-industry collusion has the potential to funnel rural resources to urban centers in the form of fuel, concentrating industrial wealth. But it may push millions of people into poverty and increase starvation-related deaths dramatically.

The agro-fuels transition suffers from a fatal flaw—there is no "new" industrial revolution. No expanding industrial sector waits to receive displaced indigenous communities, smallholders and rural workers. There are no production breakthroughs poised to flood the world with cheap food. This time, fuel will not subsidize agriculture with cheap energy. On the contrary, fuel will compete with food for land, water and resources. Corporate agro-fuels collapse the industrial link between food and fuel. The inherent entropy of industrial agriculture was invisible as long as oil was abundant. Now, food and fuel systems must shift from a savings to a checking account. Agro-Fuels lead us to overdraw. "Renewable" does not mean "limitless." While crops can be replanted, land, water, and nutrients are limited. Pretending otherwise serves the interests of those monopolizing these resources.

Agro-Fuel's appeal lies with its potential to prolong an industrial system based on oil. With an estimated one trillion barrels of oil reserves left on the planet, $100-a-barrel oil is not far off. The higher the oil prices, the more ethanol costs can rise while remaining competitive. As oil becomes more expensive, first generation agro-fuels become more lucrative, discouraging the development of second-generation bio-fuels. If oil reaches $80 per barrel, ethanol producers could afford to pay over $5 per bushel (~127 kg.) for corn, making it competitive with sugarcane. The planet's energy crisis is potentially an $80–100 trillion dollar bonanza for food and fuel corporations.

Limits—not incentives—must be placed on the corporate agro-fuels industry. If agro-fuels are to be forest and food friendly, grain, cane, and oil-palm industries require strong global management, regulation and enforcement. Strong, enforceable standards based on limiting land planted to agro-fuels are urgently needed, as are anti-trust laws powerful enough to prevent further corporate concentration. Sustainable benefits to the countryside will only accrue if agro-fuels complement local, regional and national plans for sustainable rural development.

Building Food—and Fuel—Sovereignty

The Corporate Agro-Fuels Transition is not inevitable. There is no inherent reason to sacrifice sustainable, equitable food and fuel systems to industry. Many successful, locally-focused, energy-efficient and people-centered alternatives are presently producing food and fuel in ways that do not threaten food systems, the environment, or livelihoods. The question is not whether ethanol and bio-diesel have a place in our future, but whether or not we allow a handful of global corporations to transform our food and fuel systems, destroy the planet's biodiversity and impoverish the majority of its people. To avoid this trap we must promote a steady-state agrarian transition built on re-distributive land reform that re-populates and stabilizes the world's struggling rural communities. This includes rebuilding and strengthening our local food systems, and creating conditions for the local re-investment of rural wealth. Putting people and environment—instead of corporate mega-profits—at the center of rural development requires food sovereignty: the right of people to determine their own food systems.

In both the Industrial North and the Global South, hundreds of thousands of producers and consumers are actively organizing for their right to healthy and culturally appropriate food produced through ecologically sound and sustainable methods. They are also re-building local food systems so that most of the wealth and benefits of these food systems accrue locally—not in the corporate coffers of the distant agri-foods giants. They are holding agri-foods corporations accountable for the externalities that their industry imposes on taxpayers in the form of hunger, environmental destruction and poor health from cheap, processed foods. Social movements for land reform, indigenous rights, farmer-to-farmer sustainable agriculture, ethical trade, farmers' markets, community-supported agriculture, inner-city gardens and neighborhood-food systems development, are a few examples of the widespread, multifaceted efforts for food sovereignty. Organizations like Via Campesina, Brazil's landless movement (MST), the Federation of Southern Cooperatives of African-American Farmers, and the Community Food and Justice Coalition (US), are transforming the social will from these rural and urban movements into political will—creating the change they envision.

Food Sovereignty movements are already squaring off with the agro-fuels boom. When US president George Bush arrived in Brazil to establish an ethanol partnership with President Lula, 700 women from Via Campesina protested by occupying Cargill's sugar mill in Sao Paulo. But derailing the agro-fuels juggernaut entails changing the Corporate Agro-Fuels Transition from an agrarian transition that favors industry to one that favors rural communities—a transition that does not drain wealth from the countryside, but that puts resources in the hands of rural peoples. This is a far-reaching project. A good next step would be a global moratorium on the expansion of corporate agro-fuels. Time and public debate is needed to assess the potential impacts of agro-fuels, and to develop the regulatory structures, programs, and incentives for conservation and food and fuel development alternatives. We need the time to forge a better transition —an agrarian transition for both food and fuel sovereignty.

In These Times is a journal dedicated to informing and analyzing popular movements for social, environmental, and economic justice. This article, as its title suggests, offers a balanced perspective on the ultimate efficacy of the biofuel policy, steering carefully between enthusiastic supporters and cynical naysayers. He concludes that, like so many government policies, its effectiveness will depend on how the government monitors and manages it.

2.8. "Biofuels: Promise or Peril?" David Moberg, *In These Times*

When Matt Hawkinson started growing corn in the rich farmland of western Illinois nearly a decade ago, he sold the grain for $2 a bushel, 50 cents less than it cost him to produce it. Recently, buyers have been paying him $4.35 a bushel. It's a welcome profit—even if it raises the cost of the hogs he feeds—and eliminates his need for government subsidies.

Hawkinson owes this good fortune to factories like those in the nearby towns of Galva and Pekin that turn corn into ethanol for fuel.

Yet the simple decision to make fuel from crops turns out to be anything but simple: it involves a tricky tangle of environmental, farm, trade, economic and foreign policy issues.

Biofuels—energy sources produced from dedicated crops and agricultural waste—have suddenly won wide support. The biofuel craze has been fueled by high oil prices, Mideast political turmoil, global warming fears, concern about low agricultural prices and high government subsidies, and the prospect of making money on the next big thing. Biofuels seem to promise a quick fix for worries about oil prices and supplies without the need for major technological changes. Is oil for the auto-industrial complex too expensive or fraught with problems? Just fill 'er up with biofuels.

But skeptics—on both the left and the right, including many environmentalists—argue that biofuels can't solve the world's energy problems. What's more, they argue, the biofuel solution threatens both the environment and the world's poor. In Mexico, the doubling of global ethanol production and quadrupling of bio-diesel production in the past five years has led to protests over high prices for corn tortillas. And in Southeast Asia and Latin America it has raised concerns that rainforests are being cleared to cultivate crops for fuel.

Both sides in the debate marshal studies predicting promise or peril. Ultimately, the evidence suggests that biofuels could be one valuable source of renewable energy. But for biofuels to deliver on that promise, governments will need to both tightly regulate agricultural and land-use practices, and carefully tailor trade and economic policies. Most important, the world—especially the United States—will have to greatly increase how efficiently it uses energy.

The Biofuel Allure

Biofuels seem straightforwardly attractive. Farmers capture solar energy though their crops, which take up carbon dioxide as they grow. Theoretically this off-sets the carbon dioxide released when they are burned, thus reducing the world's output of greenhouse gases (GHGs). Energy crops can be grown nearly everywhere, potentially providing income for peasants and farmers around the world. The main biofuels today are ethanol made from plant carbohydrates and sugars (like corn and sugarcane) and, to a lesser extent, biodiesel made from oilseeds (like soybeans, palm nuts, and rapeseed). Currently in development, and showing great promise, is ethanol made from woody, cellulosic plants (like switchgrass or miscanthus, as well as organic waste).

But cultivating the crops and processing them into fuel requires energy (or fossil fuel derivatives, like fertilizers), and much of that energy now comes from natural gas and coal. For years, scientists David Pimentel of Cornell and Tad Patzek of University of California at Berkeley have claimed that the energy output from ethanol made from biomass is less than the fossil-fuel energy used to produce the ethanol.

Other experts respond that their calculations of this energy balance fail to reflect the efficiencies of new facilities, overcount energy inputs and ignore the energy value of byproducts, such as the distillers' mash that animals can eat. In fact most studies show that ethanol from corn provides more energy than goes into its production, according to a 2006 review by Berkeley scientists Alexander Farrell, Daniel M. Kammen and others.

Yet in terms of global warming, the carbon balance—or contribution to reducing GHGs—is more important than the energy balance. The Berkeley review concludes that, overall, ethanol from current sources only modestly reduces GHGs.

Farming techniques and the choice of crops determine the extent to which biofuels reduce GHGs. For corn-based ethanol, the estimates range from a 36 percent reduction in GHGs to a 29 percent increase, depending on cultivation practices. The best reduction would come from using woody plants and grasses, like miscanthus and switchgrass, which could reduce GHGs by 90 percent compared to gasoline. In addition, some cellulosic feedstock plants can thrive in soils that are marginal or depleted, possibly enriching and saving the topsoil while sequestering carbon.

That is not what is happening in most of the tropics. In the near future, tropical biofuels from sugarcane and oil palm have a price advantage, and big agribusiness operators are slashing rainforests for plantations that deplete soils, reduce biodiversity and eliminate wildlife habitat. In 2006, the Worldwatch Institute reported, "If biofuels are produced from low-yielding crops, are grown on previously wild grasslands or forests, and/or are produced with heavy inputs of fossil energy, they have the potential to generate as much or more GHG emissions than petroleum fuels do." In Indonesia and Malaysia, for example, the burning of forests and peat bogs to clear land for palm oil plantations has unleashed vast quantities of carbon dioxide, overwhelming any modest GHG gains from bio-diesel.

Promise or Peril?

Energy farming also poses tough questions about how the world uses its land: Is there enough cultivable land to produce significant quantities of fuel? And won't fuel crops compete with food crops, raise food prices and hurt the world's poor?

Once again, the scientific estimates vary widely. According to World-watch, studies predict that bioenergy could sustainably provide more than twice the global energy demand and also project that "bioenergy could supply only a fraction of current energy use by 2050, perhaps even less than it does today."

The competition over use of land for food or fuel will be much greater in developing countries than in the United States, unless farmers grow energy crops on marginal lands or rely heavily on agricultural wastes. According to a December 2006 study by the International Food Policy Research Institute (IFPRI), a global think tank, producing enough ethanol to replace world gasoline demand would require five times more corn than is planted today and 15 times as much sugarcane, assuming those are the two main sources.

But the impact on food prices would depend on how the biofuel boom develops.

According to another IFPRI study, different mixtures of crops and technology improvements could raise corn prices by as much as 41 percent or as little as 23 percent by 2020. Higher grain prices will have a mixed effect: They would boost incomes of farmers throughout the world, and a large fraction of the world's poorest people are peasants. With higher grain prices, US and European farmers could sustain themselves without the current costly subsidies that lead to dumping underpriced grain on the world market, which drives down prices for peasants everywhere.

Local economies would grow and urban workers would also benefit, but probably not enough—certainly in the short run—to compensate for higher food prices. Critics worry that biofuel production will increase world hunger. But low incomes—not lack of food—are the main reason for world hunger. And the answer to that problem is to raise urban and rural workers' incomes, partly by assuring that all people have the right to organize industrially and politically.

But with big landowners and industrialists having the advantages of wealth and power, it is doubtful that farmers and peasants will reap the benefits of biofuels. David Morris, vice president of the St. Paul-based Institute for Local Self-Reliance, argues that ethanol programs in the United States must be designed to favor farmer-owned cooperatives, which have a significant but declining share of the American market.

If global trade in biofuels develops more dramatically, big business will promote biofuel exports over domestic food production in developing countries, and as a result the natural environment will be destroyed and peasants and tribal people will be forced off their lands. Some biofuel strategists, such as John Mathews, the Australian author of "A Biofuels Manifesto," argue that biofuels be certified in order to guarantee that they were produced in a socially and ecologically sustainable manner.

Fuel for Politics

US politicians of varied stripes have played up biofuels as a strategy for energy independence. But the biofuel market will continue to be influenced by petroleum prices. Ethanol is now profitable in the United States because oil prices are over the competitive threshold of $50 a barrel. But if corn prices go higher, or if oil prices drop, ethanol will be less competitive. Even now, domestic ethanol competes with Brazilian imports in large part because of a stiff tariff. And if tariffs are cut, as advocates of both free trade and cheap biofuels propose, the resulting increase in biofuel imports would undercut the goal of independence.

Though full energy independence may be illusory, increasing domestic biofuels production could significantly reduce the trade deficit. And poor, developing countries that are strapped for foreign exchange could benefit greatly from substituting home-grown fuels for imported oil.

Whether the biofuel boom benefits or harms mankind will depend on how countries regulate the agricultural and industrial practices used to produce biofuels, including how much peasants, small farmers and workers benefit from the biofuel industry.

The editors of the IFPRI study, "Bioenergy and Agriculture," conclude: "Because most of the environmental and social benefits and costs of bioenergy are not priced in the market, leaving bioenergy development entirely to the private sector and the market will lead to bioenergy production and processes that fail to achieve the best environmental and social outcomes." Public policy choices are critical.

Brazil, virtually tied with the United States as the world's largest ethanol producer, illustrates both the good and the bad. The country has introduced some policies that have helped increase the social and environmental payoffs. Initially, the government drove the development of an ethanol industry and both flex-fuel and ethanol cars. Now it promotes production of bio-diesel from crops grown on degraded, arid land in the historically poor Northeast, and it provides a seal of social responsibility for producers if the crops come from small family-owned farms. The government's ethanol policies have created 100,000 new jobs in the needy region and roughly 1 million new jobs in the whole country, while keeping 30 percent of sugarcane production in the hands of small farmers. Although sugarcane fields contribute to deforestation, cane is also planted on depleted rangeland, and the government requires than one-fourth of all plantation areas is left in natural vegetation to preserve biodiversity and natural predators of crop pests.

But huge monoculture plantations contribute to deforestation. And most of the new jobs are very poorly paid and temporary. Big corporations and large landowners are consolidating control, often pushing peasants off their land and triggering a growing rural conflict. (See "The Multinational Beanfield War.")

The biofuel potential will only be realized if governments everywhere push for energy efficiency and thereby reduce the need for massive farming for fuel. Daniel Kammen, a professor in the Energy and Resources Group at University of California, Berkeley, writes, "If the entire US vehicle fleet were replaced overnight with [plug-in hybrid electric vehicles that combine internal combustion engines with electric motors and large batteries for recharging from an outlet], the nation's oil consumption would decrease by 70 percent or more, completely eliminating the need for petroleum imports."

If the world—but especially the United States—takes advantage of existing possibilities for energy efficiency and designed biofuel policies to protect the environment as well as farmers and workers in the industry, then the potential for biofuels is rosy. If, however, we continue to leave the development of biofuels to big corporations and the free market, the biofuel dream could warp into a social and environmental nightmare.

www.inthesetimes.com

Stateline.org, an independent element of the Pew Research Center, is a non-partisan online resource for those who want to stay apprised of the activities of state governments. This post provides a balanced and informed state perspective on the prospects of ethanol.

2.9. "Ethanol Demand Outgrows Corn," Eric Kelderman, "Stateline.org"

Corn is king of renewable auto fuels, for now. But federal and state governments already are racing to find alternatives to corn as they look for ways to use ethanol to help break the nation's dependence on foreign oil.

Georgia Gov. Sony Perdue (R) announced in February that a Colorado company would build the nation's first commercial-scale ethanol plant using—not corn—but wood chips to produce 40 million gallons of fuel a year in the Peach State. A plant under construction in Louisiana is slated to produce 1.4 million gallons of ethanol annually from sugarcane waste. Tennessee has sunk $18 million into research to convert prairie grasses into auto fuel, and New York has awarded $25 million to two companies to produce more than 600,000 gallons of ethanol a year from wood chips and paper waste.

The US Department of Energy announced Tuesday (June 26) that it would spend $375 million in Tennessee, Wisconsin and California to develop more efficient ways to convert non-food crops into auto fuel. That money is in addition to $385 million the Energy Department is investing in ethanol plants that use something besides corn in California, Florida,

Georgia, Idaho, Iowa and Kansas. The six projects, announced in February, are expected to be finished within four years and be able to produce 130 million gallons of ethanol a year.

Currently, corn is the source of 98 percent of all ethanol, an alcohol that is blended with nearly half of the gasoline sold in the country to power cars and light trucks.

"In the final analysis, corn-based ethanol is practical now, but only as a transitional crop," said Robert J. Ludwig, a researcher with the Hale Group, a national consulting firm that specializes in agribusiness.

Still, these are heady times for Midwestern farmers who have been promoting ethanol since the energy crisis of the 1970s. Then, the relatively low cost of gasoline and high price of producing ethanol limited its appeal. Just 175 million gallons of ethanol were produced in 1980; by 1992, the industry crossed the 1 billion gallon mark, according to the Renewable Fuels Association (RFA), which promotes the ethanol industry.

Ethanol got a boost earlier this decade when several states began using it to meet federal Clean Air Act requirements to reduce summertime air pollution from vehicles, replacing the toxic gasoline additive MTBE (methyl tertiary butyl ether) that was found to leak into water supplies.

Now, skyrocketing gasoline prices and instability in world oil markets have intensified calls to reduce US oil imports. As a result, ethanol producers are expected to make at least 5.4 billion gallons of the fuel this year—double what was produced in 2003 and less than half of what is projected in 2009, according to the RFA.

The federal government offers a 51-cent-per-gallon subsidy for each gallon of ethanol blended with gasoline. Seven states require auto fuel in the state to contain a percentage of the largely corn-based biofuel. At least 10 give drivers a break on state gas taxes to fill their tanks with ethanol-blended gasoline, and more than 20 states are doling out tax incentives for producers to churn out ethanol made from corn or other organic materials, according to the American Coalition for Ethanol.

And the boom is expected to continue. President Bush called for the nation to reduce its gasoline use 20 percent by 2017 through a combination of higher mileage standards and expanded use of biofuels, alcohols distilled form organic matter. The US Senate recently passed a bill to require that 36 billion gallons of biofuels be used annually by 2022, with 21 billion gallons of fuel made from something besides corn. A 2005 federal energy law mandated 7.5 billion gallons by 2012.

But the limits of ethanol, especially fuel made from corn, are already in sight as the expansion of biofuels creates major shifts in the nation's agricultural markets and is being blamed for rising prices on foodstuffs from corn flakes to the milk to pour on them.

The price of corn, used primarily as feed for farm animals, has followed the growing appetite for ethanol, increasing as much as 66 percent in a year, according to the US Department of Agriculture. That's good for corn growers but raises the cost of feeding some livestock and poultry, especially outside the main corn producing states.

"Cattlemen aren't pleased," said Neil Moseman, assistant director of the Nebraska Department of Agriculture.

Beef and dairy farmers in Midwestern states that produce most of the nation's ethanol are able to feed their cattle with less expensive grains leftover from distilling that fuel. But ranchers in Texas and Oklahoma, which do not have large corn crops or produce as much ethanol, will be harder hit by high corn prices, Moseman said. In addition, hogs and poultry cannot digest the leftover grains from ethanol production, so those farmers will feel the pinch of higher corn prices, Moseman explained.

Along with making livestock feed more expensive, acres that have been dedicated to other crops or set aside for conservation now are being planted with corn, creating the biggest shift in planting patterns in the past century, said Ludwig of the Hale Group.

An annual federal report detailing farmers' planting plans estimates that corn acres will increase 15 percent over last year. Crops that likely will be supplanted by corn include rice and cotton with which US farmers are not competitive with growers in other countries, said Ludwig.

Farmers also could be induced to set aside less land for conservation or quit rotating crops on their land, sapping nutrients from the soil or causing more erosion, the US Department of Agriculture warns.

There are other hurdles to make renewable auto fuels a major replacement for gasoline over the long haul. Less than 1 percent of the nation's gas stations carry higher blends of ethanol necessary to make a significant dent in gasoline consumption, and only 2 of every 100 drivers are using cars and trucks that burn those higher ethanol blends.

All of the nation's cars can use a blend of gasoline containing as much as 10 percent ethanol. But even if all the gasoline used in a year in the United States were blended with that concentration of ethanol, the total amount of gasoline replaced would be roughly 14 billion gallons—one tenth of the roughly 140 billion gallons of gasoline used annually.

To reach the proposed federal goal of 36 billion gallons, more gas stations must sell so-called E-85, which has 85 percent ethanol and 15 percent gasoline. Only 1,232 of more than 170,000 gas stations across the country carry E-85, according to the National Ethanol Vehicle Coalition (NEVC). And the higher ethanol blend is completely unavailable in 10 states, according to NEVC's data: Alaska, Connecticut, Hawaii, Louisiana, Maine, New Hampshire, New Jersey, Rhode Island, Oklahoma and Vermont.

Although at least 26 states offer tax breaks, grants or low-interest loans to stations to install E-85 pumps, energy experts say the problem is too few vehicles capable of using the fuel. Retailers have little incentive to offer E-85 because only 6 million of the nation's 230 million cars and trucks are capable of using higher blends of ethanol.

"This is not going to happen overnight," said Larry Pearce, assistant director of the Nebraska Energy Office and a representative for the Governors Ethanol Coalition, a coalition of 36 states promoting ethanol.

The coalition is urging the federal Department of Energy to have a stronger hand in encouraging more E-85 pumps, said Pearce.

Frank O'Donnell is president of Clean Air Watch, a nonpartisan, nonprofit organization aimed at educating the public about clean air and the need for an effective Clean Air Act.

2.10. "Biofuel Backfire," Frank O'Donnell, "Tom Paine.com," October 26, 2007

It seems like only yesterday that "biofuels" was all the rage: not only has President Bush relentlessly touted increased ethanol use, but so has House Speaker Nancy Pelosi

The idea of increasing use of crops for fuel seemed to have it all—the outward virtues of reducing foreign oil use and helping the climate—and the political reality of letting both parties duke it out for the farm vote.

Not only that, but a successful biofuels mandate worked in Europe.

Or did it?

With Congress still wrestling behind closed doors over energy legislation, people are starting to take a closer look at the issue. And what they're seeing isn't pretty.

Senator Kay Bailey Hutchison, R-Texas, has stalled formal Senate and House negotiations on energy in part out of concern than more ethanol use could further drive up animal feed prices.

She's far from the only one concerned. The Washington-based International Food Policy Research Institute predicts that more use of biofuels could drive food prices 20–40 percent higher between now and 2020.

"Fuel made from food is a dumb idea, to put it succinctly," observed Ronald Steenblik, research director at the International Institute for Sustainable Development's Global Subsidies Initiative (GSI) in Geneva, Switzerland, who has studied Europe's experience with biofuels.

A follow-up analysis, released this week by my friends with the Boston-based Clean Air Task Force, ought to give everyone pause.

These researchers took an unbiased look at the European Union's effort to ramp up biofuels use. That mandate was driven primarily by farm policy (just like in the US, though we pretend otherwise), to create new markets for agricultural and forestry products.

But the Task Force found that the mandate "exacerbated some of the very problems it was designed to solve, driving up food prices, leading to increased deforestation in tropical countries, worsening global warming, and increasing imports of bio-oils."

Though reduced global warming emissions was supposed to be a side benefit of the mandate, the Task Force concluded that it actually led to the draining, clearing and burning of peat lands in Southeast Asia—making Indonesia the third largest source of global warming pollution after the US and China.

Even biofuels produced within Europe didn't produce such great results. New analyses are suggesting that increased use of nitrogen-based fertilizers and deforestation could erase any global warming gains.

This sort of talk seems to have panicked the ethanol lobby, which is accustomed to monopolizing policy discussions about fuel. Consider, for example, the salvos fired last week by Bob Dineen, president of the Renewable Fuels Association.

In rhetoric that seems borrowed from the National Rifle Association defense of assault weapons and former Vice President Spiro Agnew, Dineen assailed "nattering nabobs of negativity" and "well-funded opponents" that he charged "are engaged in a coordinated effort to protect the status quo." Asserting that "All ethanol, indeed all biofuels, are in this fight together," Dineen insinuated that anyone standing in his industry's way was a pawn of the oil industry. (A pretty ludicrous claim, by the way. The Clean Air Task Force, for example, doesn't take oil money.)

If we are going to deal with issues like this sensibly, you'd think we might want to dial down the rhetoric and carefully consider the facts. For example, that was the intention of a letter sent this week to congressional leaders from environmental and health groups, led by the American Lung Association (and including Clean Air Watch).

No one in this group voiced opposition to increased use of ethanol, but we do want to make sure the US Environmental Protection Agency has adequate authority to deal with unwanted possible consequences—such as more air pollution. The Clean Air Task Force also advocates the very sensible position of making sure we know as much as possible about the net impacts of making various sorts of biofuels.

But the latter recommendation may be too rational. For example, Sen. Barack Obama, D-Ill., has reacted to the congressional energy bill delay by joining with Sen. Tom Harkin, D-Iowa, to press for a stand-alone bill calling for more ethanol in gasoline, the vast majority of it from corn.

After all, it is only a few months until the Iowa Caucuses.

The Cato Institute and The Competitive Enterprise Institute are public policy think tanks, founded on the principles of free markets and limited government. Is it any surprise that they find the biofuel mandate totally unacceptable, though for different reasons?

2.11. "Dumb, Greedy, and Ugly," William A. Niskanen, The Cato Institute

Congress left town for its August recess with a bipartisan record that was dumb, greedy, and ugly.

The dumbest legislation of the year (so far) was the Senate energy bill. The primary provision of this bill would increase the average fuel economy of new cars, SUVs, and light trucks sold in the United States to 35 mpg by 2020, compared to the current standard of 27.5 mpg for cars and 22.2 mpg for SUVs and light trucks. Since the new fuel economy standard would apparently apply only to the average of all new vehicles, some government czar would have to set the standard for each automobile firm. The new standard, even if achieved, would not reduce fuel consumption in proportion to the increase in fuel economy, because it would reduce the fuel cost per mile and increase the total miles driven. The standard, by reducing the sales of new vehicles, would also reduce the rate at which older vehicles with lower pollution standards are replaced. The second major provision of the bill would increase the required use of biofuels from 4.7 billion gallons this year to 36 billion gallons a year by 2022. This would require more corn than is now produced in the United States, a subsidy of about $1 a gallon, and a roughly equal amount of petroleum to grow, harvest, and transport the corn and to produce and transport the ethanol. In addition, the mpg from an 85 percent ethanol-based fuel is only about 75 percent the mpg of the same vehicle using gasoline. At best, these two major provisions, at great cost, would only slightly reduce the US demand for oil with no direct effect on US oil imports. At the same time, the Senate bill would reduce the US supply of energy by authorizing new powers to investigate oil company pricing, making penalties for "price gouging," and denying approval for exploratory drilling in remote fields. Madness!

The greediest legislation of the year was the House farm bill—$25 billion of tax-financed subsidies a year, most of which will be paid to wealthy farmers that grow one of five crops, plus guarantees of high prices for a few other farm products such as milk and sugar. These measures are not necessary to assure an adequate food supply nor are they effective in reducing farm poverty. Most farm products are supplied without subsidy or price protection, and commercial farmers with an average annual income of $200,000 receive most of the farm subsidies. Not eligible for most subsidies, many small farmers are hurt by these measures, the result of lower crop prices and higher prices for farmland. Overplanting to increase subsidies leads to environmental damage. And by undermining the potential for negotiations to increase international trade, these measures raise consumer prices and restrict US exports. All of this is in addition to the huge increase in the use of biofuels required by the Senate energy bill. The supporters of the farm bill no longer make any pretense that it serves the interests of consumers and taxpayers. Brian Riedl of the Heritage Foundation concludes that "lawmakers would be hard-pressed to enact a set of policies more destructive to farmers, taxpayers, consumers, the environment, trade, global anti-poverty efforts . . . than the current farm policies."

The ugliest legislative debate of the year was over the immigration bill. Senate Republicans blocked a comprehensive immigration bill similar to that which passed the Senate last year when they were the majority party. The bill was not perfect, but it acknowledged that there are about 12 million illegal immigrants already in the United States by allowing illegal immigrant workers to apply for a new "Z-visa" by paying a $5,000 fine and a $1,500 processing fee and demonstrating a record of sustained work and no serious crime. Within eight years, the household heads could return to their former home country to apply for permanent residency but would be at the end of the line of the millions who had already applied for this status. Critics of this bill dismissed this provision as "amnesty," even though it would have been earned by paying a substantial fine and proof of a productive record. With no change in the legal status of the illegal immigrants now in the United States, we are left with the measures to secure the southern border that were approved in 2006—an ugly fence across about one-third of the border plus a substantial increase in border guards and the capacity of the detention centers. There are legitimate concerns about border security, the rule of law, and the fiscal costs of increased immigration. Nevertheless, the defeat of this bill reflects a stronger and uglier nativist sentiment in American politics than we have observed in several decades. In contrast, the United States absorbed a much higher rate of immigration a century ago, primarily from the poorer countries of Europe, without provoking such a nativist political response, and most of those immigrant families became fully assimilated Americans within a generation or so. In the meantime, of course, the United States developed a substantial welfare state, so immigrants now pose a fiscal threat that was not the case a century ago. As I concluded in this space a year ago, however: "Building a wall around the welfare state would eliminate most of the costs of increased immigration to the rest of us. Building a wall around the country, in contrast, is unnecessary, futile, and morally offensive."

2.12. "Biofuels, Food, or Wildlife? The Massive Land Costs of US Ethanol," Dennis Avery, Competitive Enterprise Institute, September 21, 2006

The high price of fossil fuels, environmental concerns, and geopolitical instability in some major oil-producing nations have spurred intense interest in the United States in alternative fuels, especially from renewable energy sources.

While popular with environmental activists, wind and solar power, because of their costs and unreliability, are not expected to grow significantly, even with massive subsidies.

Nuclear power is still viewed with suspicion, even though other countries, including France, supply a majority of their energy needs from nuclear plants.

Crop-based fuel production, especially corn ethanol, has been the main focus of interest, with government subsidies and mandates stimulating demand. Cellulosic ethanol produced from crop wastes has been heralded as the alternative fuel of the future, but it is yet to be produced in other than experimental production facilities. More recently, Brazil's example of producing ethanol from sugarcane has been presented as a model for the United States to follow.

There are significant trade-offs, however, involved in the massive expansion of the production of corn and other crops for fuel. Chief among these would be a shift of major amounts of the world's food supply to fuel use when significant elements of the human population remains ill-fed.

Even without ethanol, the world is facing a clash between food and forests. Food and feed demands on farmlands will more than double by 2050. Unfortunately, the American public does not yet understand the massive land requirements of US corn ethanol nor the unique conditions that have allowed sugarcane ethanol to make a modest energy contribution in Brazil.

The United States might well have to clear an additional 50 million acres of forest—or more—to produce economically significant amounts of liquid transport fuels. Despite the legend of past US farm surpluses, the only large reservoir of underused cropland in America is about 30 million acres of land—too dry for corn—enrolled in the Conservation Reserve. Ethanol mandates may force the local loss of many wildlife species, and perhaps trigger some species extinctions. Soil erosion will increase radically as large quantities of low-quality land are put into fuel crops on steep slopes and in drought-prone regions.

The market is already responding to the high price of oil, as investors flock to alternative fuels, including investments in cellulosic ethanol research and development. Those developments are healthy, if markets are allowed to discover the winners and losers in future alternative energy sources without government intervention through subsidies and fuel mandates, and with a clear assessment of the trade-offs that may be involved.

CorpWatch is a research organization working to foster global justice, independent media activism, and democratic control over corporations.

2.13. "Green Fuel's Dirty Secret," Sasha Lilley, CorpWatch, June 1, 2006

The town of Columbus, Nebraska, bills itself as a "City of Power and Progress." If Archer Daniels Midland gets its way, that power will be partially generated by coal, one of the dirtiest forms of energy. When burned, it emits carcinogenic pollutants and high levels of the greenhouse gases linked to global warming.

Ironically this coal will be used to generate ethanol, a plant-based petroleum substitute that has been hyped by both environmentalists and President George Bush as the green fuel of the future. The agribusiness giant Archer Daniels Midland (ADM) is the largest US producer of ethanol, which it makes by distilling corn. ADM also operates coal-fired plants at its company base in Decatur, Illinois, and Cedar Rapids, Iowa, and is currently adding another coal-powered facility at its Clinton, Iowa ethanol plant.

That's not all. "[Ethanol] plants themselves—not even the part producing the energy—produce a lot of air pollution," says Mike Ewall, director of the Energy Justice Network. "The EPA (US Environmental Protection Agency) has cracked down in recent years on a lot of Midwestern ethanol plants for excessive levels of carbon monoxide, methanol, toluene, and volatile organic compounds, some of which are known to cause cancer."

A single ADM corn-processing plant in Clinton, Iowa generated nearly 20,000 tons of pollutants including sulfur dioxide, nitrogen oxides, and volatile organic compounds in 2004, according to federal records. The EPA considers an ethanol plant as a "major source" of pollution if it produces more than 100 tons of any one pollutant per year, although it has recently proposed increasing that cap to 250 tons.

Sulfur dioxide is classified by the EPA as a contributor to respiratory and heart disease and the generation of acid rain. Nitrogen oxides produce ozone and a wide variety of toxic chemicals as well as contributing to global warming, according to the EPA, while many volatile organic compounds are cancer-causing. Last year, Environmental Defense, a national environmental group, ranked the Clinton plant as the 26th largest emitter of carcinogenic compounds in the US.

For years, ADM promoted itself as the "supermarket to the world" on major US radio and television networks like NPR, CBS, NBC, and PBS where it underwrites influential programs such as the News Hour with Jim Lehrer. Now, as it actively promotes its ethanol business, ADM has rolled out its new eco-friendly slogan, "Resourceful by Nature" which "reinforces our role as an essential link between farmers and consumers."

Despite the company's attempts at green packaging, ADM is ranked as the tenth worst corporate air polluter, on the "Toxic 100" list of the Political Economy Research Institute at the University of Massachusetts.

The Department of Justice and the Environmental Protection Agency has charged the company with violations of the Clean Air Act in hundreds of processing units, covering 52 plants in 16 states. In 2003 the two agencies reached a $351 million settlement with the company. Three years earlier, ADM was fined $1.5 million by the Department of Justice and $1.1 million by the State of Illinois for pollution related to ethanol production and distribution. Currently, the corporation is involved in approximately 25 administrative and judicial proceedings connected to federal and state superfund laws regarding the environmental clean-up of sites contaminated by ADM operations.

Friends in High Places

Environmentalists have cried foul, but they are up against the 56th largest company in the United States, as ranked by revenue in *Fortune Magazine.* ADM has more than 25,000 employees, net sales last year of $35.9 billion, with $1 billion in profits, as well as a recent 29 percent profit increase in the last quarter. The company is a global force: ADM is one of the world's biggest processors of soybeans, corn, wheat, and cocoa, which it buys from growers in the US and around the world. The company recently hired Patricia A. Woertz, an executive vice president of Chevron Corporation, as its chief executive officer.

ADM has another resource at its disposal, the considerable clout it has built up over decades of courting and lobbying Washington's power brokers. Days after the company's February expansion announcement of the coal-fired Nebraska plant, US Energy Secretary Samuel W. Bodman visited ADM's Decatur headquarters to tout its part in President Bush's Biofuels Initiative. The secretary posed for photos with then ADM Chair G. Allen Andreas and announced that the Department of Energy would offer up to $160 million for the construction of three bio-refineries to expand US ethanol production.

"Partnerships with industry like these will lead to new innovation and discovery that will usher in an era of reduced dependence on foreign sources of oil, while strengthening our economy at home," Secretary Bodman said from ADM's trade floor. Like the ADM ethanol plant in Columbus, the three bio-refineries could well be partially coal-powered, given the absence of conditions imposed by the Department of Energy.

"It's been some 30 years since we got a call from the White House asking for the agricultural industry, ADM in particular, to take a serious look at the possibilities of building facilities to produce alternative sources of energy for our fuel supply in the United States," said Allen Andreas, who was chair, chief executive and president of ADM at the time of Secretary Bodman's visit. "We are delighted to participate in any way that we can in the president's programs."

ADM and its signature project have never lacked friends in high places, despite a history of price-fixing scandals and monopolistic misdeeds. The Andreas family, which has headed up the publicly-traded company for decades, has cultivated bipartisan support through generous donations to both Republicans and Democrats. Since the 2000 election cycle, ADM has given more than $3 million in political contributions, according to the Center for Responsive Politics: $1.2 million to Democrats and $1.85 million to Republicans. These donations may have helped sustain a multitude of government subsidies to ADM, including ethanol tax credits, tariffs against foreign ethanol competitors, and federally mandated ethanol additive standards.

Politicians from the Midwestern Corn Belt are some of the company's staunchest allies. Senators Richard Durbin, Charles Grassley, and Tom Harkin, and Representative Dick Gephardt have consistently supported lavish federal tax subsidies to ethanol producers, for which ADM is the prime beneficiary. All are recipients of political action committee donations from the agribusiness behemoth. *The Wall Street Journal* has referred to the former South Dakota senator and Senate minority leader as "Archer Daschle Midland," because of his unswerving support for the interests of the company.

ADM's political heft was behind the 54 cent per gallon tariff that the US government has imposed on imports of sugarcane-based ethanol from Brazil, which is cheaper than ADM's corn-based fuel. The tariff dates back to 1980 when the CEO of ADM convinced President Carter to adopt it, according to former ADM lobbyist Joseph Karth. Iowa's Senator Grassley recently stated his intention to block any attempt to remove the tariff on lower-cost Brazilian fuel in the face of rising gas prices, stating that "lifting this tariff would be counter-productive to the widely supported goal of promoting home-grown renewable sources of energy."

Over many decades, the company has been the recipient of government largesse in the form of federal and state corn and ethanol subsidies that have totaled billions of dollars, prompting the libertarian Cato Institute to declare ADM the biggest recipient of corporate welfare in the US in 1995. ADM has been a prime beneficiary of the federal tax credit on ethanol, which the refiner can apply to the tax it pays on corporate income. First implemented in 1978, the tax credit currently stands at 51 cents per gallon of ethanol sold. The Government Accounting Office estimates the subsidies to the ethanol industry from 1980–2000 at $11 billion. As the biggest ethanol producer in the US, ADM has received the largest portion of the government's generosity.

Recent legislation has further greased the tracks of the ethanol gravy train. The Energy Policy Act of 2005's Renewable Fuel Standard stipulates that gasoline sold in the US must include a certain percentage of ethanol or bio-diesel, starting at 4 billion gallons this year and rising to 7.5 billion gallons by 2012. ADM got another boost when the federal government mandated that oil companies replace MTBE, a cancer-causing gasoline additive, with ethanol. Forty-five states have adopted policies to encourage the production and use of the fuel. ADM has responded with plans to increase its output of ethanol by 42 percent over the next three years.

When Corn is King

Subsidies and tax incentives might make public policy sense—even when they flow into the coffers of a Fortune 500 company with mega-profits—but only if corn ethanol delivers on the promise that its boosters claim: to significantly cut greenhouse emissions, protect the environment, and slow global warming.

Debate has raged for years over whether ethanol made from corn generates more energy than the amount of fossil fuel that is used to produce it. UC Berkeley's Alexander Farrell recently co-authored a comprehensive study, published in *Science*, on the energy and greenhouse gas output of various sources of ethanol. His group found that corn ethanol reduces greenhouse gases by only 13 percent, which compares unfavorably with ethanol made from vegetable cellulose such as switchgrass. "Our best guess," says Farrell, "is that using corn ethanol today results in a modest decline of greenhouse gas emissions."

Yet the enormous amounts of corn that ADM and other ethanol processors buy from Midwestern farmers wreak damage on the environment in a multiplicity of ways. Modern corn hybrids require more nitrogen fertilizer, herbicides, and insecticides than any other crop, while causing the most extensive erosion of top soil. Pesticide and fertilizer runoff from the vast expanses of corn in the US prairies bleed into groundwater and rivers as far as the Gulf of Mexico. The nitrogen runoff flowing into the Mississippi River has fostered a vast bloom of dead algae in the Gulf that starves fish and other aquatic life of oxygen.

To understand the hidden costs of corn-based ethanol requires factoring in "the huge, monstrous costs of cleaning up polluted water in the Mississippi River drainage basin and also trying to remedy the negative effects of poisoning the Gulf of Mexico," says Tad Patzek of the University of California's Civil and Environmental Engineering department.

"These are not abstract environmental effects," Patzek asserts, "these are effects that impact the drinking water all over the Corn Belt, that impact also the poison that people ingest when they eat their food, from the various pesticides and herbicides." Corn farming substantially tops all crops in total application of pesticides, according to the US Department of Agriculture, and is the crop most likely to leach pesticides into drinking water.

While banned by the European Union, atrazine is the most heavily used herbicide in the United States—primarily applied to cornfields—and the EPA rates it as the second most common pesticide in drinking wells. The EPA has set maximum safe levels of atrazine in drinking water at 3 parts per billion, but scientists with the US Geological Survey have found up to 224 parts per billion in Midwestern streams and 2,300 parts per billion in Corn Belt irrigation reservoirs.

Then there is the question of how practical it is to replace petroleum with corn-based ethanol. "There are conflicting figures on how much land would be needed to meet all of our petroleum demand from ethanol," says Energy Justice Network's Ewall, "and those range from some portion of what we currently have as available crop land to as much as five times as the amount of crop land in the US." The Department of Agriculture estimates that the Corn Belt has lost 90 percent of its original wetlands, two-thirds of which has taken place since draining for agriculture began mid-century.

"No one who's looked at this issue [from an environmental perspective] talks about using corn kernels as the only, or even major component, of the long-term solution," counters Nathanael Greene, senior policy analyst with the Natural Resources Defense Council. "Everyone assumes we'll evolve the industry from its current technology to the advanced technologies."

If that happens, it will be a marked reversal of many decades of government policy in support of Archer Daniels Midland—and the company may well wonder what it's getting for its unceasingly ample gifts to both political parties. But with the "full-throated support of the Bush Administration," in the words of the Renewable Fuels Association, a corn ethanol-dominated, ADM-led trade group, that day doesn't seem to be approaching any time soon.

www.corpwatch.org

The Washington Spectator *describes itself as a "feisty bulletin for independent-minded readers," covering the federal government and Wall Street. The piece below "exposes" what is evident to most political observers—the enormous influence of ethanol on presidential politics. Robert Bryce all but says that, but for Iowa's pivotal role in determining the parties' nominees, we wouldn't have an ethanol revolution.*

2.14. "Ethanol is the Agricultural Equivalent of Holy Water," Robert Bryce, *The Washington Spectator*

Ethanol is a magic elixir. It allows politicians and political operatives to promise voters that America can achieve "energy independence." In this new energy Valhalla, American farmers will be rich, fat and happy, thanks to all the money they will be making from "energy crops." Better yet, US soldiers will never again need to visit the Persian Gulf—except, perhaps, on vacation. With enough ethanol-blended motor fuel, America can finally dictate terms to those rascally Arab sheikhs with their rag-covered heads, multiple wives and supertankers loaded with sulfurous crude.

George W. Bush believes. In January, he declared that the US should be producing 35 billion gallons of ethanol and other alternative fuels by 2017. During a March trip to Latin America, where he signed an agreement to expand ethanol-related trade between the US and Brazil, Bush said that he was "very upbeat about the potential of biofuel and ethanol."

Not to be outdone, former North Carolina senator John Edwards declared that the US should be producing 65 billion gallons of ethanol per year by 2025. He claims that his proposed New Economy Energy Fund will "develop new methods of producing and using ethanol, including cellulosic ethanol, and offer loan guarantees to new refineries."

Even longtime ethanol foe Senator John McCain—who in the past has called ethanol "highway robbery" and a "giveaway to special interests" —has become an ethanol evangelist. Last August, during a visit to Iowa, the Republican presidential hopeful called ethanol "a vital alternative energy source not only because of our dependency on foreign oil but its greenhouse-gas reduction effects."

Every major presidential candidate has come out in favor of ethanol. So have the Democrats on Capitol Hill. Speaker of the House Nancy Pelosi wants automakers to build more ethanol-fueled vehicles and wants to see "America's farmers fueling America's energy independence."

It all sounds wonderful. But there is a bushelful of problems with ethanol, none of which fit neatly into a politician's soundbite. Of those many problems, four stand out: the massive subsidies; ethanol's inability to displace significant amounts of imported oil; its deleterious effect on air quality; and its effect on food prices.

Inconvenient Facts

First, the subsidies. Making ethanol from corn borders on fiscal insanity. It uses taxpayer money to make subsidized motor fuel from the single most subsidized crop in America. Between 1995 and 2005, federal corn subsidies totaled $51.2 billion. In 2005 alone, according to data compiled by the Environmental Working Group, corn subsidies totaled $9.4 billion. That $9.4 billion is approximately equal to the budget for the US Department of Commerce, a federal agency that has 39,000 employees.

Need another comparison? That $9.4 billion is nearly twice as much as the federal government spends on WIC, short for the Special Supplemental Nutrition Program for Women, Infants and Children, a program that provides health care and nutrition assistance for low-income mothers and children under the age of five.

Corn subsidies dwarf all other agricultural subsidy programs. The $51.2 billion that American taxpayers spent on corn subsidies between 1995 and 2005 was twice as much as the amount spent on wheat subsidies, more than twice as much as the amount spent on cotton, four times as much as the amount spent on soybeans and 96 times as much as the total subsidies for tobacco during that period.

But the ethanol lobby isn't satisfied with the subsidies paid out to grow the grain. They are also getting huge subsidies to turn that grain into fuel. According the Global Subsidies Initiative, meeting Bush's goal of producing 35 billion gallons of renewable and alternative fuels per year by 2017 will require total subsidies of $118 billion. The group claims that the $118 billion price tag "would be the minimum subsidy" over the eleven-year period. In a report released on February 9, the group said that adding in tax breaks that the corn distillers are getting from state and local governments and federal tariffs imposed on foreign ethanol (mostly from Brazil) "would likely add tens of billions of dollars of subsidies" to the $118 billion estimate.

Despite the subsidies, ethanol has always been more expensive than gasoline. Between 1982 and 2006, the price of ethanol never dropped below that of gasoline—even though ethanol contains just two-thirds of the heat energy of gasoline. That lower energy content means a car using ethanol gets worse gas mileage than one that uses gasoline.

The second problem: no matter how you slice it, ethanol production is just too small to have a significant effect on the overall energy market in the US.

Ethanol advocates talk about how domestically produced ethanol will reduce the amount of oil America imports. But by any measure, the total energy produced by America's ethanol plants borders on the insignificant. In 2006, the US produced about 5 billion gallons of ethanol. That's the equivalent of just 215,264 barrels of oil per day. For comparison, the US now consumes over 21 million barrels of oil per day. Thus, ethanol provides just one percent of total US oil consumption.

Ethanol will never make a big dent in America's oil imports. And that's true even if all the corn grown in America were turned into ethanol. The US Department of Agriculture estimates that distillers can get 2.7 gallons of ethanol out of one bushel of corn. In 2006, US farmers produced about 10.5 billion bushels of corn. Converting all that corn into fuel would produce about 28.3 billion gallons of ethanol. However, ethanol's lower heat content means that the actual output would be equivalent to 18.7 billion gallons of gasoline, or about 1.2 million barrels per day. (The US currently imports 10.1 million barrels per day.) Even if the US turned all its corn crop into ethanol, it would supply less than 6 percent of America's total oil needs.

The Grocery Tax

While Americans are breathing more polluted air due to ethanol, they are also paying more at the grocery store, a fact that leads to the fourth problem: ethanol is increasing food prices.

Last month, researchers from Iowa State University's Center for Agricultural and Rural Development released a report that looked at how ethanol production—which consumed 20 percent of America's corn crop in 2006—is affecting overall food prices. They found that increased ethanol production has resulted in higher prices on a panoply of foods, including: cheese, ice cream, eggs, poultry, pork, cereal, sugar, and beef. The researchers reported that between July 2006 and May 2007, the food bill for every American has increased by about $47 as a result of surging prices for corn and the associated price increases of other grains like soybeans and wheat. In aggregate, they concluded that American consumers will face a "total cost" for ethanol "of about $14 billion."

Let's put that $14 billion in perspective. Last year, the US produced five billion gallons of ethanol. That means that Americans are effectively paying a new tax (in the form of higher food costs) of nearly $3 for each gallon of ethanol produced. And that doesn't count any of the subsidies for corn production mentioned above or the 51-cents-per-gallon federal tax credit given to companies that blend ethanol into gasoline. Worse yet, it's not just Americans who are being fleeced. The Iowa State researchers determined that, thanks to ethanol's voracious appetite for grain, "the rest of the world's consumers [will] also see higher food prices."

What about cellulosic ethanol, the fuel that can be made from grass, wood, and straw? Al Gore claims that cellulosic ethanol will be "a huge new source of energy, particularly for the transportation sector. You're going to see it all over the place." Bill Clinton says there's enough biomass to "make cellulosic ethanol all over America." Bush, in his 2006 State of the Union speech, said that he wanted to make cellulosic ethanol "practical and competitive within six years."

Alas, cellulosic ethanol is like the tooth fairy, an entity that many people believe in, but no one ever sees. Despite years of hype, there is no significant production of cellulosic ethanol, except in very small, non-commercial distilleries. Maybe that's a good thing, because the more ethanol that's burned in American automobiles, the worse the air quality gets—a fact that leads to the third problem.

The Environmental Protection Agency's website says the agency's mission is "to protect human health and the environment." And yet when it comes to ethanol, the EPA has stated in very clear language that increased use of ethanol in gasoline will mean worse air quality in America.

Of course, that's not the official story. In an April 10 press release announcing the Renewable Fuel Standard—the federal program mandated by Congress when it passed the Energy Policy Act of 2005—EPA Administrator Stephen L. Johnson declared that the use of more ethanol "offers the American people a hat trick—it protects the environment, strengthens our energy security, and supports America's farmers." Yet on that very same day, Johnson's agency issued a fact sheet that said using more ethanol will result in major increases in the release of two of the worst air pollutants: volatile organic compounds and nitrogen oxides. The fact sheet said that "Nationwide, EPA estimates an increase in total emissions of volatile organic compounds and nitrogen oxides (VOC + NOx) [of] between 41,000 and 83,000 tons." It went on, saying, "areas that experience a substantial increase in ethanol may see an increase in VOC emissions between four and five percent and an increase in NOx emissions between 6 and 7 percent from gasoline powered vehicles and equipment."

NOx is a precursor to fine particulate, which is known to cause thousands of premature deaths each year. VOCs lead to the creation of ground-level ozone, one of the most dangerous urban pollutants. According to the EPA's website, ozone "can trigger a variety of health problems including chest pain, coughing, throat irritation, and congestion. It can worsen bronchitis, emphysema, and asthma."

The negative health effects of ethanol-blended gasoline have placed the EPA in the odd position of enforcing rules that run directly counter to its stated goals. On its website, the agency says that "reducing emissions of NOx is a crucial component of EPA's strategy for cleaner air." Nevertheless, when asked about the higher emissions related to ethanol, EPA spokesperson Jennifer Wood insisted that they are "very minimal increases." She also told me that the agency has other "tools under the Clean Air Act to reduce NOx."

Wood's claim leaves clean air advocates like William Becker of the National Association of Clean Air Agencies gasping. He said the EPA is "scoffing at a 4 to 7 percent increase in air emissions at a time when agencies across the country would do anything to achieve that kind of a reduction in VOCs and NOx." Becker's Washington-based group represents the interests of air pollution control authorities from 49 of the 50 states and several territories, as well as local agencies from 165 metro areas around the US. He said the pollution increases admitted by EPA are "a significant amount of emissions in any location in this country. And we can't just willy nilly be giving it away, particularly when states are struggling to meet current ozone standards."

The EPA's ethanol fact sheet infuriates Debbie Cook, mayor pro tem of Huntington Beach, a city located west of Los Angeles that struggles with air-quality problems. "The EPA's air quality rules in Southern California are largely a joke," Cook told me shortly after the EPA announcement. And the agency's April 10 statement touting ethanol, she says, "makes the joke worse."

It's not just the EPA that says ethanol is bad for air quality. Numerous studies have reached the same conclusion.

In 2004, the California Air Resources Board released a study saying that gasoline containing ethanol caused VOC emissions to increase by 45 percent when compared to pure gasoline. In 2006, the South Coast Air Quality Management District—the agency that oversees air quality issues for some 15 million people living in or near Los Angeles County—determined that gasoline containing 5.7 percent ethanol may add as much as 70 tons of VOCs per day to the state's air. This means that the Los Angeles area alone would account for about 25,500 tons of additional volatile organic compounds per year—or more than half of the minimum amount (41,000 tons) estimated by the EPA in its April 10 fact sheet.

In April, Mark Z. Jacobson, an engineering professor at Stanford University, published a study concluding that the widespread use of E-85 (fuel that contains 85 percent ethanol and 15 percent gasoline) "may increase ozone-related mortality, hospitalization, and asthma by about 9 percent in Los Angeles and 4 percent in the United States as a whole" when compared to the use of regular gasoline. Jacobson also found that because of its ozone-related effects, E-85 "may be a greater overall public health risk than gasoline."

Iowa Rules

Given the many problems associated with ethanol . . . why are members of Congress and presidential candidates eager to embrace it? Why has such an expensive, polluting, fuel become what one critic calls "the agricultural equivalent of holy water?" There are two plausible explanations: the value of empty—but appealing—political rhetoric; and the Iowa Imperative.

Ethanol boosters claim that ethanol is part of the prescription for energy independence—a concept that polls extremely well. The idea of energy independence appeals to a wide range of voters from the left and the right. The result: almost anything that promises to move America toward that goal—a goal that is neither achievable nor desirable because of the enormous costs it would entail—quickly garners wide support and massive subsidies.

Second, it's about Iowa, America's leading ethanol producer. Any candidate who wants to win the White House must have a good showing in the Iowa caucuses, which will be held January 14. The numbers explain the imperative: Since 2002, the amount of Iowa corn going into ethanol production has tripled. The state now has some 21 ethanol plants and another 23 either planned or under construction. About 2,500 jobs are directly related to ethanol production and another 14,000—according to IowaCorn.org—are "affected" by ethanol. Those jobs are supported by huge federal subsidies. In 2005 alone, according to the Environmental

Working Group, Iowa got $1.8 billion in corn subsidies—about $608 for every Iowan.

Given those numbers, it's hardly surprising that a January 2007 poll found that 92 percent of Iowa voters believe ethanol is important to the state's economic future. That's explains why "when politicians come to Iowa, they have to say ethanol is great," says Iowa State University political science professor Steffen Schmidt. Alas, what makes the ethanol business great for 3 million Iowans is bad for 297 million other Americans: It's bad for taxpayers, bad for air quality, bad for people who like to eat, and it will have no real effect on America's overall energy mix.

Aside from those little quibbles, ethanol truly is a miracle potion. Expect to hear more about it as the presidential campaign continues.

QUESTIONS FOR CONSIDERATION

1   The Background statement preceding the documents raises the overarching ethical concern with the new biofuel mandate: Is it appropriate to "trade food for fuel"? Is that what this bill does? How else can one look at it?

2   Historically, the federal government has served as a social engineer in the area of agriculture, by providing subsidies to crops it wants to competitively advantage. But here, the government is going one step further in literally mandating the production of a crop. Is the step from subsidy to mandate good, or even acceptable, public policy? Some may argue that this is what the autocratic Communist governments we used to decry did, utilizing a strong central authority to replace market-driven forces. Have we duplicated here what we found so unacceptable a few decades back in Russia?

3   Why has this particular policy in the Energy Independence and Security Act of 2007 received so much less media attention than the far more modest requirement that automobile manufacturers make and market cars that meet more stringent fuel efficiency standards?

4   Should the effect on foreign countries—especially economically disadvantaged and undeveloped ones where hunger and poverty are common—be considered in our own policymaking?

5   Is it troubling that our historically generous corn subsidies, to say nothing of our newly minted renewable fuels policy, are driven by presidential politics, as the last document alleges? Put more succinctly, is the fact that Iowa's caucuses are so pivotal in determining our presidential candidates defensible in light of the effect of corn surpluses on our agricultural landscape in general, the world food situation, our nation's land use policies, our growing obesity plague, and countless other manifestations? Does Iowa reach Nairobi?

Chapter 3

Corporate Average Fuel Economy Regulations (CAFE Standards)

Primary Documents

Corporate Average Fuel Economy Regulations (CAFE Standards)

3.1. "New CAFE: Higher Number, Same Problems," Bill Visnic, from Edmunds' Autoobserver.com.

3.2. "Our Positions on CAFE, Energy Security and Carbon Dioxide," The Alliance of Automobile Manufacturers, March 2007

3.3. "Boosting Fuel Efficiency Can Increase Highway Safety; Public Citizen Debunks Auto Industry Safety Canard," Public Citizen, Summary of Testimony to the Senate Committee on Commerce, Science and Transportation, January 24, 2002

3.4. "Don't Raise CAFE Standards," Jerry Taylor and Peter Van Doren, *National Review* (online), August 1, 2007

3.5. "GM workers lobbying for less-stringent CAFE rule," Doug Leduc, *Greater Fort Wayne Business Weekly*, July 27, 2007

3.6. Press Release: United Auto Workers—"UAW Supports Major Boost in Fuel Economy Standards; Compromise Bill Includes Safeguards for US Auto Manufacturing Jobs," December 5, 2007

3.7. "CAFE Kills, and Then Some: Six Reasons to be Skeptical of Fuel Economy Standards," Amy Ridenour and Payton Knight, The National Center for Public Policy Research, June 19, 2007

3.8. "Remarks from Hon. Norman Y. Mineta, Secretary of Transportation, CAFE Announcement from the US Department of Transportation," March 29, 2006

3.9. "Building a Better SUV," Selections from the Executive Summary of a Research Report, Union of Concerned Scientists

3.10. "CAFE Changes, By the Numbers," Andrew J. Kleit, *Regulation*, Fall 2002

3.11. "Testimony to the Senate Commerce Committee on Corporate Average Fuel Economy (CAFE) Standards," David L. Greene, Corporate Fellow, Engineering Science and Technology Division, Oak Ridge National Laboratory, March 6, 2007

3.12. "Resources for the Future President," Paul Portney Briefs House Senate Science Committee on Effectiveness, Impact of CAFE Standards, February 9, 2005

3.13. "Statement of Alliance President and CEO Dave McCurdy on President's Signing of Energy Bill into Law," Alliance of Automobile Manufacturers, December 19, 2007

3.14. "Greenpeace Statement on Passage of Senate Energy Bill," December 13, 2007

3.15. "House Vote Sends Landmark Energy Bill to President Bush," Statement of President Kevin Knobloch of the Union of Concerned Scientists, December 18, 2007

BACKGROUND

The Energy Independence and Security Act of 2007, signed into law on December 19, 2007, mandated the first increase in national fuel efficiency standards since they were established in 1975 in the throes of the Arab oil embargo. Specifically, the legislation provides that Corporate Average Fuel Economy requirements, popularly known as CAFE, be raised on cars and small trucks (including SUVs) to an automobile industry average of 35 mpg by 2020, an increase of 40% above the current 25 mpg.

While no specific event provided the impetus for reversing the more than three decades of efforts by environmental and energy efficiency interests to require better fuel performance from our nation's vehicles, a number of factors combined to change the climate in favor of change: our nation's continuing over-dependence on oil from countries experiencing growing unrest; the increasing national, and international, concern over global warming, to which vehicle emissions are a major contributor; the uncertainty over the consequences of terrorism; and formidable competition from foreign auto manufacturers, whose products have garnered an expanding share of the market, largely by virtue of their fuel efficiency.

Notwithstanding the financial hard times of the American auto industry, legislative and regulatory measures to require them to remanufacture vehicles to improve gasoline mileage have been fought off not only by auto and truck makers, but by conservative think tanks, organized labor (who, for much of that period, saw their interests served more by business than by the environmental community), and some, though by no means all, safety experts. Their legislative strategy of obstruction has been forcefully and effectively managed in Congress over that period by an influential and skillful tactician, Representative John Dingell, of Michigan (not surprisingly, the home state of the American auto industry). Of pivotal importance, John Dingell has been Chairman of the House Energy and Commerce Committee for almost all of the last two decades. It is to his committee that all relevant regulatory legislation is referred and reviewed, and he has held an almost autocratic power over its actions. It is interesting to note that Energy is bracketed with Commerce in the House Committee, justifying Dingell's concern with the economics of auto regulation, as well as its environmental impact. Senator Carl Levin, also of Michigan, a respected and powerful voice in his Chamber, has, of course, supported Dingell's efforts there.

The split in Rep. Dingell's Committee jurisdiction is mirrored by the split in responsibility for administering the CAFE regulations: the National Highway Traffic Safety Administration in the Department of Transportation (DOT) regulates CAFE standards, and the Environmental Protection Agency measures vehicle fuel efficiency. These divisions reflect the contending parties and issues that have perennially marked the debate over CAFE. The positions of the environmental community and energy efficiency advocates are, of course, predictable, but those opposed to changes in CAFE reflect concerns closer to DOT's concerns, as many of the documents below illustrate. They argue that significantly improved fuel efficiency can be achieved only by making vehicles smaller and lighter and therefore less safe and more likely to result in a greater number of traffic fatalities. They also contend that the retooling of cars will result in both increases in cost to consumers and/or reduced profits for their makers, a factor with great political force given that almost 10% of the jobs in the US are dependent on the automotive industry. And all of this for small increments of efficiency that will be eaten up by the wasteful consumer habits that reduced operating costs will encourage. Rather the DOT would prefer economic incentives for more sophisticated technological investments. All of these arguments though are asserted, and rebutted, in the following documents.

One final note: Virtually all the media have represented the CAFE provisions of the Energy Independence and Security Act as mandating their increase to 35 mpg by 2020 from the current 25 mpg, but that is not entirely accurate. The legislation includes a provision that authorizes the DOT to issue "attribute-based" standards to insure that increased fuel efficiency does not come at the expense of automotive safety. This means that different mileage standards would apply to different classes of vehicles based on their attributes, principally size. The Transportation Research Institute at the University of Michigan concludes that an attribute-based CAFE would mean lower standards for automakers, or a range of standards from 33 mpg to 38 mpg. These, in turn, may result in greater gains in market share and profits for Detroit. As is the case so often with complicated legislation and, particularly with its implementing regulations, "the devil is in the details." This is, no doubt, one of several obscure concessions made to Rep. Dingell and his constituents that account for his grudging support.

DOCUMENTS

Founded in 1999, the SUV Owners of America is a non-profit consumer organization supporting the rights and serving the interests of SUV, pickup, and van owners. The following document reflects a distinctly suspicious attitude toward the new mandate.

3.1. "New CAFE: Higher Number, Same Problems," Bill Visnic, from Edmunds' Autoobserver.com

The US House of Representatives finally approved a massive energy bill whose cornerstone is the long-debated increase of fuel economy standards to a 35 miles per gallon average for both passenger cars and light trucks by 2020.

Trouble is, just when auto companies, politicians and environmental interests seem able to agree the public insists on something resembling "action" regarding auto fuel economy, the bill faces an almost certain roadblock in the Senate—not to mention a threatened veto from President Bush—because it retains a provision to reduce tax breaks for Big Oil and mandates large utilities produce at least 15 percent of their energy from renewable sources.

Both are measures eco-evasive Bush and Republican stalwarts say derail any prospects of the bill's passage in the Senate.

Deal or No Deal?

The House's sudden puckishness in the face of certain Senate opposition brings to a screeching halt what appeared to be the fast-tracking of an uneasy compromise to move forward with the proposal for the new 35-mpg Corporate Average Fuel Economy measure.

For weeks, Congressional leaders tooted the trumpets of compromise in proclaiming the serious hike in CAFE was imminent. Although the co-called "bumper sticker" number of a combined 35 mpg average is a marked increase over the respective 27.5 mpg and 22.2 mpg those vehicles are expected to attain today, most industry sources say any forthcoming deal is more about political expediency than relieving the nation's dependence on foreign oil.

There will be tangible benefits, some of them immediate, if the proposed new vehicle fuel economy standards eventually are agreed upon by Congress and the overall energy bill is signed by President Bush.

But "the devil will be in the details," says Ron DeFore, communications director for SUV Owners of America.

The most important of those details:

- Light trucks reputedly will continue to enjoy lower fuel-economy targets than passenger cars, although trucks must be figured into each automaker's overall fleet average. Thus the definition of what constitutes a "truck"—and who crafts that definition—will be exceedingly important.

"As long as there is differentiation (between cars and trucks), there's always going to be a game," says Anthony Pratt, also a senior analyst at Pricewaterhouse Cooper's Automotive Institute.

Some of the vehicles that have famously driven through the same loophole in today's Corporate Average Fuel Economy regulations include Chrysler's PT Cruiser, advantageously classified as a truck for CAFE purposes because it has removable rear seats, and Subaru's Legacy Outback, which earned the company scorn when it deliberately fiddled with the redesigned '05 car's ground clearance and other details so that that National Highway Traffic Safety Administration, which administers CAFE, would call a "truck" what clearly is a car.

- It also appears any new fuel-economy legislation will continue to offer automakers the ability to win extra CAFE credits for producing "flex-fuel" vehicles capable of running either on gasoline or E-85, which is 85 percent ethanol and 15 percent gasoline—a fuel that ostensibly reduces dependence on foreign oil and is proven to cut emissions.

Retaining flex-fuel CAFE credits reportedly was staunchly defended by many politicians. Some industry sources suggest it is the presence of the ethanol credit that has enabled several automakers—chiefly the US domestics—to meet CAFE standards over the past several years.

The House version of the bill—which passed on Dec. 6 by a 235-181 margin—contains a provision to boost ethanol production to 36 billion gallons by 2022, a 700 percent increase from today's levels.

The Alliance of Automotive Manufacturers says that as of March this year, there were about six million flex-fuel vehicles on the road. And with good reason: thanks to a bizarre formula for calculating these vehicles' fuel economy, each flex-fuel vehicle earns its maker an outsized claim towards meeting CAFE. That is the reason many automakers spend perhaps as much as $100 per vehicle to endow some of their highest-volume models with flex-fuel capability.

An example from the blog of a former automotive engineer: a pickup truck with combined fuel economy rating of 18.6 mpg, if outfitted as a flex-fuel vehicle, is credited as a 31-mpg truck for CAFE purposes.

Currently, automakers can pump out enough flex-fuel vehicles to boost their full-line CAFE by as much as 0.9 mpg (from 1993 to 2004, it was 1.2 mpg). This doesn't sound like much until the CAFE performance of a few of the largest producers of flex-fuel vehicles is examined. In 2006, the most recent year for complete figures, the light-truck fleet standard was 21.6 mpg; Chrysler and GM's final truck CAFE squeaked in at 21.7 mpg. Nissan finished at 21.9 mpg, Ford at 21.1 mpg. Clearly, earning an extra 0.9 mpg makes a difference.

Most critics say the phantom promise of flex-fuel vehicles comes from the fact the preponderance of them rarely, if ever, are fed the fuel—largely because it would be all but impossible: of the approximately 170,000 fuel stations in the US, only about 1,200 offer ethanol. The fuel is not available at all for retail sale in seven states. And there has been controversy regarding how much the nation's intake of foreign oil actually is reduced by using the domestically produced E-85.

35 MPG No Engineering Picnic

The targeted 35-mpg overall standard "is not insignificant," says Dan Montague, also a senior automotive analyst at PWC's Automotive Institute. "E-85 credits will help to compensate for the fact it's difficult to get there."

The PWC analysts and DeFore of the SUVOA, a group that essentially has campaigned against CAFE standards of any type, saying such regulation essentially distorts market forces, say the inevitable "remixing" of vehicle fleet to meet the 35-mpg standard won't come any faster or any less painfully because of new legislation.

And that pain will be most felt, they say, by domestic automakers because their current fleet mix is biased 57 percent toward light trucks. Meanwhile, sales for the so-called New Domestics (import automakers, essentially) currently are weighted a much more manageable 36.7 percent toward trucks.

Consumers ultimately will pay for the new 35-mpg standard "through a drastically increased price of the vehicle," says DeFore. His group estimates the cost could be $7,000–$8,000 extra for an average-sized car.

Remixing of US Market Inevitable

PWC's Pratt says with gasoline commonly exceeding $3 per gallon, "Are we at a place where consumers are willing to pay for fuel efficiency?" He says it appears buyers are discernibly choosing more fuel-efficient vehicles, noting this year's marked downturn in sales of large pickups and many truck-based SUVs. He says it seems obvious "recreational" truck purchasers have abandoned the segment.

The PWC analysts say the more immediate effects will include an accelerated use of more efficiency-enhancing powertrain upgrades, such as direct injection and advanced transmissions. And they say diesel engines could be a valuable tool, what with its potential to immediately improve fuel economy by as much as 25 percent or more. Analysts and many major suppliers say diesel could capture as much as 12–14 percent of the US market within 10 years.

If a bill is passed that contains the fuel-economy measures, it appears it will be, for now, more about political expediency than actual improvements.

"Perhaps it's a step forward," suggests Montague. "But CAFE is not altogether efficient. It's not really working.

"Remixing (of the car-truck ratio) is partially going to happen," he adds. "But people won't give up their truck-based vehicles. They will demand those vehicles are more efficient."

PWC's analysts also say automakers ultimately have agreed to the proposed standard because "they've accepted the fact this is a done deal."

It's a long time until 2020, and those suspicious of all motives in the debate say the appeasing nature of the fuel-economy deal—never mind the separate battle raging over Big Oil's taxes and renewable-electricity mandates—simply means all sides are willing to agree publicly while buying time for behind-the-scenes maneuvering to more favorable conditions.

Or waiting for a political and environmental majority in America that is at least a paler shade of green.

The Alliance of Automobile Manufacturers is a trade association of nine car and light truck manufacturers, including Ford, GM, Toyota, and Volkswagen. Here it argues for assistance in developing alternative and advanced technology vehicles as opposed to CAFE standards.

3.2. "Our Positions on CAFE, Energy Security and Carbon Dioxide," The Alliance of Automobile Manufacturers, March 2007

As an introduction, it is the view of the Alliance of Automobile Manufacturers that energy security is a priority to all Americans, and the auto industry must aggressively pursue its innovation agenda. Automakers are already investing significantly in advanced technology vehicles powered by electricity, biofuels, diesel, hydrogen and compressed natural gas. Still, autos are only one part of the energy security picture. We are already a "carbon-constrained" industry and one that is heavily regulated. Broader-based policies addressing fuels and the growth and use of renewable low carbon fuels by consumers need to be explored as well. To be effective, these policies must incorporate all stakeholders, including alternative energy suppliers, the R&D community, the investment community, government at all levels, and especially consumers. To be successful, the goal of reducing petroleum consumption must be viewed as a shared responsibility.

http://www.autoalliance.org/fuel/fuel_whitepaper.php

Public Citizen is a non-profit, consumer advocacy organization promoting, among other causes, clean and safe energy sources and safe and healthy environmental protections. Here, Joan Claybrook, formerly Administrator of the National Highway Traffic Safety Administration, rebuts the auto administration's contention that fuel efficiency threatens public safety.

3.3. "Boosting Fuel Efficiency Can Increase Highway Safety; Public Citizen Debunks Auto Industry Safety Canard," Public Citizen, Summary of Testimony to the Senate Committee on Commerce, Science and Transportation, January 24, 2002

Public Citizen, Summary of Testimony to the Senate Committee on Commerce, Science and Transportation, January 24, 2002

WASHINGTON, DC—Contrary to assertions by auto manufacturers, boosting fuel economy standards will not lessen highway safety and likely would save lives, Public Citizen told congressional lawmakers today.

Vehicle size and crash protection design are the key factors in safety, Public Citizen President Joan Claybrook said in testimony presented to the Senate Committee on Commerce, Science and Transportation. Claybrook was the administrator of the National Highway Traffic Safety Administration from 1977 to 1981.

Although the auto industry has promoted a myth that heavier vehicles are always safer, they are not, Claybrook said. In fact, some lighter cars have a lower driver death rate than some heavy vehicles. For example, the GM Suburban four-wheel drive has a higher death rate than the Honda Civic. The key issue is vehicle crashworthiness, she said.

Not only do sport utility vehicles (SUVs) have high rollover rates, more handling problems and are often less crashworthy, but they cause more damage to smaller vehicles in crashes. Nor do fuel economy standards cause increased fatalities. Fuel economy is achieved primarily by techno-logical improvements and to a small extent by weight reduction, which occurs only in heavy vehicles (it is not cost-efficient to reduce the weights of light cars). Thus, new fuel economy standards would create a fleet of vehicles with fewer disparities in weight, which is safer for everyone on the road.

"The auto industry has argued, time and again, that raising fuel economy standards will adversely impact safety by causing the increased production of smaller vehicles or by reducing vehicle weight," Claybrook said. "In fact, there is no evidence that establishes [this]. . . . The use of the timeworn safety canard by the industry is a cynical attempt to frighten consumers and Congress to deflect new fuel economy requirements, and appears most appallingly hypocritical when we consider that the industry itself has acted to obstruct safety improvements over the last 35 years."

Claybrook noted that over the years, the industry has fought mandatory air bag laws on cost grounds and fought side impact and fuel system standards. It is now battling to prevent effective dynamic rollover tests, an improved roof crush standard and requirements for a tire pressure monitoring system, which would save fuel economy and improve safety . . .

CAFE standards have not been updated above the 1985 requirement, despite better technology and the increasing dominance of SUVs on the highways. One major deficiency in the current CAFE program is that it holds light trucks to a lower fuel economy standard than passenger cars. While this distinction may have been valid in 1975, when light trucks were not widely used as passenger vehicles, it is now badly outdated, Claybrook said.

The Union of Concerned Scientists last year released a report showing that technologies exist to make today's vehicles far more fuel efficient while keeping vehicle manufacturing cost-effective and having no negative impact on safety. These technologies include changing tire tread designs, increasing the use of aluminum and plastics, and allowing engines to turn off rather than idle.

Claybrook called for the following actions by Congress, which she said are necessary because the auto industry will not boost fuel efficiency or act to improve safety on its own:

- Require NHTSA to set new safety standards for rollover crashworthi-ness protection and limits on aggressivity, which could prevent thou-sands of deaths and injuries. The rollover protections should include a dynamic roof crush standard, roof energy absorbing protection to reduce injuries from contact with the roof, safety belt pretensioners that are triggered in a rollover crash, improved seat structure to keep occupants in position during a roll, side impact protection air bags that are triggered in a rollover crash;

- Close the light truck loophole in the CAFE standards. Fuel economy standards should be raised to 40 mpg for cars and light trucks over 10 years, starting with the model year 2005;
- Increase the accuracy of testing procedures used to predict fuel economy performance;
- End the dual-credit program, in which manufacturers are rewarded for building vehicles that can theoretically run on alternative fuels. In reality, only one percent of the miles driven in these vehicles are ever powered by alternative fuels;
- Eliminate CAFE's "carryback" provision, which allows a manufacturer that fails to meet its CAFE requirement to submit a plan for improving vehicle fleet efficiency in three future years. This invites abuse and dishonesty by the manufacturers by effectively delaying the deadline by which manufacturers must meet their fuel economy targets;
- Clarify a provision that precludes state-run "feebate" programs, in which manufacturers and consumers are rewarded for selling cars that are more fuel efficient than required; and
- Immediately appropriate $5 million for fuel economy.

The National Review *is a journal representing the conservative viewpoint. This piece represents a forceful argument attacking a whole range of issues supporting CAFE.*

3.4. "Don't Raise CAFE Standards," Jerry Taylor and Peter Van Doren, *National Review* (online), August 1, 2007

Everybody in Washington wants to force the auto industry to make more fuel-efficient cars and trucks. President Bush wants to require new vehicles to meet federal standards (to be determined) based on how heavy they are. The Senate wants to mandate that every car, pick-up truck, and SUV sold in 2020 average a fuel efficiency of at least 35 miles per gallon—far more aggressive than the 27.5 mile per gallon standard now in place for passenger vehicles. The House could offer an amendment on fuel standards from the floor on Friday. Either way, we'll find out later this week what's in store.

Would the market produce "too little" conservation without corporate average fuel efficiency (CAFE) standards? At first glance, no. The "right" (that is, efficient) amount of gasoline consumption will occur naturally as long as fuel markets are free and gasoline prices reflect total costs. In fact, a review of market data by Clemson University economist Molly Espey and Santosh Nair found that consumers actually *overvalue* fuel efficiency. That is, they pay more up front in higher car prices than the present value of the fuel savings over the lifetimes of the cars.

But driving imposes costs on others that aren't reflected in fuel prices, like environmental degradation. Because gasoline prices do not reflect total costs, consumption is higher than it ought to be. Congress is therefore doing the economy a favor by mandating increased increments of energy conservation, right?

The Argument is Clever, but Wrong

Increasing CAFE standards will not decrease the amount of pollution coming from the US auto fleet. That's because we regulate emissions per mile traveled, not per gallon of gasoline burned. Improvements in fuel efficiency reduce the cost of driving and thus increase vehicle miles traveled. Moreover, automakers have an incentive to offset the costs associated with improving fuel efficiency by spending less complying with federal pollution standards with which they currently over-comply.

Those two observations explain calculations from Pennsylvania State economist Andrew Kleit showing that a 50 percent increase in CAFE standards would increase total emissions of volatile organic compounds by 2.3 percent, nitrogen oxide emissions by 3.8 percent, and carbon-monoxide emissions by 5 percent.

Another rationale for CAFE standards is that gasoline purchases send money to foreign terrorists who kill and maim with our dollars. Energy conservation, according to many, is our "ace in the hole" against al Qaeda and its ilk.

If there were a relationship between our "energy addiction" and Islamic terrorism, one would expect to find a correlation between world crude oil prices and Islamic terror attacks or mortality from the same. But there is no statistical relationship between the two. Terrorism is a very low-cost endeavor and manpower, not money, is its necessary determinant. That explains why even the lowest inflation-adjusted oil prices in history proved no obstacle to the rise of Islamic terror organizations in the 1990s.

While it's true that nasty regimes like Iran are getting rich off our driving habits, the extent to which oil profits fuel its nastiness is unclear. After all, Pakistan is a poor country with no oil revenues, but it had no problem building a nuclear arsenal. The same goes for North Korea. Iran without oil revenues might look like Syria. Venezuela without oil revenues might look like Cuba. In short, while rich bad actors are probably more dangerous than poor ones, oil revenues don't seem to make much difference at the margin.

Finally, we're told that CAFE helps secure our energy independence. But the amount of oil we import is related to the difference between domestic and foreign crude oil prices. Reducing oil demand may reduce the total amount of oil we consume, but it will not reduce the degree to which we rely on foreign oil to meet our needs.

Regardless, tightening CAFE standards would have little impact on any of these alleged problems. If the Senate's proposed CAFE standard of 35 mpg by 2020 were to become law, it would reduce oil consumption by, at most, about 1.2 million barrels a day. Given that the Energy Information Administration thinks world crude oil production would be 103.8 million barrels a day by 2020, the reduction would be 1.2 percent of global demand and result in a 1.3 percent decline in price; nowhere near enough to defund terrorists, denude oil producers of wealth, or secure energy independence.

Congress has no business dictating automotive fuel efficiency. That's a job for consumers, not vote-hustling politicians. There are no problems for CAFE standards to solve. Hence, they shouldn't be tightened; they should be repealed.

This newsletter promotes the involvement of GM workers in an effort against more rigorous CAFE standards reflecting, and marshalling, workers' concerns.

3.5. "GM workers lobbying for less-stringent CAFE rule," Doug Leduc, *Greater Fort Wayne Business Weekly*, July 27, 2007

A General Motors Corp. newsletter has gone out to all employees of its Fort Wayne Assembly Plant, encouraging them to contact members of Congress about fuel economy standards that could reshape their futures.

The truck plant employs more than 3,000 who make full-sized Chevrolet Silverados and GMC Sierras. Its production workers are represented by United Auto Workers Local 2209.

The plant is supplied by more than 450 businesses, including several in northeast Indiana. It averaged about 62 trucks per hour last year, or close to 1,000 per day from two production shifts. But new Corporate Average Fuel Economy, or CAFE, requirements Congress is considering could threaten that production level.

The company and the UAW are working alongside other organizations with auto-industry ties to drum up support for H.R. 2927, also known as the Hill-Terry CAFE alternative, which would boost fuel economy by as much as 40 percent over the next 15 years. . . .

House action on fuel economy standards could come by the end of July. Speaker Nancy Pelosi, D-Calif., and other lawmakers publicly have stated that they are supporting a more severe CAFE hike approved by the Senate in June: a 35-mpg minimum combined car/truck standard.

To meet that Senate standard and other more stringent proposals, automakers say they would be forced to significantly downsize their vehicles to carry less cargo and fewer people. That also would compromise safety, they argue.

In addition, automakers say unrealistic standards would significantly raise vehicle prices. New fuel-saving technologies, such as hybrid or diesel engines, would add $2,000 to $5,000 to the cost of a vehicle. Or they may simply eliminate certain models altogether.

The Hill-Terry CAFE alternative—named for Reps. Baron Hill, D.-Ind., and Lee Terry, R-Nev.—boosts current standards to between 32 to 35 mpg by model-year 2022. Unlike the Senate bill, the Hill-Terry bill permits separate CAFE standards for different classes of vehicles such as cars, trucks and sport-utility vehicles.

Proponents say the Hill-Terry measure not only gives automakers enough lead time to develop the technology needed to meet the new standards, but it balances fuel economy increases with vehicle diversity, safety concerns and affordability.

Earlier this month, the proposal received the support of the National Automobile Dealers Association, and vehicle dealers from across Indiana met with members of Congress to lobby for it.

Hill-Terry "really has gained a lot of support, pretty much across both sides of the isle," said Greg Martin, a GM spokesman in Washington, DC. "It stretches the industry, but doesn't do it at the cost of jobs and to the consumer." . . .

US Rep. Mark Souder, who represents the Fort Wayne area, has voiced opposition to the more restrictive fuel economy standards.

In June, he condemned the Senate's action to increase fuel efficiency standards on cars and light trucks to 35 miles per gallon by 2020. The Senate passed the measure by voice vote as part of a broader energy bill.

"The Senate action is potentially devastating to northern Indiana's economy," Souder said in a statement. "This Democrat-led initiative could cripple our GM plant—sending more jobs overseas—which has me particularly worried about pensions and health care benefits for thousands of Hoosiers.

"It could also whack our towable RV and boat industries. It's pretty hard to tow an RV or boat without a pickup, SUV or other large vehicle."

Souder said he supported a bipartisan compromise that recognized the differences between light trucks and cars.

The United Auto Workers, like most unions representing labor, historically opposed CAFE standards, fearing a threat to jobs. But a number of key provisions in the enacted bill, enumerated below, provided the assurances they needed, and, like "attribute-based standards," may have provided just the support needed to reverse the result.

3.6. Press Release: United Auto Workers—"UAW Supports Major Boost in Fuel Economy Standards; Compromise Bill Includes Safeguards for US Auto Manufacturing Jobs," December 5, 2007

UAW Supports Major Boost in Fuel Economy Standards; Compromise Bill Includes Safeguards for US Auto Manufacturing Jobs

The UAW "strongly supports" new fuel economy provisions in energy legislation being considered by Congress, UAW President Ron Gettelfinger said today.

"The UAW strongly supports this historic bill, which contains aggressive but still achievable fuel economy requirements," said Gettelfinger. "It will help consumers and the environment, and at the same time protect US jobs."

The new provisions on corporate average fuel economy (CAFE) require significant increases in the fuel economy standards for passenger cars and light trucks. By 2020 the average fuel economy for all cars and light trucks will have to achieve an average of 35 miles per gallon for the entire industry. This will guarantee substantial savings in gas consumption, thereby enhancing US energy security and reducing greenhouse gas emissions.

"There are no off ramps or other gimmicks," said Gettelfinger of the compromise legislation. "The new rule cannot be gamed to avoid the higher requirements."

At the same time, Gettelfinger said, the new CAFE standards contain key features which were strongly supported by UAW members and their families during the discussions that led to the compromise legislation. These include:

- Strong anti-backsliding language to require automakers to produce smaller, more fuel-efficient vehicles in the United States. This will protect the jobs of tens of thousands of American workers who assemble and produce parts for these vehicles.
- A continuation of the distinction between passenger cars and light trucks in the CAFE program. Requiring different rules for these different types of vehicles will ensure that light truck production and jobs are not adversely impacted by the new rules.
- An extension and then gradual phaseout of flex-fuel credits under the CAFE program. This will continue the incentive for auto companies to produce these vehicles, while helping moderate the transition to tougher fuel economy standards.
- Assistance to auto manufacturers for retooling facilities to produce hybrid and advanced diesel vehicles and their key components. This

will accelerate the introduction of these more fuel-efficient vehicles, while helping ensure that cars and trucks of the future are built in this country, creating jobs for American workers.

Gettelfinger applauded House Speaker Nancy Pelosi and Senate Majority Leader Harry Reid, along with House Energy and Commerce Committee Chair John Dingell, D-Mich; Senate Energy and Natural Resources Committee Chair Jeff Bingaman, D-NM, and Senate Commerce, Science and Transportation Chair Daniel Inouye D-Hawaii, for their role in crafting the new CAFE provisions.

"These legislative leaders were able to achieve a historic breakthrough on CAFE legislation because they listened to members of our union," said Gettelfinger. "UAW members want to save fuel and protect the environment—and we also want to preserve good-paying US manufacturing jobs. The new CAFE rules accomplish all of these objectives."

The National Center for Public Policy Research is a research and communications foundation advancing free-market solutions to public policy problems. Its characteristic Q & A format is designed to be attractive to "sound bite" journalists and talk show hosts.

3.7. "CAFE Kills, and Then Some: Six Reasons to be Skeptical of Fuel Economy Standards," Amy Ridenour and Payton Knight, The National Center for Public Policy Research, June 19, 2007

Background

. . . An expected reduction in gasoline usage is the most common reason cited for raising CAFE standards. It is not clear, however, that CAFE standards are particularly helpful in reducing gasoline use. Meanwhile, there are significant disadvantages to the standards, especially the harsh—and very likely unattainable—52 mpg level for both cars and light trucks as proposed in the Energy Bill, which the auto manufacturers and the UAW say could possibly be a death knell for the domestic auto industry.

Ten Second Response

CAFE standards already result in the deaths of approximately 2,000 Americans every year, since smaller cars are less crashworthy. By failing to acknowledge this in their policymaking, Congress has cost thousands of Americans their lives. Now Congress is poised to compound the dangers by raising CAFE standards still further—so much so, it may kill the domestic auto industry itself.

Thirty Second Response

CAFE standards have little impact on greenhouse gas emissions, and the environmental benefits of increasing CAFE standards are frequently overstated. Their impact on human health is more certain: CAFE standards have resulted in tens of thousands of deaths since their adoption. Furthermore, raising CAFE standards at this time—particularly to the draconian level of 52 mpg for both cars and light trucks—would significantly harm auto manufacturing jobs in the US, raise vehicle prices, and reduce vehicle choices for families and for those who use vehicles for towing and moving goods.

Discussion

Opponents of increasing CAFE standards raise the following concerns:

1) Increasing mpg reduces the per-mile cost of operating vehicles, which increases the number of miles driven, thus reducing or eliminating any CAFE benefit. Jerry Taylor and Peter Van Doren of the Cato Institute explain why this is the case:

> Energy efficient appliances reduce the costs of operation. This might not be a big deal when it comes to, say, the television set (we won't watch more TV just because it costs a little less to turn on the set). But for appliances like air conditioners that make all the difference during peak demand periods, energy efficiency reduces the marginal cost of energy services and thus increases—not decreases—energy consumption. This is a well-known phenomenon called the "rebound effect." The same goes for automobile fuel efficiency. Environmentalists argue that increasing the miles per gallon of the cars we drive would save more energy than increased drilling could produce. But the data show that fuel consumption goes up whenever automobile fuel efficiency goes up. Nearly all the gains in fuel efficiency disappear once we account for the demonstrable increases in driving that such investments produce.

James Taylor, editor of the Heartland Institute's *Environment News*, cites supportive data:

> [USA Today columnist John] Merline noted people drive their vehicles more when increased fuel economy makes the price per mile cheaper. "The number of miles driven by passenger cars and light trucks climbed 104 percent between 1975 and 2000, according to the Department of Transportation," noted Merline.

A 2001 study conducted by the National Research Council (NRC) reached the same conclusion. According to the NRC, CAFE "reduces the fuel cost per mile of driving, thereby encouraging faster growth in vehicle travel than would otherwise be the case."

"NHTSA neglects the adverse effects from the increased driving induced by the proposal," agreed Randall Lutter and Troy Kravitz in a February 2003 study released by the AEI-Brookings Joint Center for Regulatory Studies. "By lowering the costs of driving, NHTSA's proposal increases vehicle miles traveled, thereby boosting traffic accidents and congestion. The increase in the costs of accidents and congestion fully offsets and probably outweighs the social benefits resulting from greater fuel economy."

Writing in the *Wall Street Journal* in 2001, Kimberly A. Strassel observed, "[s]ince 1970, the United States has made cars almost 50% more efficient; in that period of time, the average number of miles a person drives has doubled."

2) CAFE standards are dangerous. In 2002, the National Academy of Sciences released a report, "Effectiveness and Impact of CAFE Standards 2002," concluding that since CAFE standards were imposed in the US in 1975, an additional 2,000 deaths per year can be attributed to the downsizing of cars required to meet CAFE standards.

In 2001, Charli E. Coon, J.D. of the Heritage Foundation wrote:

> The evidence is overwhelming that CAFE standards result in more highway deaths. A 1999 USA TODAY analysis of crash data and estimates from the National Highway Traffic Safety Administration and the Insurance Institute for Highway Safety found that, in the years since CAFE standards were mandated under the Energy Policy and Conservation Act of 1975, about 46,000 people have died in crashes that they would have survived if they had been traveling in bigger, heavier cars. This translates into 7,700 deaths for every mile per gallon gained by the standards.

3) CAFE increases are less likely to reduce gas consumption than are gas tax increases. In a 2002 essay published in the *Los Angeles Times*, the Cato Institute's William A. Niskanen and Peter Van Doren noted, "since the CAFE standards were introduced, the average fuel economy has increased by 114% for new cars and by 56% for new light trucks, but the US consumption of imported oil has increased from 35% to 52%." Niskanen and Van Doren recommended that if reducing gas consumption is the goal, an increased gasoline tax is more likely to get the job done: "In contrast to a tax on gasoline, CAFE standards are an imperfect and inefficient method of signaling drivers about the true costs of the gasoline that they consume."

The Congressional Budget Office took a similar view:

This issue brief focuses on the economic costs of CAFE standards and compares them with the costs of a gasoline tax that would reduce gasoline consumption by the same amount. The Congressional Budget Office (CBO) estimates that a 10 percent reduction in gasoline consumption could be achieved at a lower cost by an increase in the gasoline tax than by an increase in CAFE standards. Furthermore, an increase in the gasoline tax would reduce driving, leading to less traffic congestion and fewer accidents. This analysis stops short of estimating the value of less congestion and fewer accidents and, therefore, does not draw any conclusions about whether an increase in the gasoline tax would be warranted. However, CBO does find that, given current estimates of the value of decreasing dependence on oil and reducing carbon emissions, increasing CAFE standards would not pass a benefit-cost test.

4) CAFE standard increases will harm domestic automakers and employment in the domestic auto industry. As National Center for Public Policy Research Senior Fellow Eric Peters writes:

> The legislation differs from previous fuel economy standards in that it would apply to both passenger cars and "light trucks"—a category of vehicle that includes pick-ups, SUVs and minivans—and which has up to now been held to a separate (and less stringent) fuel economy standard of 21.5-mpg vs. 27.5-mpg for passenger cars.
>
> As a result, [legislation to increase CAFE standards] would disproportionately hurt American car companies, which have their profit centers in large pick-ups and SUVs—while giving a competitive leg-up to imports, which make most of their money selling smaller, inherently more economical passenger cars.

It's much easier to tweak the design of a compact or mid-sized front-wheel-drive passenger car with a four or six-cylinder engine that already gets 32 mpg to the 35 mpg mark than it is to get a full-size, V-8 powered truck or SUV from 20-something mpg to 35 mpg. Thus, the impact of the [legislation to increase CAFE standards] will hurt American car companies most where they are especially vulnerable—at a time when they can least afford another legislative knee-capping. GM, Ford and Chrysler have all posted alarming losses recently, even as the quality and appeal of their vehicles has been on the upswing. Hitting them with a 35-mpg fuel economy edict would have the same effect as sucker punching someone already laid low by the flu. Furthermore, more stringent CAFE standards will make new cars more expensive, which will depress sales generally.

5) Some individuals, families and businesses need the large vehicles a

CAFE standard increase will tend to drive out of the market for towing or storage capacity or simply to transport their families. Laws requiring parents to transport children—in some states, children up to eight years of age—in approved child safety seats effectively reduces available seating in the back seat of most small (and many mid-sized) sedans to two persons. For safety reasons, transporting a third child in the front seat is inappropriate in most vehicles, and is illegal in some areas, making larger vehicles all but mandatory for many families with children.

6) The argument that increasing CAFE standards will reduce global warming is grossly overstated. Even if greenhouse gas emissions due to human activities are significantly, and harmfully, raising global temperatures, which remains a subject of debate, increasing CAFE standards would have scant impact. As Charli E. Coon, J.D., of the Heritage Foundation wrote in 2001:

> Nor will increasing CAFE standards halt the alleged problem of "global warming." Cars and light trucks subject to fuel economy standards make up only 1.5 percent of all global man-made greenhouse gas emissions. According to data published in 1991 by the Office of Technology Assessment, a 40 percent increase in fuel economy standards would reduce greenhouse emissions by only about 0.5 percent, even under the most optimistic assumptions.

Norman Mineta was Secretary of Transportation for most of this Administration's term. In this statement, he addresses, and reflects, some of the earlier thoughts about CAFE standards, especially as they may apply to light trucks. Perhaps this is part of an effort to head off the more stringent standards that eventually emerged.

3.8. "Remarks from Hon. Norman Y. Mineta, Secretary of Transportation, CAFE Announcement from the US Department of Transportation," March 29, 2006

. . . I am in Baltimore this morning because this city's highways, bridges, and tunnels are among the most congested in the nation. And a good deal of that traffic comes in the form of pick-up trucks, sport utility vehicles, and minivans.

Commuters here understand how important these light trucks are to maintaining our way of life, our mobility, and our economic vitality. But Marylanders also understand that we have to act now to end our addiction to foreign sources of oil, and they are not intimidated by big challenges.

It is of course our President who set the goal of reducing our dependence on foreign sources of oil to make America more secure. So I am here today to announce the Department of Transportation is doing its part—with tough new fuel economy standards designed to make the eight and a half million light trucks sold each year in this country more fuel efficient.

These new standards, which are called the Corporate Average Fuel Economy standards (CAFE), represent the second time that the Bush Administration has increased the mileage requirements for light trucks and the first complete reform of this program since it was created in 1979.

The standards will reduce our fuel consumption by encouraging automakers to bring the same energy and innovation to fuel economy that they have been applying to vehicle design, safety, and product reliability for decades.

The new standards represent the most ambitious fuel economy goals for light trucks ever developed in the program's 27-year history. And more importantly, they close the loopholes that have long plagued the current system.

Much has changed in seven months since our initial proposal. So the rules that I am announcing today include significant improvements that strengthen the proposal that I first outlined last August.

First, the final standards include individual miles-per-gallon goals for all passenger trucks sold in the United States. That is because the current approach to light truck standards is too easy to get around. There is no incentive in the current structure to encourage automakers to apply fuel-saving technology to their largest and most profitable vehicles.

Under the new CAFE system, manufacturers will have to add fuel-saving technology to all passenger trucks. Not only is this good for fuel economy, but it is also good for safety. Our new standards will encourage automakers to use cutting-edge fuel-saving technology instead of making weaker, lighter vehicles that put passengers at risk during crashes.

We also worked hard to make sure that no single SUV gets a free pass under these new standards. So we have included for the first time ever the largest sport utility vehicles on the market today—those that weigh between 8,500 and 10,000 pounds—in our final standards starting in 2011.

Just by including theses large sport utility vehicles, we have increased fuel savings by ten percent, more than 250 million gallons a year.

Finally, the new fuel economy standards strengthen the miles-per-gallon targets for all light trucks.

We took a good, close look at automakers' plans, examined new technology that is in use or under development—like hybrids and the latest generation of diesel-burning engines—and decided that we could ask more of the manufacturers than we proposed last August.

This was no easy decision. But seven short months have taught us that we can and we must save more fuel.

In August, we proposed the highest ever light truck targets of 24 miles per gallon, up from the current average of 21.6.

We have now asked even more from automakers by including 240,000 of the world's least fuel-efficient SUVs. This means that, for some light trucks, the fuel-economy target will be 28.4 miles per gallon, higher than today's standard for passenger cars.

Many of the changes to the CAFE program will be mandatory beginning in 2011. Automakers that can and want to move faster can opt into our reformed program earlier.

Regardless, the changes in the new standards will have a significant impact on the way that companies produce, design, and market their light trucks. And our schedule allows manufacturers enough time to make the adjustments needed so that they can comply with the new standards.

By the time that our reforms are fully in place, these new light truck standards will save two billion more gallons of fuel than our earlier proposal, for a total savings of 10.7 billion gallons.

We are focusing our efforts today on light trucks because that is where we believe that we can achieve the most savings in the shortest period of time.

In addition, as part of the Energy Bill that President Bush signed last summer, Congress directed the Department to study ways to improve fuel economy standards for all passenger cars sold in the United States. We are working on that project, and expect to send a report to Congress this August.

Saving fuel is as important to our national security and economic vitality as it is to preserving the environment. President Bush understands that and is committed to encouraging the kind of measures that will reduce our reliance on foreign oil. . . .

The Union of Concerned Scientists is a science-based non-profit working group tasked with a broad mission to develop responsible changes in government policy, corporate practice, and consumer choices.

3.9. "Building a Better SUV," Selections from the Executive Summary of a Research Report, Union of Concerned Scientists

SUVs are marketed to consumers as a safe and rugged alternative to the station wagon. The reality, however, is that automakers have offered consumers unsafe SUVs that place a heavy burden on both pocketbooks and the environment. In 2002, 42,815 people lost their lives in US highway fatalities—the highest level since 1990. SUVs and pickups accounted for more than 60 percent of the increase. At the same time, the fuel economy of light trucks (SUVs, pickups, and minivans) fell to its lowest level since 1981, forcing the average light truck owner to pay more than $11,000 for gasoline over the life of the vehicle. This poor fuel economy contributes to a growing dependence on oil, rising imports, and a transportation sector that emits more global warming emissions than most countries release from all sectors combined. Consumers want and deserve better. This report provides a blueprint for using existing technologies to build a better SUV —one that can save lives, money, and gasoline while providing consumers with the same size and performance they have today.

Fuel Economy and Pollution Loopholes

SUV sales increased by a factor of 20 between the early 1980s and 2002, and now represent one out of every four new car sales in the United States. Despite the dramatic rise in light truck sales and their primary use as passenger vehicles rather than work vehicles, SUVs, pickups, and minivans are allowed to meet a much lower fuel economy standard than cars. As a result, the average light truck's fuel economy was about 30 percent lower than the average car in 2002. This translates into nearly $3,200 more spent on gasoline over the truck's life, assuming a conservative gas price of $1.40 per gallon. In addition, the average model year (MY) 2002 light truck produced 40 percent more emissions of the heat-trapping gases that cause global warming and roughly 1.5 to 5 times more nitrogen oxide emissions (a key smogforming pollutant) than cars.

Safety Pitfalls

Consumers may perceive SUVs to be safer than cars, but the overall fatality rate for SUVs was actually eight percent worse than cars in 2000. Furthermore, in single-vehicle accidents resulting in rollovers, the fatality rate for SUVs rises to nearly three times that for cars. Rollover fatalities in SUVs and pickups accounted for the majority of the increase in all occupant fatalities in 2002.

SUVs and pickups also drive up the fatality rates in other vehicles because of their heavy, stiff frames, which act like battering rams in collisions with other vehicles. The added height of SUVs and pickups makes matters worse by allowing the truck to ride up over a car's bumper, negating many of that vehicle's safety features. Despite these problems, neither the government nor the automakers have established standards or taken significant steps to reduce rollovers and make SUVs less dangerous to others on the road.

Building a Better SUV

Building a better SUV means offering consumers a vehicle they will want to buy—one that saves lives, money, and gasoline while providing the same performance they have come to expect. To demonstrate the safety and fuel economy potential of light trucks, the Union of Concerned Scientists developed a blueprint for a new SUV. This blueprint relies on improvements that could be made using existing safety and fuel economy technologies, all of which are on the road today in the United States, Europe, or Japan. . . .

Building Better Cars and Light Trucks

For the past 15 to 20 years, automakers have focused on building bigger and more powerful cars and trucks, and consumers now have vehicles with plenty of size and hauling power. But they also have vehicles that fail to provide the safety and fuel economy Americans want and deserve. The technologies we used to design a better SUV can also be incorporated into cars, minivans, and pickups to give consumers better choices. Light trucks with these improvements could match the current fuel economy standard for cars (27.5 mpg) by MY 2008, cutting our oil use by 800,000 barrels per day in 2015. Putting all of these technologies to work in both cars and trucks would result in safer highways and new vehicles that could reach 40 mpg by 2014. This would increase US oil savings to two million barrels per day in 2015.

Automakers have the necessary technologies in hand to spend the next decade and beyond focused on saving thousands of lives and billions of dollars at the pump every year.

The Cato Institute is a libertarian think tank advocating free markets and small government. It attacks a number of the assumptions of CAFE's proponents, but especially its effect on consumer behaviour.

3.10. "CAFE Changes, By the Numbers," Andrew J. Kleit, *Regulation*, Fall 2002

Last march, the US Senate considered a proposal by Sen. John Kerry (D-Mass.) to raise the Corporate Average Fuel Economy (CAFE) standards for cars and light trucks by 50 percent. Kerry and other proponents of stricter standards had the support of a July 2001 report by the National Research Council (NRC) that called for significantly higher standards, as well as the backing of many major newspapers. The events of September 11 and the subsequent resurgence of violence and political uncertainty in the Mideast added to the momentum in favor of new fuel efficiency standards. But a coalition of Republicans and auto-state Democrats defeated the Kerry measure by a decisive and surprising 62–38 vote. To the casual observer, the decision may have seemed a defeat of the public interest by special interests. In fact, it was a victory for economic common sense. As many economists and other policy experts have argued, the CAFE standards save very little gasoline, increase car buyers' costs and lower their benefits, increase pollution and auto fatalities, and shift revenue away from US automakers to foreign firms. Instead of raising the fuel efficiency standards, policymakers would better address any externalities associated with gasoline by raising the gas tax . . .

Compliance

If a manufacturer does not comply with the CAFE standards, it is subject to a civil fine of $55 per car/mpg. For example, if a manufacturer producers one million cars with a sales weighted mpg of 26.5 mpg, that firm could be subject to a fine of $55 per car/mpg X 1 million cars X 1 mpg, or $55 million.

Foreign automakers view the fine as a tax. Thus, BMW and Mercedes-Benz, for example, have routinely paid CAFE fines. In contrast, American firms view the standards as binding because their lawyers have advised them that, if they violate CAFE, they would be liable for civil damages in stockholder suits. The fear of civil suit is so strong that even Chrysler, which is owned by the German firm Daimler-Benz, will not violate the limits. Because the "shadow tax" of the CAFE constraint (the cost of complying with the standards rather than paying the fine) can be much more than $55 per car/mpg, the effects of CAFE standards are much larger on US automakers than foreign firms.

Gasoline Externalities

In a free market, consumers equate the price of a commodity (the "internal" cost) with the marginal value of its consumption. In the absence of any external costs like air pollution or traffic congestion, the marginal value of a gallon of gas to consumers equals its price. No public benefit would arise from reducing the consumption of gasoline, under that scenario. However, if external costs do exist, economic theory recommends that the appropriate policy response is to increase the price to consumers to equal the marginal cost of production plus the cost of the externality. That way, the consumer must consider the full cost of the commodity when he purchases and uses it.

That leads to an important question: Does gasoline consumption create external effects that consumers do not currently pay for? As part of its research on CAFE, the NRC estimated that the external costs associated with the consumption of a gallon of gasoline are approximately 26¢ per gallon. The NRC reached that figure by estimating that the combustion of the gas produces 12¢ worth of adverse global climate effects, 12¢ worth of detrimental oil-import effects, and 2¢ worth of undesirable changes from pollution emissions from refineries. The cost estimates are subject to several criticisms.

With respect to climate change, there is a wide range of uncertainty about measuring the relevant externality. Previous estimates have placed it between 1¢ and 4¢ a gallon, implying the NRC may have overestimated the cost by a factor of at least three. The oil-import effects estimate can be criticized for ignoring the theory of comparative advantage, which holds that those who can produce a certain good at the lowest cost should be the ones to produce it. Thus, it makes far more sense for oil to be produced in Saudi Arabia at $2 a barrel rather than Alaska at $20 a barrel. Granted, some argue that reducing US consumption of imported oil would make the United States economically more secure, but that assertion ignores the fact that the market for oil is worldwide and we cannot isolate ourselves from any price shock.

Despite those criticisms, let us assume that the NRC estimates are correct. The policy implication is that government should affix a 26¢ externality tax on a gallon of gasoline. Of course, gasoline already is taxed significantly, but under federal law most of the funds from the existing tax are used to build and maintain roadways, and therefore should be viewed as user fees rather than attempts to combat externalities. Those taxes, ironically, work to encourage more driving and gasoline usage. An externality tax should be assessed in addition to the road-way tax, to cover the external costs produced by the gasoline. The revenue generated from the tax should then be spent on projects other than road construction. CAFE supporters claim that such a tax is politically infeasible.

I disagree with that opinion; the federal government, every single state in the union, and all developed foreign countries of which I am aware have gasoline taxes. The average tax (federal and state combined) on gasoline in the United States is currently 41¢ per gallon. Democratically-elected European governments have much higher taxes. Hence, it does not seem that an additional tax on gasoline is politically unfeasible.

Problems with CAFE

Ignoring concerns over feasibility, CAFE proponents claim that increasing the fuel efficiency standards has the added advantage of creating net benefits apart from any reduction in the external cost of gasoline use. The NRC report goes so far as to assert that higher standards would actually pay for themselves, with the increased costs more than offset by reduced fuel consumption—yet another "free lunch" from Washington, DC. Contrary to those claims, it appears that stricter standards would save very little gasoline. There are three basic reasons for that:

• CAFE has only a limited effect on the production of "gas-guzzlers."

- CAFE leads to increased driving.
- CAFE keeps older cars with lower gas mileage on the road.

Gas-guzzlers

The CAFE standards affect the mix of vehicles produced by a manufacturer, but not the overall production of any particular type of car. That is important to remember because, as explained earlier, domestic firms will feel constrained by the new standards but foreign firms will not. The constrained US firms will be forced to increase their fuel efficiency, leaving an undersupply in the large-car market. In turn, foreign firms will move into that market and begin producing vehicles with lower fuel efficiency. Though the cars will have a slightly higher price because of CAFE fines, they likely will still appeal to consumers, so the overall mix of cars being sold will not change nearly as much as what CAFE proponents expect.

Foreign automakers stand to draw a lot of profits away from US firms if stricter CAFE standards are adopted. Honda and Toyota, for example, have fleet averages now that likely would satisfy any new standards that Congress might pass, hence the automakers would have no disincentive to try for a larger share of the US large-car market. (In fact, they may feel they need to move into that market because US automakers will be moving into the small-car market.) Even if the foreign automakers' fleet averages would not satisfy the new standards, the automakers likely would pay the relatively small mileage fines in order to have a larger share of the market.

More driving

CAFE standards may reduce the consumption of fuel per mile, but they also increase the overall amount of driving. Because the standards lower the per-mile cost of operating a car, drivers have less financial incentive to drive less. Vehicle use is just like any other market in which demand is responsive to price: A decrease in cost results in an increase in aggregate use. The latest estimates are that for every 10 percent increase in fuel efficiency, people increase their driving by two percent. Those trends indicate, again, that the fuel savings from tighter CAFE standards will be less than what proponents believe.

Old cars

By raising the cost of new cars, cafe standards provide a disincentive for old-car owners to trade in their lower gas-mileage vehicles for new, more-efficient ones. That, in turn, increases gasoline consumption by older cars because they will be staying on the road instead of being taken to the scrap yards.

So, yet again, stricter CAFE standards will have less of a gas-saving effect than what proponents claim.

Other problems

CAFE standards not only save very little gasoline, they increase air pollutants such as volatile organic compounds (VOC), oxides of nitrogen (NOX), and carbon monoxide (CO). The increases occur because the standards do not alter a car's grams/mile of emissions and thus do nothing to alter pollution levels directly. Because the pollution from a car is a direct function of the number of miles it is driven, and people in more fuel-efficient vehicles drive more, the net result from an increase in CAFE standards is an increase in automobile pollutants.

Increased CAFE standards also result in more auto fatalities. As the NRC panel conceded in its report, compliance with stricter standards means that automakers lighten their cars. Lighter, smaller cars, in turn, mean more fatalities from automobile accidents.

Finally, CAFE standards are, in large part, unworkable because demand can shift much more quickly than a manufacturer's ability to alter the fuel use of its vehicles. For example, it would take a firm three to five years to re-engineer its cars so that, at current demand levels, the fleet would satisfy a new standard. But consumers can change their buying habits in an extremely short period of time and can buy a mix of cars very different than what automakers expected. Automakers, through no fault of their own, could face short-run CAFE problems that they could address only through "mix-shifting"—selling fewer large cars and more small cars by raising prices on the former and lowering them on the latter. Because mix-shifting annoys consumers and reduces industry employment, the government has little choice but to grant the automakers relief, or else the politicians will permit serious unemployment and economic harm. These considerations further indicate that the benefits of new CAFE standards will be less, and the negative effects more, than what proponents believe. . . .

Conclusion

Proponents of stricter CAFE standards, including the authors of the recent NRC report, claim that increasing the CAFE standards is the policy equivalent of a free lunch. But fuel-efficiency standards are an extremely poor policy tool. If enforced, they would reduce consumer welfare and motorist safety, harm the environment, and increase the profits of foreign firms. Worst of all, they do not save gasoline very effectively. If policymakers wish to reduce energy consumption, they should tax gasoline consumption. It is that simple. Unfortunately, altering the CAFE standards is a politically attractive policy to invoke to reduce gasoline consumption's external costs. Because of that attractiveness, there is little debate on the real issues involved in energy consumption.

David L. Greene is a scientist with the Oak Ridge National Laboratory. His testimony provides an independent scientific analysis supporting fuel economy standards, and introducing an alternative protocol, "feebates." He also raises, and briefly discusses, the question of whether Congress or the administrative agencies should set the standards.

3.11. "Testimony to the Senate Commerce Committee on Corporate Average Fuel Economy (CAFE) Standards," David L. Greene, Corporate Fellow, Engineering Science and Technology Division, Oak Ridge National Laboratory, March 6, 2007

. . . The views I express today will be entirely my own and do not necessarily reflect the views of Oak Ridge National Laboratory or the Department of Energy.

Energy Challenges

Our nation and our world face crucial energy challenges. Our nation's oil dependence costs our economy hundreds of billions of dollars each year and undermines our national security (Greene and Ahmad, 2005). The threat to the global environment from human-induced climate change fed by increasing emissions of carbon dioxide from the combustion of fossil fuels becomes clearer with each passing day. With demand for mobility growing rapidly around the world, sustainable sources of energy for the world's growing mobility demands must be found. There is no quick, easy solution. Strong, comprehensive, sustained policies are required. Significant technological advances are also essential. The fuel economy policies we address today are by themselves not enough to solve these energy challenges. But they are the cornerstone of any sufficient strategy.

We Can Do This

Fuel economy standards have been successful in the past, not just in this country but around the world. They can take many forms. The EU has industry-wide voluntary standards. Japan and China have mandatory weight-based standards. The United States has mandatory Corporate Average Fuel Economy (CAFE) standards. What all these standards have in common is that they have successfully raised the energy efficiency of motor vehicle fleets and saved enormous amounts of energy without significant negative side-effects. Our own CAFE standards brought about a 50%

increase in on-road fuel economy over a period of 20 years. This improvement saves American consumers more than 50 billion gallons of gasoline every year. . . .

How High Should We Go?

Fuel economy standards should be set at a level consistent with the urgency of our energy problems, at or an appropriate distance beyond what can be achieved cost-effectively with proven technologies that do not require significant changes in the size and performance of light-duty vehicles. Timing is also an important consideration. Manufacturers should be given sufficient lead time to redesign their entire product lines (approximately 10 years). In this way the full impact of proven fuel economy technologies can be realized and manufacturers can be given a clear, long-term goal around which to plan.

The National Research Council (NRC) Committee on the Impacts and Effectiveness of CAFE Standards, on which I was privileged to serve, defined the "cost-efficient" level of fuel economy as the level at which the marginal present value of fuel savings to the consumer of the next increment in fuel economy exactly equals the marginal cost of technology added to the vehicle to produce those savings (NRC, 2002). Further, the Committee's definition allowed no change in the size, weight, or performance of vehicles over a base year level. In my opinion, fuel economy standards should be set at least as high as the cost-efficient level but not a great deal higher . . .

Why doesn't the market produce this level of fuel economy without being compelled by fuel economy standards? I addressed this question in my January 7, 2007 testimony to the Senate Energy Committee. Like the market for most other energy using consumer durable goods, the market for automotive fuel economy is not efficient. At the time of vehicle purchase, consumers do not fully value future fuel savings and therefore manufacturers, in general, do not make vehicles as energy efficient as they would if the market itself were efficient. It is more effective to sell cars based on other features that excite car buyers. And, of course, few new car buyers will voluntarily and on their own initiative pay more for the public benefits of reduced US oil dependence or greenhouse gas emissions. . . .

In June of 2006, in response to a request from Senators Obama, Lugar and Biden, I calculated cost-efficient levels of light-duty vehicle fuel economy increases at higher gasoline prices than assumed in the NRC (2002) report. . . .

As with all such analyses, there are some caveats. The NRC study is now five years old, and there have been significant technological developments since its publication. Some of the technologies used to construct the

NRC fuel economy cost functions have already been adopted in existing vehicles but have been used to increase power and weight rather than fuel economy. On the other hand, important new technologies have also been developed. Second, at fuel costs above $3.50 per gallon the indicated cost-efficient fuel economy levels are beyond the range of what could be achieved using the fuel economy technologies considered by the NRC study. . . .

The cost-efficient analysis assumes constant light-duty vehicle weight and performance. Fuel economy technology can also be used to increase horsepower and weight while holding fuel economy constant. Setting fuel economy standards involves an implicit judgment about the importance of having even heavier and more powerful vehicles than we have today versus reducing oil dependence and mitigating greenhouse gas emissions.

The cost-efficient analysis is limited to existing, proven fuel economy technologies. There is no doubt that technological advances will be made over the next ten years. This fact allows decision makers to have greater confidence that the targets set can be achieved without harm to the automobile industry or to motorists. Indeed, when the NRC committee finished its study just five years ago, it concluded that neither hybrid nor clean diesel engines could be considered proven technologies. Today there are a dozen hybrid models to choose from and clean diesels will soon be available. The cost-efficient method does not rely on technological progress but it does expect it.

Market-Based Alternatives to CAFE

Fuel economy standards are not the only effective way to realize greater fuel economy. Feebates are a way to emphasize the value of reducing petroleum via the purchase price of vehicles rather than future fuel savings. Feebates give a rebate to purchasers of low-fuel consumption vehicles and impose a fee on buyers of high-fuel consumption vehicles. While feebate systems can take many forms, perhaps the most appropriate formulation bases the rebate or fee on fuel consumption (gallons per mile), thereby giving equal value to every gallon of fuel saved.

Feebate systems consist of a pivot point and a rate. Vehicles whose fuel consumption is below the pivot point receive a rebate while vehicles with fuel consumption above the pivot point are charged a fee. There can be a single pivot point or different pivot points for different types of vehicles. The rate specifies the additional value of saving fuel. Feebate rates on the order of $1,000 to $1,500 per 0.01 gallons per mile should achieve fleet average fuel economy improvements of 30% to 50% (Greene et al., 2005). The feebate rate determines the incentive to use fuel economy technology to increase fuel economy. The pivot point determines which vehicles gain (receive a rebate) and which vehicles lose (pay a fee).

Feebates have two important advantages over fuel economy standards. First, they are a continuing incentive to adopt energy efficient technologies and use them to increase fuel economy. Once a fuel economy standard has been met, there is no additional incentive for manufacturers to increase fuel economy beyond the value of future fuel savings to consumers. A feebate system (especially if indexed for inflation) provides a continuing added incentive. There is always a rebate to be gained or a fee to be avoided. Second, feebates put a cap on the costs manufacturers will have to incur to increase fuel economy. Manufacturers are required to meet fuel economy standards regardless of the cost. There is no reason why a manufacturer would spend more to gain a rebate or avoid a fee than its value. Thus, the feebate rate puts a cap on the economic costs that might be incurred to increase fuel economy.

The chief disadvantage of feebate systems is that they do not guarantee that a desired level of fuel economy improvement will be achieved. Feebates depend on manufacturers and consumers efficiently trading off the higher cost of fuel economy technology and the value of rebates or fees. Since both affect the purchase price of a vehicle, there is good reason to expect markets to respond efficiently, but there is no guarantee.

Today, we have half of a feebate system for passenger cars in the form of the gas-guzzler tax. There is no comparable policy for light trucks. I can think of no good reason for taxing inefficient passenger cars but not light trucks. Furthermore, half of a feebate system is less than half as effective as a full feebate system. I urge you to consider a complete well-formulated feebate system for all light-duty vehicles. Should you decide not to implement a complete feebate system, I would urge you to abolish the gas-guzzler tax for passenger cars in favor of higher fuel economy standards for all light-duty vehicles.

What Form?

Critics of the CAFE system have raised many objections to it over the past 30 years. Two criticisms have been especially potent in preventing progress: CAFE is unfair. CAFE is unsafe. The first is accurate. The second is incorrect. I have addressed the safety issues in other testimony and other publications (Greene, 2005; Greene and Keller, 2002; Greene, 2007). Regardless of one's viewpoint on these two issues, the reformed CAFE standard adopted by the National Highway Traffic Safety Administration (NHTSA) for light trucks nullifies both criticisms. It adjusts each manufacturer's standard according to the size mix of vehicles it produces. It removes any incentive for downsizing that an unreformed CAFE system might create. At the same time, it keeps nearly all significant fuel economy technologies in play. It also creates the opportunity to finally eliminate the distinction between cars and light trucks in a unified set of footprint-based standards. I congratulate the staff of NHTSA for this important innovation. . . .

Who should Decide?

An important issue that has received too little analysis is who should set the fuel economy standards? Should it be the Congress or the Executive Branch? If it is the executive branch, should it be the Department of Transportation, the Department of Energy or the Environmental Protection Agency? In 1975, Congress set ambitious standards for passenger cars and left the establishment of standards for light trucks to the NHTSA. The result was less ambitious standards for light trucks. Yet over the past few years, NHTSA has raised the light truck standards twice by modest but meaningful amounts and has instituted important changes in the form of the standards. Congress has not raised the passenger car standards in more than 30 years. In my opinion, a one-time increase in fuel economy standards will not be adequate to address the problems of climate change and of oil dependence. A 50% increase in fuel economy by 2020 would need to be followed by an increase of 100% over current levels by 2030.

I don't claim to know who should set fuel economy standards but I do have some observations that I believe are relevant. First, oil dependence is a problem that we "solved" temporarily and incompletely 20 years ago. And when we "solved" the problem we seemed to lose interest in the policies necessary to keep it solved. And so it has come back. We will be struggling with the problem of climate change, in my opinion, for decades, much as we have done with urban air pollution. Indeed, climate change appears to be even more difficult and has a much longer time horizon. Twenty years from now, I think that it will still be clear that we have not solved the problem of climate change and that we must keep working at it. In my view, this argues for locating the authority over fuel economy standards with the agency that has the greatest interest in and responsibility for addressing climate change.

Congressional Guidance is Needed

If Congress elects not to set fuel economy targets itself, it is absolutely critical that Congress give clear and strong guidance about the importance of fuel economy standards to addressing the problems of oil dependence, greenhouse gas emissions and sustainable energy for transportation. There are many ways that strong guidance could be given. It could take the form of statements about the importance of the problems fuel economy standards help solve. It could be in the form of recommended targets.

Regardless of the form of its guidance, Congress should clearly express to the regulating agency how important increasing fuel economy is to solving our oil dependence problem, mitigating carbon dioxide emissions to reduce the probability of dangerous climate change, and developing sustainable energy sources for transportation. Congress' guidance should be clear and emphatic enough to sustain progress when some might think the oil dependence problem is solved. It should give clear direction to regulators about the importance of mitigating greenhouse gas emissions versus continuing the horsepower race. As the 2002 NRC report pointed out, Congress has both the authority and responsibility for establishing the priority of these societal goals.

Resources for the Future is a non-profit, non-partisan research organization focusing on the economic and social science implications of energy, environment, and natural resources. Here, its President, who was Chair of the National Research Council's Committee that issued the oft cited report on the consequences of fuel economy standards, issues a statement that counsels a rethinking of the issue in light of recent political events.

3.12. "Resources for the Future President," Paul Portney Briefs House Senate Science Committee on Effectiveness, Impact of CAFE Standards, February 9, 2005

... Portney, chair of the National Research Council's Committee on Effectiveness and Impact of CAFE Standards, noted that, upon reflection, the committee's 2001 report may have been too conservative in its fuel economy recommendations.

> "Hybrid vehicle sales have grown faster than anyone expected," he said. "Similarly, considerable progress is being made in the development of much cleaner diesel engines. It might be possible to meet more stringent fuel economy standards at lower costs than the committee foresaw in 2001."

Portney mentioned that, in addition to these developments, a number of factors with considerable impact on this issue have occurred since the committee published the report.

> "In August of 2001, we simply could not have imagined the impact the horrific events of September 11 would have on our thinking about the consequences of US oil consumption and our growing dependence on imported oil from nations that are unstable or may bear us ill will."

Portney also noted that oil prices have risen significantly since the report was published, due to rapidly growing demand for oil in the developing world and slower growth in production. "These factors, coupled with impressive developments in hybrids and diesel power, have created a greatly different world than the one the committee anticipated when the report was written," he stated.

However, Portney also pointed out that research on the "rebound effect," or additional miles motorists drive in vehicles that get better fuel economy, since the time the 2001 report was written suggests that tighter CAFE standards may also carry some negative effects that could be significant.

> "New factors have cropped up since 2001 that might weigh in on both sides of the debate to tighten CAFE standards," he stated. "Any deliberations over the program in the future should bear all these factors in mind."

Following are a number of brief statements of those who participated in the debate over enactment of the new CAFE standards, on the occasion of the bill's signing.

3.13. "Statement of Alliance President and CEO Dave McCurdy on President's Signing of Energy Bill into Law," Alliance of Automobile Manufacturers, December 19, 2007

The Alliance of Automobile Manufacturers is pleased that a new federal fuel economy standard has been signed into law. We believe this tough, national fuel economy bill will be good for both consumers and energy security. It is critical that automakers and consumers have the certainty that this national, 50-state fuel economy law provides.

Importantly, this landmark agreement establishes nationwide fuel economy requirements for the next 12 years and beyond. For the first time in more than 30 years, Congress has weighed in and established aggressive fuel economy standards that balance important environmental, energy security, safety and economic considerations. Automakers are moving forward to tackle the challenges that these new requirements will demand.

This legislation will result in a 40 percent increase in fuel economy and 30 percent reduction in carbon dioxide emissions from new automobiles, enhancing our energy security while at the same time addressing climate change.

This historic legislation would not have been possible without the efforts of auto workers, dealers, suppliers, user groups and industry allies in the business community—whose leaders and members participated in this process.

3.14. "Greenpeace Statement on Passage of Senate Energy Bill," December 13, 2007

WASHINGTON—Responding to the Senate's passage of The Energy Independence and Security Act of 2007, Kate Smolski, Global Warming Legislative Coordinator for Greenpeace USA, issued the following statement:

"Faced with two of the most critical issues of our day—global warming and oil dependency—the Senate has responded by legislating on behalf of special interests rather than Americans and the future of the planet.

"Weak fuel efficiency standards and the elimination of key renewable energy provisions may get a bill passed but they will not deliver the clean energy future this country needs. Lack of leadership from the Senate Democrats has cheated the American public and given the polluting fossil fuel companies a fat Christmas bonus.

"Greenpeace urges Congress to come back next year and pass significant legislation to curb global warming. Our children and grandchildren deserve no less. And voters in 2008 will be watching."

3.15. "House Vote Sends Landmark Energy Bill to President Bush," Statement of President Kevin Knobloch of the Union of Concerned Scientists, December 18, 2007

In an overwhelming 314 to 100 vote, the House today passed historic energy legislation that raises fuel economy standards for the first time in 30 years, boosts energy efficiency standards, and requires a significant increase in biofuels production. The Senate approved the legislation late last week, and President Bush has indicated that he will sign the bill into law before the end of the year.

According to analysis by the Union of Concerned Scientists (UCS), the bill's fuel economy and renewable fuel standards combined will save the country 2.3 million barrels of oil a day in 2020—more than what the United States currently imports from the Persian Gulf. The fuel economy provisions alone will create 149,300 jobs, and save consumers $22 billion at the pump every year starting in 2020, even after paying for the fuel-saving technology needed to meet the standards. In addition, the fuel economy standards will prevent more than 190 million metric tons of global warming emissions in 2020.

The following is a statement by UCS President Kevin Knobloch:

"For too long, America has been starved for leadership on energy policy. Today, Congress has overcome the obstacles that have blocked progress for more than 30 years. This law is a very significant, concrete and long overdue step forward. No energy legislation has ever done more for

America's security by saving oil and curbing global warming pollution. The fuel economy mandate will breathe new life into a faltering domestic auto industry, prodding Detroit to design and build much more efficient vehicles that consumers are hungry to buy.

"With today's vote we begin our journey to solve global warming and achieve energy independence. We can get there by enacting a national renewable electricity standard, passing economy-wide climate legislation, and preserving existing federal and state authority to regulate global warming pollution."

QUESTIONS FOR CONSIDERATION

1   The CAFE issue poses thorny questions about the efficacy of instituting technological solutions to problems that have significant social dimensions. For example, energy experts are quick to point out that automobile engines have, in fact, improved in efficiency over recent decades. However, these efficiencies have been undermined, even erased, by corresponding increases in vehicle weight and power. Is it therefore appropriate to require automakers to meet more stringent fuel economy standards?

2   Is your answer to this question affected by the fact that automakers disproportionately advertise their larger, low-mileage models because the profit margin on them is greater?

3   Is it good public policy to focus on automobile efficiency independent of other policies that could decrease gasoline consumption, such as reduced speed limits and their stricter enforcement, or greater restrictions on wasteful idling? Are automakers being asked to compensate for behavior largely out of their control?

4   Opponents of stricter CAFE standards point to the fact that the smaller and lighter vehicles they would promote are more dangerous. But dangerous to whom? Are the occupants of other, smaller vehicles on the road in greater peril in the event of a collision? And don't vans and sport utility vehicles obstruct the vision of drivers of sedans?

5   Is it a stretch to allege that reducing gasoline consumption would foster greater security by reducing our petroleum imports?

6   If there is an urgency to the factors justifying reduced gasoline consumption, why make 2020 the target date for the new standards? Is long-lead time one of the concessions that proponents of CAFE needed to make to get the bill enacted? Is it too cynical to suggest that lawmakers want credit for appearing to do the right thing, but don't really want to fully accept the political consequences of such a policy?

Chapter 4

The Cap-and-Trade Protocol

BACKGROUND

Though global climate change has been recognized as a real and potentially catastrophic threat to the health and welfare of the planet for many decades, only recently has it captured the attention of the national media, an anxious public, and US government officials. Part of the reason is that many of its consequences have become starkly apparent, even photogenic, and, worse, seen as accelerating. These perceptions have been confirmed by a succession of increasingly dire predictions from the Intergovernmental Panel on Climate Change, the world's preeminent authority on this ecological phenomenon. But it was not until 2007 that Congress, under prodding from interests across the political spectrum, began to feel the urgency of controlling carbon emissions. The introduction, in October 2007 of America's Climate Security Act, S-2191, was the first major piece of legislation to seriously address the problem.

The tipping point may well have been the decision of the US Supreme Court in a landmark case, *Massachusetts v. EPA*. In this case, the Court, finding that CO^2 was an air pollutant under the Clean Air Act, effectively charged the Environmental Protection Agency with developing a policy to minimize heat-trapping gases threatening the environment. But the task of developing such a national program was properly the responsibility of Congress, and the two prime sponsors of S-2191, Senators Lieberman and Warner, acknowledged as much and responded to the call. Despite the extensive period of time during which the issue lay veritably dormant, at least as a public policy matter, tackling climate change now reflects the urgency it has long deserved. S-2191 has put the matter on the table, and it now seems likely that climate threatening practices will get prompt and comprehensive attention.

The protocol embodied in America's Climate Security Act is generally referred to as "cap-and-trade," and it has almost immediately secured wide support. It is not difficult to understand why. It continues the regulatory trend away from the heavy-handed standard setting and strict enforcement protocol known as "command and control," implemented very successfully by EPA during its first two decades, and toward a more favored policy that allows markets to signal appropriate environmental behavior. An example of a pure market program, favored by a substantial percentage of economists and free-marketers, is the imposition of a carbon tax, which directly rewards or discourages behavior, allowing individual actors the freedom of choice. The government would then gradually increase the tax over time, and secure increasing increments of improvement.

"Cap-and-trade" is something of a hybrid. In its bare essentials, the government would set an overall authorized limit on greenhouse gas emissions (a "cap") for which permits would be issued, though that limit would be ratcheted down over time to insure reduced emissions. The credits would then be granted by the government, or purchased or auctioned. The rigidity of "command and control" would be replaced by a market-friendly freedom on the part of industrial actors to trade credits among themselves. Those who find ways to reduce carbon output could profit from selling their rights to those who need all, or more, of their allotment. It therefore allows businesses to drive solutions, even profit from them. Inevitably, a market price for carbon would be established, rather than having a tax imposed by a regulatory agency.

As noted earlier, the "cap-and-trade" protocol enjoys wide support. A program administered by EPA in the 1990s to control emissions of sulfur dioxide to address acid rain was very successful, though operated on a much smaller scale. A comparable program has been administered in Europe for several years, though with mixed results. A counterpart program was even part of the Kyoto agreement in 1997. Even before the introduction of S-2191, cap-and-trade was made part of the Regional Greenhouse Gas Initiative forged by a consortium of northeastern states to address their region's carbon emissions. It was also one of the recommendations contained in the Mayors Climate Protection Agreement entered into by over 750 local governments. So S-2191 starts its legislative journey with a broad base of support.

That support, however, is not unequivocal or unanimous. Many of the interest groups represented below offer recommendations for refinement or reservations to be recognized. And some, of course, are downright opposed. Perhaps the most interesting political aspect of its reception is that it uncharacteristically splits usually cohesive policy alliances. Neither the business community nor the environmentalists are uniformly behind its enactment, at least not without substantial amendment or refinement. S-2191 entered 2008 with a good chance to be the first major Congressional enactment dealing with global climate change.

DOCUMENTS

The two prime sponsors of America's Climate Security Act, S-2191, set out their broad objectives for the legislation. Senator Joe Lieberman enumerated several of the urgent adverse health and environmental consequences, stressing particularly its potential effect on our grandchildren. Senator John Warner pointed specifically to the importance of dealing with climate change as a national security issue. He also identified the decision in Massachusetts v. EPA as a spur to the legislative branch of government to join the Executive in an effort to deal with greenhouse gas emissions.

4.1. Press Release: "Lieberman and Warner Introduce Bipartisan Climate Legislation," October 18, 2007

Washington DC—Senators Joseph I. Lieberman (ID-CT) and John W. Warner (R-VA), chairman and ranking Member of the Senate Subcommittee on Private Sector and Consumer Solutions to Global Warming and Wildlife Protection today introduced a bill that would achieve substantial, long-term cuts in US greenhouse-gas emissions.

On its own, the America's Climate Security Act (ACSA) is projected to reduce total US greenhouse-gas emissions by as much as 19% below the 2005 level (4% below the 1990 level) in 2020 and by as much as 63% below the 2005 level in 2050. Lieberman and Warner presented their new bill as the core of a new federal program that Congress should pass to avert catastrophic global climate change while enhancing America's energy security.

"With all the irrefutable evidence we now have corroborating that climate change is real, dangerous, and proceeding faster than many scientists predicted, this is the year for Congress to move this critical legislation," said Lieberman. "If we fail to start substantially reducing greenhouse gas emissions in the next couple of years, we risk bequeathing a diminished world to our grandchildren. Insect-borne diseases such as malaria will spike as tropical ecosystems expand; hotter air will exacerbate the pollution that sends children to the hospital with asthma attacks; food insecurity from shifting agricultural zones will spark border wars; and storms and coastal flooding from sea-level rise will cause mortality and dislocation."

"In my 28 years in the Senate, I have focused above all on issues of national security, and I see the problem of global climate change as fitting squarely within that focus," said Warner. "Today we introduced a balanced bill. Senator Lieberman and I found a good, sound, starting point that sends a significant signal that the US is serious about taking a leadership role in reducing its greenhouse gas emissions."

. . .

"It is imperative that our nation acts now to address the concerns over growing greenhouse gas emissions, while carefully addressing the effects it could have on working families and our economy," said Coleman. "The Lieberman-Warner America's Climate Security Act meets this need by taking a responsible approach to greenhouse gas reduction that will not undermine our economy, which is why I am pleased to be an original co-sponsor. Climate change is not a problem we can leave to our children to solve. I am confident this bill will not only protect our environment, but protect our children."

"The science is clear and compelling—we must act to control and reduce greenhouse gas emissions," said Senator Harkin. "This bill is an excellent starting point for formulating a national climate change strategy. I am especially pleased that it recognizes the critical role that the agricultural sector can play in that strategy through reductions in farm emissions and sequestration of carbon in soils."

"The solution to this serious problem is not inaction," said Senator Elizabeth Dole. "We must ensure clean air for future generations, and this is a responsible, market-driven approach that strengthens our economy, competitiveness and security."

"Climate change is one of the most daunting challenges we face and we must develop reasonable solutions to reduce our greenhouse gas emissions. That is why I am pleased to be an original co-sponsor of the Lieberman-Warner America's Climate Security Act. This bi-partisan bill presents a practical, economically-sound approach to reducing America's greenhouse gas emissions 70 percent over 2005 levels by 2050," said Senator Susan Collins.

In July 2007, The Environmental Protection Agency (EPA) found that if the US achieves emissions reductions of the magnitude mandated by ACSA, then—making conservative assumptions about the pace of emissions reductions in the rest of the world—the concentration of greenhouse gases in the atmosphere will remain below 500 parts per million (ppm) at the end of this century. According to the Intergovernmental Panel on Climate Change, keeping the concentration below 500 ppm will avoid a high risk of global warming that would cause severe impacts.

America's Climate Security Act controls compliance costs by allowing companies to trade, save, and borrow emission allowances, and by allowing them to generate credits when they induce non-covered businesses, farms, and others to reduce their greenhouse gas emissions or capture and store greenhouse gases.

The Act invests set-aside emissions credits and money raised by the auction of such allowances in advancing several important public policies, including, but not limited to:

- Deploying advanced technologies and practices for reducing emissions;
- Protecting low- and middle-income Americans from higher energy costs;
- Keeping good jobs in the United States; and
- Mitigating the negative impacts of any unavoidable global warming on low- and middle-income Americans and wildlife.

Several key environmental groups, companies, and other organizations, including the National Wildlife Federation, Environmental Defense and the National Resources Defense Council, have expressed support for ACSA.

Larry Schweiger, President and CEO, National Wildlife Federation:

> "This is a bipartisan breakthrough on global warming that takes us a giant step closer to a historic vote in the United States Senate. I commend Senator Lieberman and Senator Warner for drafting a strong bill to protect wildlife from global warming."

John Rowe, Chairman and CEO, Exelon Corporation:

> "As an early and vocal advocate for climate change legislation, Exelon applauds the bipartisan leadership of Senators Lieberman and Warner to introduce a bill that will help reduce greenhouse gas emissions to address global warming as soon as possible. The legislation represents another important step towards developing the bipartisan consensus necessary to enact legislation this Congress. We are especially pleased that the bill recognizes the need to protect electricity consumers by allocating part of the allowances to local utilities for the benefit of their customers."

Steve Cochran, National Climate Campaign Director, Environmental Defense:

> "Lieberman and Warner have paved the way for a historic committee vote on a bill that promises to make great strides toward climate security and economic growth. Thanks to their thoughtful approach we're moving beyond talk and quickly toward action."

Steven Kline, Vice President for Corporate Environmental and Federal Affairs, PGE Corp:

> "We believe America's Climate Security Act provides a solid starting point for constructively advancing a comprehensive, national response to and policy on climate change. Senators Lieberman and Warner have developed a thoughtful proposal that recognizes the urgent need for action by designing a program to achieve significant emission reductions from all sectors of the economy. The bill includes provisions that prioritize energy efficiency and technology development and deployment, as well as innovative ideas to protect electricity consumers, manage overall program costs, and provide states with the resources to help address the unique needs of their communities and citizens as we transition to a low-carbon economy and adapt to a changing

environment. America's Climate Security Act takes significant steps toward recognizing that a national program must balance the economic, technology, and environmental challenges of combating climate change."

Frances Beinecke, President, Natural Resources Defense Council:

"The introduction and planned markup of America's Climate Security Act by Senators Joe Lieberman (I-Conn.) and John Warner (R-Va.) represents an important step forward in the overdue process to enact comprehensive, mandatory global warming legislation. Committee consideration of this legislation will help move us toward the substantial reductions in global warming pollution we need to protect our climate. The bill also recognizes the need to direct proceeds from the pollution allowance market to important policy objectives, including promoting clean energy solutions, protecting the poor and other consumers, ensuring a just transition for workers in affected industries, and preventing impacts abroad that lead to conflicts and threats to security."

The Members of the Association of Fish & Wildlife Agencies:

"[O]ur organizations, representing millions of American sportsmen and sportswomen, thank you again for working with us to help address the challenge of climate change by both reducing emissions of greenhouse gases and providing important new resources to assist fish and wildlife survive in the face of this unprecedented challenge."

4.2. "Sen. Warner Opening Statement for Subcommittee Hearing on 'America's Climate Security Act,' " October 24, 2007

Wednesday, October 24, 2007

Senator Lieberman, my fellow subcommittee members, and distinguished witnesses, I am proud to begin the America's Climate Security Act's journey through the legislative process today with this subcommittee hearing. . . .

In brief, it is my view that America cannot afford to continue to stay on the sidelines. We need to get on the field. Our government has three co-equal branches of government, and one of these, the judicial branch, has spoken. In April, the United States Supreme Court ruled that greenhouse gases are air pollutants. The executive branch favors a voluntary approach to reducing greenhouse gas emissions. Now is the time for the legislative branch to begin movement on a well-conceived mandatory greenhouse gas emissions reduction program. I am eager to see the Senate take the lead. And I look forward to the House proceeding . . .

If our full committee completes its markup before the United Nations Framework Convention on Climate Change Conference of Parties in Bali in December, the US will emerge as a leader. It will send a rare signal from 1 ½ branches of government.

In short, I want to see the United States credibly enter the realm of world leadership on this issue producing legislative action here at home.

The bill before us relies heavily on the pioneering work done here by many. I point to the accomplishments of the first President Bush, as he broke the logjam on the Clean Air Act amendments by campaigning on the issue in 1988. His Administration presented the idea of a cap-and-trade system, one that has worked effectively in the Acid Rain Program. My friend, Senator Baucus helped hone and usher the amendments through this body, and today, the success of the Acid Rain Program speaks for itself.

To underscore the urgency of the economic and energy situation facing our nation now, one need only look at a recent permit denial for a power plant in Kansas. Last week, the Kansas Department of Health and Environment cited carbon dioxide emissions as the reason for rejecting an air permit for coal-fired power plants.

Furthermore, nationally, plans for at least 16 plants have been scrapped this year with another 76 plans on hold with a very uncertain future. This is why Congress needs to move, so the private sector has certainty.

These actions have significant economic impacts.

How are we going to meet our power needs for economic growth in this country if we do not provide the regulatory certainty to enable that growth?

Our country relies on power fueled by our nation's largest natural resource: coal. In order to create the certainty needed for further investments to occur in the power sector, in order to meet our country's growing energy needs, a federal regulatory structure for greenhouse gases needs to be enacted.

I thank the subcommittee members, all of whom Senator Lieberman and I met with personally. In the pages of our bill are many of the ideas brought to our attention in those meetings. We may not always agree on how to address the issue of climate change, but this bill is intended to provide the vehicle by which the Senate will work its will on this pressing challenge before us.

I look forward to the continued dialogue and to hearing the views of today's witnesses.

The Union of Concerned Citizens is a broad, science-based coalition of scientists, students, and citizens that conducts research and promotes civic action to solve environmental problems by changing government policy, corporate practice, and consumer behavior.

While it doesn't speak specifically to S-2191, the following document argues for the need for an effective cap-and-trade program.

4.3. "We Need a Well-Designed Cap-and-Trade Program to Fight Global Warming," Rachael Cleetus, Union of Concerned Scientists

Union of Concerned Scientists

The debate over global warming has finally shifted from whether it is indeed happening (it is) and if human activity is causing it (it is) to what we need to do to avoid the worst consequences of climate change. If we stabilize atmospheric concentrations of global warming emissions at or below 450 parts per million (ppm) of carbon dioxide (CO_2) equivalent, we have a 50 percent chance of preventing the Earth's average temperature from rising 3.6 degrees Fahrenheit (2 degrees Celsius) above pre-industrial levels. Scientific evidence suggests this would avoid some of the worst, irreversible consequences of global warming.

According to a Union of Concerned Scientists (UCS) analysis, even with aggressive action by industrialized and developing countries, the United States would have to cut its emissions by at least 80 percent from 2000 levels by 2050.

This daunting task will require countries to quickly deploy clean energy technologies and develop new low-carbon technologies, using a combination of policies to help spur these activities. Foremost among them is a well-designed cap-and-trade program, which would put a price on carbon emissions that reflects the costs of global warming. This must be coupled with strengthened efficiency standards, incentives, and public investment in clean technologies and infrastructure. A carbon tax—which has attracted some attention recently on Capitol Hill—also could be part of the solution, but it would not guarantee necessary emissions reductions without an emissions cap in place.

How a Basic Cap-and-Trade Program Works

Under a cap-and-trade program, the federal government would establish an economy-wide cap on emissions, measured in metric tons of CO_2 equivalent, and tighten that cap over time. It then would issue "emissions allowances" that correspond to a specific number of metric tons of carbon. The total number of allowances would match the cap.

The program would require electric utilities, refineries, and other sources of global warming pollution to have an allowance for each ton of their emissions. Polluters would acquire allowances during the initial distribution or by trading for them in an "allowance market." This market would enable polluters that are able to reduce their emissions relatively cheaply to sell allowances to those that are unable to do so, thereby establishing a market price for carbon. The program would create an incentive for polluting facilities to implement the most cost-effective emissions reduction options and, by putting a price on global warming pollution, encourage investments in new low-carbon technologies.

Key Elements of a Well-Designed Cap-and-Trade Program

All cap-and-trade programs are not equal. Only a well-designed program would achieve the necessary emissions reductions and protect the environment and the economy. The key elements are:

- Stringently capping emissions, with firm near-term goals. As discussed above, the United States must reduce its global warming pollution emissions at least 80 percent below 2000 levels by 2050 to avoid the worst effects of global warming. Delay in taking action would require much sharper cuts later, making it much more difficult and costly to meet the necessary target. A near-term goal of a 15 percent to 20 percent reduction from current levels by 2020 is essential.
- Including as many economic sectors as possible. The cap should cover all major sources of emissions, either directly or indirectly. They include electric utilities, transportation, and energy-intensive industries, which together comprise some 80 percent of US global warming pollution, as well as fossil fuel emissions from the agriculture, commercial and residential sectors.
- Including all major heat-trapping gas emissions. Those include carbon dioxide (CO^2), methane ($CH4$), nitrous oxide (N^2O), hydrofluorocarbons (HFCs), perfluorocarbons (PFCs) and sulfur hexafluoride (SF6). Emissions of different gases could be combined according to their global warming potential using the CO^2-equivalent method.
- Auctioning all (or a substantial majority of) allowances rather than giving them away to emitters. An allowance auction would allow the market to set the price of carbon, and it would be the most efficient and equitable way of distributing allowances. Giving away too many allowances would distort the market and could result in windfall profits for polluters.
- Using auction revenues for the public good. The government should invest auction revenues in clean, renewable energy technologies and energy efficiency measures. Revenues also could compensate low-income families, provide transition assistance to workers or economic sectors that are disproportionately disrupted by the program, and help communities adapt to the unavoidable effects of global warming.
- Excluding loopholes that undermine the integrity of the program. To be effective, a cap-and-trade program should not include a "safety

valve" setting a maximum price for allowances and requiring the government to sell unlimited allowances to polluters once that price is hit. This would undermine the integrity of the emissions cap, and reduce the incentive for investments in clean technology.

- Including strict criteria for cost-containment mechanisms such as off-sets and borrowing. Offsets would allow regulated polluters to purchase emissions reductions from unregulated sectors or countries that do not have caps, instead of reducing an equivalent amount of their own emissions or buying allowances from other regulated facilities. (For example, a regulated electricity generator could pay an unregulated landfill company to capture its methane emissions and use those emissions reductions to "offset" their own.) Borrowing would allow facilities to emit more global warming pollution if they promise to make sharper emissions cuts later.

  Offsets and borrowing could lower the cap-and-trade program's short-term costs for polluters. However, by postponing emissions reductions from major emitting sectors, they would delay much-needed technological innovation and jeopardize the program's long-term goals. Any offsets should meet rigorous standards to ensure the activities are permanently removing carbon from the atmosphere beyond what would happen in a business-as-usual scenario. Borrowing should not reach unsustainable levels that threaten the program's viability.

- Linking with similar programs. There are important economic advantages to linking a domestic cap-and-trade regime with those in Europe and other regions that have adopted a stringent emissions cap. Doing so would require the US program's design to be compatible with these other regimes.

Lessons from Existing Cap-and-Trade Programs

In 2005 the European Union implemented a cap-and-trade program, the EU Emissions Trading System (EU ETS), covering 27 countries. In its first phase, which ends this December, the program covered the electric power and major energy-intensive industrial sectors. The program has been criticized for setting overly generous caps for polluters and giving away most allowances, resulting in huge windfall profits for power generators. The EU is making adjustments for the next phase of the ETS, which extends from 2008 through 2012. A US cap-and-trade program should learn from the EU's experience and implement strong design principles from the outset to avoid these mistakes.

Any federal cap-and-trade system also could borrow from examples here in North America. The Regional Greenhouse Gas Initiative (RGGI), which will begin in January 2009, is a cap-and-trade program designed to reduce emissions from the electric power sector in ten Northeast and Mid-Atlantic States. California has set a cap of reaching 1990 levels of global warming pollution by 2020, and is moving to implement a suite of policies, including an emissions trading system, to achieve that goal. Meanwhile, six Western states and two Canadian provinces have launched the Western Climate Initiative to develop a regional cap-and-trade regime, and several Midwestern states are proposing similar programs as part of climate change legislation.

At the federal level, the acid rain program provides a good model of a successful cap-and-trade program that has greatly reduced power plant emissions of sulfur dioxide (SO^2) and nitrogen oxides (NOx), the pollutants that cause acid rain and smog. . . .

Cap and Trade Alone is not Sufficient

A cap-and-trade program alone would not be sufficient to meet the challenge of climate change. While a cap-and-trade policy would address the failure of the market to account for harm to the climate, it cannot by itself provide sufficient incentives for the technologies and other measures that will be needed to establish a true low-carbon economy. The government must implement parallel policies alongside a cap-and-trade regime to ensure development and deployment of the full range of clean technologies. These policies include requiring utilities to generate a higher percentage of their electricity from renewable energy sources, requiring automakers to increase vehicle fuel economy standards, stronger energy efficiency policies, incentives for investments in low-carbon technologies, and policies encouraging smart growth. Studies have shown that a comprehensive approach including these parallel policies would lower the price for allowances, cut emissions, and save consumers money by lowering their electric and gasoline bills.

What about a Carbon Tax?

A well-designed cap-and-trade program has an important advantage over a carbon tax. The former would require the specific emissions reductions necessary to avoid dangerous climate change, while a carbon tax by itself cannot guarantee any particular level of emissions reductions. Moreover, a cap-and-trade program would more easily dovetail with similar existing and proposed regimes in other countries and regions. For example, allowing developing countries to sell carbon credits in a cap-and-trade program from tropical deforestation emissions reductions would provide a powerful incentive to address the source of some 20 percent of global warming pollution emissions.

Nevertheless, a carbon tax, like a cap-and-trade program, would use the power of the market to achieve cost-effective emissions reductions, and both would generate revenues that could be used for the public benefit. It may be possible for the two policies to co-exist and complement one another. For example, a cap-and-trade program could cover most economic sectors where emissions can be capped at centralized sources, such as power plants. A carbon tax could provide incentives for emissions reductions in sectors where it is more difficult to establish a cap, such as transportation, where emissions are more dispersed through the stages of fuel production and consumption.

Any effective US climate strategy must cut global warming pollution deeply enough to avoid the worst effects of climate change, which means at least 80 percent below 2000 levels by 2050. Emissions trading and carbon taxes are both tools we can used to achieve these reductions, as are technology standards, incentives, and public investment in clean technology and infrastructure. What's most important is that we move aggressively to address the climate crisis, and that we begin the transition to a low-carbon economy right now.

Environmental Defense, a major advocacy organization, was the earliest and most ardent advocate for a cap-and-trade protocol in general and S-2191 in particular. Its almost unqualified support has incited what some have called a "green civil war" with sister groups who, while acknowledging the need for a federal program to control carbon emissions, have serious reservations about this particular program. Fred Krupp, ED's Executive Director, makes the case in his testimony before the Senate Committee on Environment and Public Works.

4.4. "Statement by Fred Krupp of Environmental Defense Regarding 'America's Climate Security Act' Submitted to the US Senate Committee on Environment and Public Works," November 15, 2007

November 15, 2007

I am honored to be here with you today as this Committee deliberates America's Climate Security Act. There is no more important legislation that this Committee will ever consider than comprehensive climate change policy. . . .

America's Climate Security Act contains all of the essential elements needed in legislation for the US to begin to tackle the problem of global climate change. If the members of this committee remember one thing from my testimony today—it should be this—we must pass comprehensive climate legislation now. Our economy, our environment, and our morality compels it—and if I am back here three years from now—still calling on this Committee to pass legislation—then all who are in this room today will have failed. We would have lessened our chances of preventing the most dangerous consequences of climate change and we would have raised the costs to the economy of meeting the challenge.

In my testimony today, I want to make five points: 1) why time is of the essence, 2) that America's Climate Security Act has the right framework to tackle climate change, 3) that we have the technology we need to get started, 4) that the carrots and sticks in America's Climate Security Act will prompt international action, and finally, 5) I will comment on a couple of amendments that I believe are worth special notice.

1. There is no time for delay.

If the legislation is enacted and takes effect in 2012, the emissions caps would result in an annual reduction of emissions of just under 2% per year and, for covered sources, arrive at a reduction of 15% below current levels by 2020. But what happens if we delay enacting legislation by two years? Just two years of delay—holding everything else constant—has major consequences. As you can see in the diagram behind me, in order to result in the same amount of cumulative emissions by 2020 (and with climate change, it is the cumulative emissions that matter), a two-year delay will require that emissions fall by 4.3% every year—over twice as quickly! Instead of a reduction of 15% in the annual emissions for the year 2020, two years of delay means 2020 emissions have to be reduced by 23%—just to get to the same place. The worst thing we can do for our economy and our environment is to do nothing at all, the second worst thing we can do is to delay, even just by two years.

2. America's Climate Security Act has the right framework to address the challenge of climate change in a way that makes sense for the environment, entrepreneurs, and the economy.

The Act sets strong early targets. As I have mentioned earlier, these targets are important to the environment and the economy. Aggressive early year targets increase our ability to avoid a greater than 2° increase in warming and the consequences that would bring. The early targets will jump start the entrepreneurial energy we need to deploy current technology and develop even better technology. The Act contains long-term targets that provide assurance to our grandchildren and our financial markets that we will stay committed to the task.

A recent report by the University of Maryland reviewed data and studies on the economic impacts of climate change and the costs of inaction. The review finds that economic impacts of climate change will "occur throughout the country, [and] economic impacts will be unevenly distributed across regions and within the economy and society." Just to highlight one finding of the report, it "found that negative climate impacts will outweigh benefits for most sectors that provide essential goods and services to society." The review finds that

> New York State's agricultural yield may be reduced by as much as 40%, resulting in $1.2 billion in annual damages. Expected water shortages in California's Central Valley are likely to affect the agricultural sector in the area. Agriculture around the San Antonio Texas Edwards Aquifer region is likely to suffer a similar fate. The regional impact may reach losses of $3.6–6.5 billion by 2030 and $6.75–10.13 billion by 2090. Even those farms and regions that temporarily benefit from altered environmental conditions (e.g., carbon fertilization and extended growing season) risk economic losses if temperatures exceed those preferred by the crops they currently produce. Climate change will also trigger increases in energy demand for cooling and will out-pace declines in heating requirements. For example, electricity demand in Massachusetts may increase by 40% in 2030 because of climate change alone, most of which will occur in summer months and require significant investment in peak load capacity and energy efficiency measures. Nationwide, the required investment may exceed $300 billion by the middle of this century. Given the long lead times of capacity expansion in the energy sector, little time remains to act on anticipated warming trends.

In addition to safeguarding the environment, the Act protects the economy in many ways. First, it uses the time-proven mechanism, cap-and-trade, that allows regulated entities access to the lowest cost emissions reductions possible. Cap-and-trade provides a whole range of cost management mechanisms that allow companies a wide choice in managing their compliance with emissions limits. Companies can

- make emissions reductions at their own facilities,
- purchase allowances from other facilities whose cost of reductions are even lower (so much so that they can "over-comply" and sell their excess allowances to others), and
- optimize plant development schedules and maintenance and can "bank" and "borrow" emissions allowances to fit into those schedules.

As experts have written "enhanced environmental performance can be attributed to the increased flexibility associated with emissions trading. Where emission reduction requirements are phased in and firms can bank emission reductions—as was the case in the Lead Trading, Acid Rain, ABT, and Northeast NOx Budget Programs—the achievement of the required emission reduction has been accelerated."

Companies can also purchase offsets from American farmers. They can earn credits by reducing international forest destruction. The ability to sell excess allowances creates an incentive for inventors and entrepreneurs to develop and deploy new technologies. All of these processes work together to allow us to meet our challenge at the lowest possible cost.

3. Some question whether we have the technology to meet the emission requirements of the Act. It is natural to ask: How will we get there? How can we accomplish the deep reductions in global warming pollution that science tells us we must achieve, and that this bill would require?

The good news is that we know how to cut emissions today, with proven technologies.

- **Energy efficiency.** Based on programs already in place at the state level, the National Action Plan for Energy Efficiency has estimated that by 2025 we will be able to reduce carbon dioxide emissions by over 400 million tons a year simply by using energy more wisely. [And in many cases, conserving energy ends up saving consumers money.]
- **Farms and forests.** The US EPA estimates that activities such as improved forest management, agricultural soil carbon sequestration, and methane and nitrous oxide mitigation could cut emissions by 620 million metric tons a year by 2015 at a cost of under $15 per ton—and that figure would double at prices of $30 a ton. (See Attachment 2 for a summary of EPA's findings.)

Just putting those numbers together yields over one billion tons of reductions a year. This is more than a third of the way (or more precisely 35%) to the abatement required in the year 2025.

And that is just the tip of the iceberg. The next generation of coal-fired power plants will have "carbon capture and sequestration" technology available to them. While that may sound far off, in fact all of the components have been tested and are in place. Gasification technology has been available for decades. And oil and gas companies are already pumping CO^2 into geologic reservoirs as part of enhanced oil recovery. The only reason we have not deployed these technologies widely for electric power generation is that there has been no financial incentive to do so. Placing a cap on carbon will change all that.

I could list all of technologies available today from wind power—which is exploding across the Plains and the West—to more efficient vehicles like the hybrid diesel vehicles being built in Ohio—to low-carbon fuels being developed in Tennessee and other states—to the substitution of chemical processes at plants in Delaware—to methane management for farms all across America. The list goes on and on. And putting a cap on carbon will bring even more technologies to market.

4. America's Climate Security Act has a system of carrots and sticks to prompt action from major emitting developing countries.

The first carrot is the opportunity for participation in the US greenhouse gas emissions market. If emitters in other countries would like to sell allowances that they earn in their home countries into the United States emissions market, then those countries will have to meet the practices and standards called for in this Act. Another important carrot is the International Forest Carbon provision. Every year, the cutting and burning of the world's tropical forests causes 20% of greenhouse gas pollution worldwide, irrevocably destroying the richest repositories of biological diversity on the planet, and impoverishing the hundreds of millions of people who depend on forests for their livelihoods—all because the forest is worth less alive than it is dead. This Congress can change all of this and, for the first time, give living forest economic value for tropical nations and forest peoples, by allowing tropical countries that make real, verifiable reductions of their national deforestation emissions to sell those reductions in our carbon market.

A stick is present in what is commonly referred to as the Bingaman-Specter provision because it mirrors what is in the Low Carbon Economy Act of 2007 (S-1766). This provision would prompt action to ensure that the emission reductions of ACSA are not undone by emissions associated with imported products manufactured in major emitting uncapped nations. The bill's authors recognize that our domestic greenhouse gas reduction program will move forward in a world grappling with the realities of globalization and its impacts on the US. As the USCAP Call for Action states: "[C]are should be taken that policies do not merely push emissions from US facilities to overseas plants, ultimately there must be an international program for addressing climate change and its impacts. US action to implement mandatory measures and incentives for reducing emissions should not be contingent on simultaneous action by other countries. Rather, we believe that US leadership is essential for establishing an equitable and effective international policy framework for robust action by all major emitting countries."

Recognizing that poorer nations might not be able to cap and cut emissions as quickly as the United States, but that we cannot address the global warming problem effectively unless all major emitting nations do cut emissions, the bill first calls for new international agreements engaging all major emitting nations in cutting their emissions. If negotiation of these new agreements proves unsuccessful, the bill would, after a certain time period, level the environmental and competitiveness playing field by requiring that imports of products produced in uncapped nations submit emissions allowances sufficient to cover the emissions incurred by the production of those products abroad.

As part of a comprehensive framework, a combination of these kinds of carrots and sticks makes sense. However, if we want nations with less capacity, fewer resources, and more problems to take serious action to cut GHG emissions, then we as a nation must act forcefully and without equivocation. Let's show them how to do it credibly and effectively and set a reasonable timeframe for their comparable action.

5. We strongly support moving the bill forward in its current form and will oppose amendments that would weaken the bill.

As the bill moves forward to Senate floor and through the legislative process, there are issues that we hope Senators will continue to work on:

i) The best science we have today indicates that we will need to make economy-wide emissions reductions of 80% by 2050. The bill's science review (sometimes called "lookback") provisions, can be amended to ensure that new scientific information generated in the future is not only evaluated but also leads directly to action with minimal delay. The EPA should be given the authority to take additional actions if the science reviews mandated by the bill demonstrate that the bill's emissions targets will not be met.

ii) Senator Whitehouse has discussed an amendment to establish an Ocean Trust as part of the adaptation assistance provisions in the bill. Elevated CO_2 levels are projected to profoundly impact the health of the oceans, which provides about 20% of the world's protein, and the coasts, where over half the US population now lives. The bill amendment will help our fisheries and oceans adapt to ocean acidification, increasing water temperatures, and rising sea levels, by establishing a dedicated funding mechanism for on-the-ground efforts to protect and restore ocean and coastal ecosystems. Establishing such an oceans trust was a priority recommendation of the US Commission on Ocean Policy created by Congress—and I thank Senator Whitehouse for his efforts here.

iii) International-adaptation provisions should not be limited solely to national-security considerations and resources provided for international adaptation should be increased. Currently, ACSA would provide international adaptation funding only where such expenditures are deemed "necessary to enhance the national security of the United States," specifically to "assist in avoiding the politically destabilizing impacts of climate change in volatile regions of the world." While national security is one appropriate consideration in this context, it is not the only one. Many of the world's poorest peoples will be adversely affected by climate change that is, to a significant degree, of America's making.

We will oppose amendments that would:

1) Weaken the targets and timelines of the bill.
2) Include any price cap (or so-called "safety-valve"). A safety-valve set at any price would gut the environmental targets in the bill and would prevent investors from making the commitments needed to develop and deploy needed technology.
3) Further restrict the use of offsets. We believe high-quality offsets can play an important role in reducing emissions quickly, providing new revenue streams for farmers, and lowering costs for regulated entities and yield important environmental benefits.

The Pew Center on Climate Change brings together business leaders, policymakers, and scientists to address the immense complexities of climate change in a way that is both effective and economically viable. The Pew Center joins Environmental Defense as vigorous supporters of this legislation.

4.5. "Statement on Reducing US Greenhouse Gas Emissions Cost-Effectively from Hon. Eileen Claussen, President, Pew Center on Global Climate Change, Submitted to the United States Senate, The Environment and Public Works Committee," November 15, 2007

The Pew Center strongly supports reporting the America's Climate Security Act of 2007 from the committee on the schedule that you have announced, and looks forward to working with you and the rest of the Congress as the bill goes through the process. I would like to discuss several reasons for recommending that you move forward with this bill.

Cap-and-trade is the most cost-effective way of reducing greenhouse gas emissions Senators, the bad news is that climate change poses real risks to our nation's security, economy and environment, and that these risks will grow dramatically if we do not begin to reduce our greenhouse gas emissions now. The good news is that the market-based mechanisms found in the America's Climate Security Act of 2007 will allow us to address this problem cost-effectively and in a way that enhances US competitiveness.

Unlike most emissions this committee deals with, greenhouse gas emissions are essentially fungible. Greenhouse gases mix quickly throughout the atmosphere, which means that wherever you can reduce a ton of greenhouse gas emissions—whether from a car, a factory, or a power plant; whether in Los Angeles, London, or Lagos—the benefit to the climate is the same.

In most of our other environmental laws, Congress directs EPA to dictate how much of a given pollutant a facility can emit or which pollution control technology to use. We do not have to take that approach with greenhouse gas emissions. Instead, by using a cap-and-trade program, Congress can set the overall greenhouse gas reduction goals and let the emitters decide for themselves how to achieve the environmental goals of the program at least cost. When we used a market-driven approach in the acid rain program, it provided the best environmental result at the lowest overall cost to our economy. This does not mean that achieving our climate security goals will be cost-free, just that the cost can be kept as low as possible—and far less than the cost of not acting.

An Economy-Wide Program will be More Cost-Effective than Sector-by-Sector Programs

The Pew Center supports the proposal to apply the cap-and-trade program to all large sources of greenhouse gas emissions simultaneously. Congress has seen several proposals to cap and trade emissions from power plants only. Similarly, Congress has seen several proposals that address the transportation sector only, for example, by reducing the carbon footprint of transportation fuels. Certainly, such a sector-by-sector approach can work, but it will be more expensive and slower than an economy-wide approach.

The most cost-effective approach is to bring power plants, factories and transportation together in one market, where all can benefit from the efficiencies and technological breakthroughs available in any sector at a given time. With an economy-wide program, we do not have to await the deployment of a single solution—such as carbon capture and sequestration, for example—to begin cost-effective reductions. The Pew Center's research with leading companies demonstrates that there are numerous cost-effective and even cost-saving reductions available now from off-the-shelf technologies and fuels. This is especially true in reducing non-CO_2 emissions from industrial processes, increasing industrial and building energy efficiency, increasing the use of low-carbon fuels, and improving vehicle efficiency. In the medium and longer term, steeper reductions will be made possible through deployment of more advanced technologies, such as highly efficient vehicles, improved nuclear power plants, renewable energy combined with enhanced electricity storage capacity, and carbon capture and storage (CCS). An economy-wide trading program will draw these technologies into the marketplace when they are ready, reducing the burden on any one sector, reducing the cost to the economy as a whole, and providing the broadest incentive possible for early emission reductions and technology innovation.

The America's Climate Security Act uses other important measures to lower the cost of greenhouse gas reductions as well. The bill allows companies to offset some of their emissions with reductions from sources not covered by the program. Allowing the use of offsets motivates emission reductions throughout the economy from sources too small or dispersed to be specifically targeted by the program. Companies would also be allowed to use credits from the markets of other countries, thus making use of the global fungibility of greenhouse gases and expanding the scope of the program. Again, the larger the program, the lower the cost. We see opportunities to increase the use of these measures even beyond what is already in the bill.

A greenhouse gas cap-and-trade program will enhance US competitiveness. The America's Climate Security Act will enhance US competitiveness. Given what the peer-reviewed science tells us about climate change, we must move quickly from our current economy to one in which our greenhouse gas footprint shrinks even as our standard of living increases. That will require a profound worldwide technological revolution. The United States can and should be leading that revolution, and positioning itself to reap the economic benefits associated with decreased dependence on foreign oil and increased export potential of low carbon technology. We currently are not leading, however, and federal R&D subsidies alone will not change that. An appropriate price on greenhouse gas emissions, in combination with "technology push" policies, will.

Some have asserted a false dichotomy between the need for mandatory climate policy, on the one hand, and support for climate-friendly technology, on the other. In fact, a well-designed mandatory climate policy that leverages the power of the market is essential for driving deployment of climate-friendly technology. When combined with subsidies for specific technologies, it is the most cost-effective method of driving deployment. Government would have to spend roughly ten times the amount in incentives alone in order to achieve the same environmental result as a price signal coupled with incentives. The America's Climate Security Act wisely combines mandatory greenhouse gas constraints and technology subsidies.

I would like to mention three other important issues before I conclude: how to deal with transportation, the use of allowance allocation as a tool, and the need for cost certainty and reliability.

Reducing Emissions from the Transportation Sector

Transportation emissions account for roughly one-quarter of total US emissions and are growing rapidly. Reversing that trend is essential, and can only be done by: (1) increasing vehicle efficiency, (2) reducing vehicle miles traveled (VMT), and (3) reducing the carbon footprint of transportation fuels. The America's Climate Security Act would include transportation fuels in the cap-and-trade program, providing a price signal that would promote all three—especially if complemented by the other measures currently being proposed by the White House and Congress to increase vehicle efficiency and promote low-carbon fuels, and with VMT-reduction measures, such as those in the Transportation Equity Act.

Using the Allocation Process to Aid Transition

While the use of a well-designed cap-and-trade program ensures the lowest overall cost, many important sectors of the economy will face real transition costs that can and should be dealt with through the allowance allocation process. Allocation, contrary to the impression some stakeholders may be creating, has no effect on the greenhouse gas reductions mandated by the cap. Given this, we should use the allocation process, in the early years of the program, to address the legitimate transition costs some sectors will face as we move to a low-greenhouse gas economy.

Take coal-based electricity, for example. Coal is cheap and plentiful, and the United States is going to use it for the foreseeable future. Even if we did not, China and India would, so rapid development and deployment of climate-friendly technologies is essential. The best hope, at the moment, lies with carbon capture and sequestration, which most experts believe will take at least a decade to deploy throughout the power sector. While we need not wait until then to begin cost-effective reductions, it would be appropriate to allocate initially a significant amount of allowances to this sector to help with transition. The bill does this and also appropriately uses bonus allowances and a clean coal technology program funded out of auction proceeds to accelerate CCS deployment and speed and smooth the transition. There is a similar need for transition assistance in other sectors of the economy, most particularly energy-intensive industries that face significant foreign competition. As the need for transition assistance diminishes, the allocation of free allowances should phase out, which the bill does as well.

In addition, the bill includes provisions to mitigate any effect the program may have in increasing energy prices, especially for low- and middle-income Americans. A significant percentage of the proceeds from the auction have been dedicated to help these consumers and to help states assist their residents.

Addressing Price Volatility and Cost Containment

Some stakeholders fear that, in the early years of the program, the market price of an allowance might be volatile and might swing too high too rapidly. Similarly, concerns have been raised about market liquidity, hoarding of allowances, and manipulations of the market.

In addition to the cap-and-trade itself, which provides for flexibility in meeting the environmental target, this legislation includes powerful cost containment mechanisms, including banking and borrowing. Allowing firms the ability to bank excess allowances or credits for future use helps firms manage the normal swings of the market. Allowing firms access to offset credits further lessens the danger of supply shortages, which in part create this price volatility. The bill also draws from the excellent work of Senators Warner, Landrieu, Graham and Lincoln and the Nicholas Institute at Duke University in establishing a Carbon Market Efficiency Board, which can gauge market activity and step in should unexpected problems arise. We look forward to working with the authors of this bill, Chairman Boxer and others, as the bill moves forward to refine measures to provide additional assurances of a smoothly functioning market, so long as they do not undermine the integrity of the greenhouse gas emissions cap.

Conclusion

In conclusion, the America's Climate Security Act of 2007 is an excellent foundation for an environmentally effective, cost-effective greenhouse gas reduction program. Continuing to move it through the legislative process will engage important stakeholders whose contributions will improve the bill. We applaud the committee's work to date, and urge the committee to report the bill.

Physicians for Social Responsibility was founded with the goal of halting nuclear proliferation in the 1960s, but has since expanded its mission to redress, among other medical and public health issues, global climate change and the toxic degradation of the environment. While PSR welcomes the debate on global warming legislation, it sees grave health threats in the pending bill, specifically its generous allowances for coal-fired power plants and its identification of the nuclear industry as a beneficiary of its subsidies.

4.6. "Lieberman-Warner Global Warming Legislation Provides Vehicle for Important Senate Debate," Physicians for Social Responsibility, December 5, 2007

(Washington, DC) The Senate Environment and Public Works Committee moved global warming legislation to the full Senate today, marking a significant development in the effort to curb greenhouse gas emissions. The Lieberman-Warner bill, S-2191 as amended by the chair, was reported out of the committee with few amendments and likely will be considered by the full Senate in 2008.

"While the reductions in greenhouse gases represented in the bill are significant, we hope efforts to strengthen the bill on the Senate floor will be successful," said Dr. Michael McCally, Executive Director of Physicians for Social Responsibility. "The allowances for coal-fired power plants are too generous, and language was added to the bill that identifies nuclear as a beneficiary of subsidies. These are serious flaws."

The bill seeks to reduce current emissions by more than 15 percent by 2020 with additional reductions nearing 60 percent by mid-century.

PSR seeks more rapid reductions in these emissions and fewer allocation giveaways to dirty power sources, primarily coal.

"Coal plants produce more than carbon dioxide. PSR cannot support any efforts to promote more coal facilities that emit sulfur dioxide, nitrogen oxides, mercury and other pollutants that harm human health. There is no such thing as clean coal technology as long as it allows plants to dump millions of tons of pollutants into the air," added McCally.

PSR sees global warming as one of the gravest threats to human health and security. Millions are expected to suffer from water and food shortages worldwide, while heat waves, incidences of disease and threats from severe weather will increase in the US.

The staunchest opponent of S-2191, and the prime foe of Environmental Defense in the "green civil war," is Friends of the Earth. While in subsequent statements, FOE has allowed that Committee amendments improved the introduced version of the bill, the group nevertheless regards the protocol as providing a windfall for "polluters," a view shared by some of its sister organizations as well as free-market environmentalists. The following document justifies the charge.

4.7. "Windfalls in Lieberman-Warner Global Warming Bill: Quantifying the Fossil Fuel Industry Giveaways," Friends of the Earth, October 2007

In the attempt to set the United States on a course to mitigate our global warming emissions, Senators' Lieberman (I-Conn.) and Warner (R-Va.) America's Climate Security Act of 2007 gives hundred of billions of dollars away to corporate polluters. All in all, nearly a half a trillion dollars is allocated directly to the fossil fuel industry, over half of which goes to coal. In addition, approximately $324 billion in auction revenue is given away to the coal industry. In total, the fossil fuel industry receives approximately $800 billion through in America's Climate Security Act of 2007.

The Making of a Windfall

The Lieberman-Warner America's Climate Security Act of 2007 creates a regulatory system that caps the amount of global warming emissions that covered entities can emit. The cap is gradually reduced over a period of time leading into 2050. Under the cap, each emitter receives permits, or allowances, from the federal government for specified amounts of global warming emissions. The total amount of allowances is equal to the amount of global warming emissions permitted under the cap. Any unused permits may be traded (sold) to entities requiring more permits than their allotted share.

One natural effect of limiting the supply of emission rights through permits is that it imbues the permits with real economic value—it turns them into a vehicle for buying and selling the right to pollute. With current United States global warming emissions totaling more than 7.3 billion metric tons of greenhouse gases annually, the total economic value of these permits could be tremendous.

A recent survey of economic literature by the Congressional Budget Office suggests that global warming emissions permits could be worth between $5 to $65 per metric ton. Friends of the Earth's analysis uses figures from the Environmental Protection Agency's Analysis of the Climate Stewardship and Innovation Act of 2007. The EPA's analysis states that between 2015 and 2050, the price of one of these permits would increase from an average of $14 to $78 per ton of carbon dioxide equivalent greenhouse gas emissions leading into 2050.

The Lieberman-Warner bill caps global warming emissions from approximately 73 percent of the economy, responsible for 5.2 billion tons of global warming emissions. A cap initially set at this emissions level would create permits worth more than $72 billion in the first year of the program, and $3.6 trillion throughout the program's lifetime, using the value per ton of carbon identified by EPA.

How does the Windfall Work?

The way in which the federal government hands out these valuable permits will determine whether companies receive a windfall or if the money benefits the public at large.

There are two clear options for how the federal government distributes the permits. The government can either give companies or sectors the permits for free, or it can auction or sell the permits. Allocating the permits, or giving the permits away for free, essentially hands the value of the permit from the government to the company at zero cost to the company. It is then up to the company to choose how to use the economic value of the permit. According to the Congressional Budget Office, "giving away allowances could yield windfall profits for the producers that received them by effectively transferring income from consumers to firms' owners and shareholders."

Auctioning the permits allows the federal government to capture the economic value of the permit and use the revenue for public benefit or other use. The revenue could be used to help consumers offset increases in energy prices that result from the program, to invest in renewable energy and energy efficiency, or to provide assistance to communities in the US and in developing countries to help them adapt to the impacts of global warming. According to the same Congressional Budget Office report, "selling emission allowances could raise sizable revenues that lawmakers could use for various purposes, which would lower the cap's total cost to the economy."

Windfalls in Lieberman-Warner America's Climate Security Act

The Lieberman-Warner America's Climate Security Act of 2007 allocates, or simply gives away, 50 percent of these permits over the lifetime of the program, starting with 82 percent in 2012 and ending with 27 percent in 2050. All-in-all, between 2012 and 2050, 66 billion pollution permits, valuing $1.5 trillion, would be given away.

While many of the permits are given away to "public benefits," a large amount of the permits are given to the very industries that are responsible for global warming; 38 percent of allocated permits are gifted to the fossil fuels industry over the lifetime of the program. Overall, the fossil fuels industry would be given permits worth $436 billion. Of this, over $268 billion could go exclusively to the coal industry.

The remaining 50 percent of the permits would be auctioned for sale. Some of the revenue from these sales is then distributed to different environmental and social causes that ease the impacts that climate change causes.

Regrettably, the fossil fuel industry benefits here as well; 15 percent of the revenue from auctions could go to the fossil fuel industry over the life of the bill, from funds for "advanced and sequestration of carbon." Carbon sequestration technology is specific to the coal industry, and therefore, this equates to approximately a $325 billion giveaway to the coal industry over the life of the program. In addition, $522 billion is allocated to the "zero- and low-carbon energy technologies" fund in the bill. The fund allocates money based on a reverse auction, and as currently written, does not clearly articulate which energy technologies would benefit from this program. This fund was not included in our final analysis because renewable energy and energy conservation will be able to compete for these funds. Although some of the auction revenue *does* discourage global warming pollution, it still benefits the fossil fuel industry, which causes many environmental and social problems in addition to greenhouse gas emissions, both nationally and internationally.

Conclusion

A cap-and-trade system will create winners and losers in the marketplace. Unfortunately, if America's Climate Security Act of 2007 is written into law, the biggest polluters will become the biggest winners, with a massive windfall for the fossil fuel industry that totals nearly $800 billion. Polluters should have to pay for their pollution, not be rewarded for it.

One-hundred percent auctions are a better approach. Such auctions would penalize pollution—and new revenues could be used to help Americans become more energy efficient (and save money), to speed our transition to clean, alternative energy sources, improve low-carbon transportation infrastructure, and to help impoverished communities around the world adapt to the challenges posed by global warming. In September Sen. Lieberman said a 100 percent auction was "on the table." With 100 percent auction on the table, Congress can prevent this massive corporate giveaway.

In his statement on the Lieberman-Warner subcommittee markup, Carl Pope, Sierra Club Executive Director, steers a course between support of a federal protocol to address climate change and endorsement of this particular version of it. He affirms that it purports to accomplish Sierra's two objectives—preventing catastrophic global warming and stimulating a clean energy revolution—but, like FOE, objects to the allowances it accords to polluters.

4.8. "Significant Improvements Needed to Lieberman-Warner Bill, Sierra Club Looks to Full Committee Markup to Strengthen Bill," Statement of Carl Pope, Sierra Club Executive Director, November 1, 2007

We are pleased that today's subcommittee markup included incremental changes to improve the bill and we will continue to work vigorously to strengthen this proposal as it moves forward. While we support moving the bill into full committee, it unfortunately still falls far short of what science requires and what economic fairness demands and thus we cannot yet offer our support for the bill. Just as bold action is needed to address the challenge of global warming, bold changes will need to be made to this legislation before we are able to support it. Our support is not contingent upon perfection, but rather on whether a bill offers us a reasonably good chance of achieving our widely shared goals: preventing catastrophic global warming and bringing a clean energy future to life.

It is essential that we get markets moving immediately to begin reducing our emissions and speed our transition to the clean energy economy. This can only be achieved by setting a strong, science-based short-term target—a 15–20 percent reduction in total emissions by 2020. The bar must also be set where science demands in the long run—a reduction of 80 percent by 2050. Our window of opportunity to avoid catastrophic changes to our climate is rapidly closing—perhaps faster than any of us previously imagined—and this bill's targets do not match up with the current challenge that scientists have lain before us.

Polluters must pay for the damage they do to our climate—period. This bill continues to give hundreds of billions of dollars in allowances to polluters for far too long and also returns a significant portion of the proceeds from the allowances that are auctioned off right back to those same polluting industries. Instead of private windfalls, we must have a 100 percent auction or allocation for the public benefit to give us the funds we need in order to ensure a just transition for workers, protect consumers from rising energy costs, and make the investments in new technology needed to make the new clean energy economy a reality.

Senator Boxer has provided exemplary leadership on this issue and has stated a goal of improving the bill. We very much look forward to working with her and other members of the committee to produce a bill that is sufficiently strong to address the challenge before us. Barring these significant changes, we do not believe that this bill should be enacted.

It was probably Matt Stoller of Open Left.com who first applied the term "green civil war" to the divisions among the ranks of environmental advocacy groups on this legislation. In his post on the Open Left website, he takes up the politics of their differences, and the strategies that should be pursued.

4.9. "The Green Civil War Needs to Begin," Matt Stoller, "The Open Left," October 17, 2007

Here's the DLC green group Environmental Defense:

> Senators Joe Lieberman and John Warner tomorrow will introduce comprehensive, bipartisan climate change legislation that would cap and cut US greenhouse gas emissions while protecting the economy and American consumers.

And here's the more progressive Friends of the Earth:

> Global warming legislation expected to be introduced tomorrow could provide giveaways worth hundreds of billions or even trillions of dollars to polluting industries, according to an analysis of a draft of the legislation conducted by Friends of the Earth.

Here's Grist's David Roberts:

> This is, in a sense, the same old strategy question that comes up all the time. Do you, like FOE, act as an outside agitator, draw lines in the sand, and try to pressure the political process? Or do you, like ED, worm your way inside the process, schmooze the big players, and

strive to insure that the final bill is as good as it possibly can be under the circumstances?

If you say "we need both," gold star for you.

I love David's writing, but I don't agree with this as a matter of politics. Insider-outsider strategies are critical to move policy, but what Roberts is describing is not an insider-outsider strategy. He is describing a parasite. Environmental Defense is justifying a large corporate giveaway under the rubric of environmentalism, and the rest of the green community is letting ED get away with it.

In terms of the policy, Environmental Defense is alone here. The green groups are remarkably polite to each other, as most of them started in the 1970s convinced that protecting the environment was a value system. At the time, it might have been. Today, the question is how to manage a commons, and these groups just don't agree with each other. There is no movement around the environment anymore, there are progressives, corporatists, and deniers, all fighting over a large multi-trillion dollar and rapidly shrinking commons. The lack of robust internal debate among green groups means that ED's Fred Krupp can nonetheless speak for "the environmental movement," scoop up his corporate money, and throw everyone else to the curb.

A letter on carbon allowances implicitly protesting the bill came out in September from Clean Water Action, Defenders of Wildlife, Earthjustice, the League of Conservation Voters, the National Audubon Society, the National Environmental Trust, the National Tribal Environmental Council, the National Wildlife Federation, the Natural Resources Defense Council, Oceana, Physicians for Social Responsibility, The Sierra Club, Union of Concerned Scientists, US Public Interest Research Group, and the Wilderness Society all agree, to a greater or lesser extent with Friends of the Earth. They don't like the bill, or the giveaway, but judging by tomorrow's coverage, you wouldn't know it.

ED is using its brand as an environmental group to push against progressive solutions to global warming. In prisoner's dilemma parlance, it is "defecting" from the rest of the community to get what it wants, which is insider influence and corporate money. The argument from ED will be that corporations are part of the solution, which is of course true, though not in the way they mean.

We're long overdue for a real green fight. And if these groups won't do it, ED is going to win until there's an internal revolt from the progressive dissidents within and outside of the environmental community.

The environmental community is not alone in supporting government involvement in climate change mitigation. Indeed, the US Climate Action Partnership, a cooperative effort of more than two dozen major corporations and a half-dozen environmental organizations was undertaken precisely to lobby the Administration to develop and enact a cap-and-trade program to address what it concedes is a real and potentially devastating problem. Accordingly, it strongly supports S-2191.

4.10. "US Climate Action Partnership Launches Ad Campaign," October 4, 2007

The United States Climate Action Partnership (USCAP) today launched an advertising campaign to advocate for national legislation that includes market approaches to mandatory reductions in greenhouse gas emissions. The first wave of advertising will run through the end of this year, and will include print and radio spots.

. . . The ad emphasizes the growth in USCAP's diverse membership and outlines key policy recommendations, including:

- Enacting an economy-wide cap-and-trade law,
- Creating an emissions inventory,
- Allowing credit for early action; and,
- Establishing policies to accelerate the development of low- and zero-emitting technologies, such as carbon sequestration.

The ad lists by name all six of the environmental organizations and 27 corporations that comprise the current membership of the group. The ad was created by Sawyer Miller Advertising and Powell Tate.

"The time to act on climate change is now," said Peter O'Toole, Director of Public Relations for General Electric. "The launch of USCAP's advocacy campaign underscores the commitment our diverse coalition has made to addressing climate change. USCAP's advertising campaign urges Congress to enact legislation that would allow market forces to help lower greenhouse gas emissions."

David Yarnold, Executive Vice President for Environmental Defense, said: "US leadership on this issue is essential to establishing a fair and effective global framework to deal with climate change. We know enough to act and America has an opportunity to lead. We hope these ads will be a catalyst for Congress to establish comprehensive market-based legislation, including a mandatory cap-and-trade system."

. . . USCAP is a landmark coalition of six environmental NGOs and 27 businesses that has called on Congress to quickly enact legislation setting long-term emissions reductions targets, with a nationwide cap-and-trade approach and other complementary policies. USCAP hopes its recommendations will minimize the large-scale adverse effects of climate change for humans and the natural environment.

Driven by top executives of the member organizations, USCAP has operated by consensus-based approach, seeking to balance interests across industries and regions to create the best economic path to reducing greenhouse gas concentrations.

USCAP members represent a broad cross-section of the US economy, including: the transportation sector, financial services, mining and metals, oil and gas, manufacturing, chemicals, energy and electric power, agribusiness, health care, food and beverage, pharmaceuticals, buildings, and construction equipment.

Collectively, USCAP companies have total revenues of nearly $2 trillion and a combined market capitalization of more than $2.2 trillion. Member companies employ more than 2.7 million workers—with operations in all 50 states and nearly every country in the world. The non-governmental organizations, leaders in environmental and conservation issues, include a combined membership of more than two million worldwide.

In January, USCAP issued its solutions-based report, titled *A Call for Action*, laying out the following six key principles:

- Account for the global dimensions of climate change;
- Recognize the importance of technology;
- Be environmentally effective;
- Create economic opportunity and advantage;
- Be fair to sectors disproportionately impacted; and,
- Recognize and encourage early action.

USCAP has also recommended that Congress establish short- and mid-term emission reduction targets; a national program to accelerate technology research, development and deployment; and approaches to encourage action by other countries, including the developing world. . . .

On the other hand, other business interests oppose the bill, splitting the business community much like the environmental community is divided. Of the representatives of smaller, more focused interests the most broad-based is the Chamber of Commerce, which is concerned with its potential effect on jobs and the environment, and would like to see more promotion of greenhouse gas reducing technologies like nuclear energy and clean coal. The National Mining Association represents coal, metal, and mineral interests. The Association sees in its burdens on coal increases in consumer prices for electricity among other economic consequences. Similarly, the Alliance for Energy and Economic Growth, a coalition of energy producers and consumers, fears the measure would cause higher and more volatile energy costs, cost jobs, and otherwise damage the economy with questionable carbon reductions.

4.11. "The Chamber of Commerce Statement on the Lieberman-Warner Bill"

Dear Chairman Boxer and Ranking Member Inhofe:

The US Chamber of Commerce, the world's largest business federation representing more than three million businesses and organizations of every size, sector, and region, strongly opposes S-2191, the "Lieberman-Warner Climate Security Act of 2007."

As Chamber President and CEO Thomas J. Donohue previously communicated in testimony to your Committee on June 28, 2007, the Chamber hinges our support for climate legislation on whether it satisfies five core principles: it must (1) preserve American jobs and the economy, (2) address the international nature of global climate change, (3) promote accelerated technology development and deployment, (4) reduce barriers to development of climate-friendly energy sources, and (5) promote energy efficiency measures. The Chamber opposes S-2191 because it fails to satisfy several of these principles.

First, S-2191 fails to preserve American jobs and the domestic economy. As Dr. Anne Smith of global research firm CRA International stated to the Committee on November 8, 2007, S-2191 could cost America 3.4 million additional jobs, a $1 trillion decline in GDP, and a doubling of wholesale electricity prices between now and 2050. The bill requires American companies to undertake dramatic emissions reductions regardless of whether its economic competitors do the same, at least prior to the year 2019. As utilities are forced to move off coal, Dr. Smith predicts that natural gas demand for electricity generation will increase by as much as 66 percent over the next 20 years. By then much of the United States' energy-intensive industry could be gone, having either shut down or moved overseas. The chemical industry has already largely moved overseas because it cannot compete in the world market while complying with domestic energy constraints and emissions controls; how many other American businesses will be forced to follow suit?

Second, S-2191 does not adequately address the international nature of global climate change. The domestic emissions constraints imposed by S-2191, without corresponding long-term cutbacks in greenhouse gas emissions from other nations (particularly developing nations), will not only fail to make the required impact on levels of greenhouse gases in the atmosphere, but could also irreparably harm the country's ability to compete in the global market. Any long-term climate change action plan absolutely *must* include developing nations such as China and India. Chinese emissions are projected to increase 119 percent and Indian emissions 131 percent between 2004 and 2030. Without engagement by developing nations, the carbon constraints imposed by S-2191 would penalize domestic businesses attempting to compete in the world market while non-participating developing nations continue to get a free ride.

Third, S-2191 does not promote greenhouse gas reducing technologies —such as clean coal and nuclear energy—at a substantial enough level or a fast enough pace to compensate for the bill's aggressive emissions constraints. Dr. Margo Thorning of the American Council for Capital Formation testified before your Committee that US per capita emissions would have to be reduced about 25 to 35 times greater than what occurred from 1990 to 2000 to meet the targets of S-2191, and the technologies simply do not exist to reduce emissions to this extent without severely reducing the growth of the US economy and employment. With respect to clean coal, Title IV of the bill does attempt to use a percentage of early- and annually-auctioned credits to fund low-carbon and zero-carbon energy technologies, but this meager step is not nearly enough. According to *The Future of Coal*, a report released in March 2007 by a consortium of faculty and energy experts at MIT, it will take a $5 billion, ten-year program to research, develop, and demonstrate on a realistic scale the technology necessary to capture and store carbon dioxide from coal-fired power plants. And coal, despite the efforts of many in Congress, is not going anywhere: the Energy Information Administration (EIA) projects electricity generation from coal to rise from about two trillion kilowatthours (kWh) today to well over three trillion kWh by 2030. With such little funding for research, carbon capture and sequestration technology will not be cheaply or readily available to entities covered by S-2191 by the time the caps are in place and begin to decrease annually. Coal is vital to the United States' energy future, and paltry funding for clean coal technology is completely unjustifiable. Moreover, while coal receives paltry funding under S-2191, nuclear power receives no funding whatsoever: S-2191 fails to support in any way the research, development and expansion of new nuclear power facilities. In fact, the word "nuclear" does not appear in the text of the 303-page bill even *once*. Such obvious oversight of a clean and safe energy technology that will be absolutely necessary in a carbon-constrained environment is yet another reason the Chamber cannot support S-2191.

Finally, S-2191 does very little to reduce barriers to development of climate-friendly energy sources. In the regime imposed by S-2191, clean coal and nuclear power will not be readily available to meet our energy needs. And if the recent death sentence for the Cape Wind project is any indication, the US may not even be able to site or permit renewables. That leaves natural gas as the only legitimate replacement option for electricity generation. But S-2191 has no mercy on natural gas, either (and was recently amended to add an "upstream" cap on emissions from natural gas processors, crippling natural gas users even more). Increased natural gas production costs from the bill could result in decreased investment and the shutting down of marginal natural gas wells. S-2191 would likely exceed the less stringent Lieberman-McCain bill, S-280, which had been projected to reduce US natural gas production by up to 11 percent by 2030. Moreover, a recent study by Pennsylvania State University found that EIA has over-estimated natural gas supply and under-estimated corresponding demand in the electric power sector, calling into serious question whether natural gas can handle the demands of industrial, commercial and residential consumers if legislation like S-2191 forces the United States to move off coal.

For these reasons, the Chamber opposes S-2191.R.

4.12. "The National Mining Association Statement on the Lieberman-Warner Bill"

Madame Chairman and Ranking Member Inhofe:

The National Mining Association (NMA) is ready and prepared to work with you, members of the Environment and Public Works Committee and all interested senators on a constructive technology-based policy framework to address climate change. However, NMA is opposed to the "America's Climate Security Act" (S-2191).

NMA represents more than 325 companies involved in all aspects of the mining industry including coal, metal and industrial mineral producers, mineral processors, equipment manufacturers, state associations, bulk transporters, engineering firms, consultants, financial institutions and other companies that supply goods and services to the mining industry.

As a general matter, it is not economically feasible to meet the greenhouse gas (GHG) emissions reductions proposed under S-2191 without the technologies to achieve them. S-2191 fails to adequately provide for the development, demonstration and commercial deployment of advanced clean coal and carbon capture and storage (CCS) technologies that will enable the continued utilization of America's most versatile, abundant and affordable energy resource—coal.

Coal powers more than 50 percent of US electricity generation, with the US Energy Information Administration forecasting that number to grow to 57 percent by 2030. The reasons are simple—the United States possesses more than 240 years worth of coal reserves, and on an output basis, our nation has more energy reserves in coal than Saudi Arabia has in oil. The abundance, availability and affordability of coal when compared to other energy resources also explains why consumer electricity costs are low in regions where it is the predominant fuel source for generation. Policies that disrupt the ability of generators to use coal for electricity production will necessarily and adversely impact consumer electricity rates and costs. The economic consequences of S-2191, as acknowledged by Sen. Joe Lieberman (I-Conn.) during subcommittee markup, will be enormous. Indeed, an independent analysis performed by Charles River and Associates discussed before your committee shows staggering costs to the economy and working families.

S-2191 further lacks a general cost-containment mechanism to avoid harm to the economy and consumers. Nor does the bill account for meaningful participation from major economic trade competitors such as China and India, among others. The bill also lacks the needed regulatory and liability framework necessary to accelerate the deployment of commercial-scale CCS technologies.

The US mining industry has long advocated technology-based solutions for mitigating greenhouse gas emissions. Advanced clean coal and CCS technologies offer the most promising near-term solutions to this issue because they will allow us to continue to use affordable coal-based electricity generation to power America. And yet S-2191 fails to provide sufficient and sustained funding to assist in the public-private partnerships needed to help develop, demonstrate and deploy these critical technologies on a commercial scale.

For these reasons, we oppose S-2191 and urge the committee to develop policies that accelerate the research, development, demonstration and deployment of clean coal and CCS technologies that will ultimately prove far more effective in reducing greenhouse gas emissions globally than the proposal presently before the committee . . .

4.13. "The Alliance for Energy and Economic Growth Statement on the Lieberman-Warner Bill"

Dear Chairman Boxer and Ranking Member Inhofe:

The Alliance for Energy and Economic Growth (AEEG), a broad-based coalition of more than 1,200 companies and organizations representing energy producers and consumers, supports the goal of addressing global climate change in a manner that protects US jobs and economy, but is very concerned that the Senate plans to move forward with S-2191, the "Climate Security Act," without adequately considering the consequences such legislation will pose to the American economy. S-2191 imposes major new requirements on American business and industry without sufficiently funding the research, development and commercial deployment of essential new technologies or protecting American consumers and the competitiveness of US industry. The result would be significantly higher and more volatile energy costs for US consumers, considerable harm to the economy, and millions of lost American jobs, with questionable impact on global greenhouse gas concentrations.

The Committee heard analyses of the economic costs of S-2191 at hearings on November 8, 2007. Dr. Anne Smith of CRA International testified that S-2191 could cost America 3.4 million additional jobs, a $1 trillion decline in GDP, and a doubling of wholesale electricity prices, all by the year 2050. Dr. Margo Thorning of the American Council for Capital Formation stated that US per capita emissions would have to be reduced about 25 to 35 times greater than what occurred from 1990 to 2000, and the technologies simply do not exist to reduce emissions to this extent without severely reducing the growth in the US economy and in employment.

As the statements of Dr. Smith and Dr. Thorning make clear, the emissions reduction schedule in S-2191 would place the American economy at significant risk. Yet, in the face of these startling economic analyses, and without the economic impact estimates of S-2191 requested from Energy Information Administration and Environmental Protection Agency by Senators Lieberman and Warner, the Committee intends to push forward with a markup of the bill this week.

AEEG instead recommends harmonizing emissions reduction requirements with the availability of existing and emerging, lower and non-carbon technology options, which could reduce these costs and mitigate more severe economic disruptions. We support policies to promote the accelerated development, demonstration and global deployment of climate-friendly technologies, and we want to work with you to remove financial and regulatory barriers that stand in the way of harnessing America's ingenuity in energy technology.

AEEG also worries that S-2191 will dramatically increase the demand for natural gas for the purpose of power generation, and domestic natural gas producers will not be able to meet this demand. Limitations on access to America's natural gas resources have caused domestic natural gas producers to struggle to keep up with the demand of American consumers. With huge portions of the natural gas resource base off limits to environmentally responsible production, supply would be unable to keep pace with the additional demands created by the cap-and-trade system created by S-2191. We fear that the result will be vastly increased costs to consumers and businesses in every part of the country. Moreover, the inclusion of natural gas residential and commercial customers in the program will further increase their energy bills. AEEG strongly recommends that any climate change program address the need to free up the new natural gas supplies that will be essential to reaching our climate change goals.

We also are concerned that the bill does not include an effective cost-containment safeguard. Rather, S-2191 establishes a "Carbon Market Efficiency Board" (Board) with limited authority to adjust the ways in which a regulated entity can meet its annual compliance obligation by expanding offsets or by borrowing and paying back allowances. The Board would select certain facilities for modest relief in the short term, but this approach is fraught with uncertainty, fails to establish a clear price signal, and merely postpones economic hardship. Inclusion of a mechanism to give confidence in the cost of cap-and-trade legislation is essential to managing and containing costs in a manner that protects US jobs and provides for economic growth.

AEEG believes that Congress should support policies that strengthen our global competitiveness and avoid imposing costly greenhouse gas emissions regulatory programs without the participation of developing nations, such as China and India. This is necessary to prevent outsourcing of jobs and the export of emissions overseas, ensure that total global emissions are reduced and that the economic burdens associated with climate change are borne equitably. We are concerned that S-2191 requires US companies to undertake dramatic emissions reductions regardless of whether its economic competitors do the same, at least prior to the year 2019. By then, much of the United States' energy-intensive industry could be gone, having either shut down or moved overseas.

Finally, climate change legislation should establish consistency among regional and state greenhouse gas reduction efforts. Consistency is necessary to reduce regulatory uncertainty and increase the efficiency and effectiveness of climate change policy, yet S-2191 fails to address this issue as well.

For these reasons and others, we believe that S-2191 would impose substantial penalties on the US economy, consumers and working families, and would do little to ensure technology development and global participation essential to achieving meaningful reductions in greenhouse gas emissions. We thank you for your consideration and look forward to working with you towards achieving a workable and effective solution to global climate change concerns. . . .

The Competitive Enterprise Institute is a non-profit think tank advocating free enterprise and limited government. Not surprisingly it opposes S-2191, but, interestingly, on much the same ground as Friends of the Earth—its vulnerability to fraud.

4.14. "Cap-and-Trade: A System Made for Fraudsters," Iain Murray, Competitive Enterprise Institute

Ever since Enron decided that carbon trading would "do more to promote Enron's business than almost any other regulatory initiative," informed observers have been wary of the idea.

Yet the idea of creating a new commodity by capping emissions of greenhouse gases and issuing tradable permits to produce the emissions has gained ground as hysteria over effects of global warming has grown.

Now, two separate investigations have demonstrated why carbon caps and trading are bad ideas, and why they were so attractive to Enron.

In the first, the Congressional Budget Office analyzed the effects of cap-and-trade on American households. In the European version of the scheme that has been in operation since 2005, the permits are given away to firms. Some businesses are very much in favor of this, because it gives them an opportunity to reap windfall profits, as has happened in Europe.

As the CBO found, "Because most of the cost of the cap would ultimately be borne by consumers, giving away nearly all of the allowances to affected energy producers would mean that the value of the allowances they received would far exceed the cost that they bear." So while energy companies benefit, the consumer suffers higher costs.

If the allowances are sold, individual companies benefit less, as they have to pay for the allowances in the first place. But even if there is some compensation in the form of a reduction in payroll or corporate taxes, most of the population still suffers reduction in household income.

Fraud Revealed

The poorest fifth of the population suffers worst, losing about 3% of its take-home household income. The richest fifth, on the other hand, increase its take-home pay. Only if there is some carbon welfare bureaucracy to administer rebate payments do lower-income families benefit, but that almost triples the cost to the economy as a whole.

All of this, moreover, is the effect of a very modest cut in emissions in the year 2010, certainly not enough to have any impact on warming temperatures. Some sectors of the economy would likely be hit extremely hard—like the 80,000 people who depend on coal mining for their living.

If that weren't enough to suggest that cap-and-trade would be a bad idea even if it worked as advertised, the *Financial Times* has now revealed that where it is being tried it is inefficient, fraudulent or both.

The newspaper's investigations have revealed "widespread failings in the new markets for greenhouse gases, suggesting some organizations are paying for emissions reductions that do not take place. Others are making big profits from carbon trading for very small expenditure and in some cases for clean-ups they would have made anyway."

A particularly galling example relates to chemical giant DuPont, which invites people to pay $4 per ton to reduce emissions from a Kentucky plant, yet the equipment that reduces the gases is actually relatively cheap.

More Emissions?

My organization's investigations earlier in the year revealed DuPont's preferred strategy would realize a return in investment of around 900% for its emissions reductions so far. Yet this isn't new money—it's the consumer and taxpayer that are filling DuPont's pockets for very little in return.

This is one of the reasons why economists such as Ross McKitrick of the University of Guelph in Canada refer to cap-and-trade schemes as creating a "carbon cartel." Friends of the Earth agrees, calling DuPont's actions "greenwash."

Even worse, though, is the potential for fraud. The *Financial Times* found there is a risk that people might buy carbon credits for carbon reduction that does not exist.

Another significant risk relates to companies selling the same credits several times over. Large companies such as BP have found it difficult to find enough projects that passed its quality control standards. Individuals and smaller companies are much more vulnerable to the fraudsters and charlatans.

There's even a chance that trading will increase emissions. The *Sunday Times* of London recently revealed that an Indian factory had made more than $600 million from selling emissions credits after investing just $3 million in new equipment that eliminates emissions. With that profit windfall, it will be building a new factory that will emit a refrigerator gas called HFC-143a, which is over 1,300 times more potent than carbon dioxide as a warming agent. As perverse incentives go, that one's a doozy.

Carbon trading is excellent for the fraudster, good for the robber baron, ineffective for the environment, bad for the economy as a whole and disastrous for the poor. No wonder Enron liked it.

Finally, Steve Milloy is publisher and manager of a website—junkscience.com—debunking most environmental science and the public policies it promotes. In this post, Milloy attributes the recent activism around global warming to the Supreme Court decision in Massachusetts v. EPA, *and attributes their support of S-2191 to greed. He castigates the major financial and industrial giants for supporting cap-and-trade for the economic benefits they can reap from it.*

4.15. "Global Warming and the Supremes," Steve Milloy

The Supreme Court attempted to insert itself in the global warming debate this week with its decision in *Massachusetts v. EPA*, which gives the Federal Environmental Protection Agency authority to regulate greenhouse gas emissions from motor vehicles.

"This is a landmark decision," former Clinton administration EPA Chief Carol Browner said on PBS' "The News Hour with Jim Lehrer."

Unfortunately for the court and Ms. Browner, but fortunately for the rest of us, its decision will have little, if any, practical impact on the ever-intensifying climate controversy.

The controversy began on Oct. 20, 1999, more than a year after the Clinton administration signed the Kyoto Protocol, when 19 environmental activist groups petitioned the Browner-led EPA to regulate greenhouse gas emissions from automobile tailpipes.

But the global warming-believing Browner failed to act on the petition as of the November 2000 presidential election, possibly presuming that an ensuing Al Gore administration, which she likely would have been part of as a long-time Gore acolyte, would grant the petition and commence a rulemaking.

But when Gore's presidency was thwarted by the December 2000 Supreme Court decision in *Bush v. Gore*, the Clinton EPA scrambled in its waning days to launch a regulatory process for regulating carbon dioxide from automobile tailpipes, issuing an eleventh-hour "request for [public] comment," one week before the inauguration of President Bush.

Though President Bush rejected the Kyoto Protocol, his EPA nonetheless continued the regulatory process, ultimately denying the petition in September 2003.

The Bush EPA said that it did not believe it had the authority to regulate greenhouse gases from tailpipes and, even if it did, such regulation would be unwise at the time, and the petitioners, now joined by several states and local governments, including Massachusetts, sued the EPA.

Before we get to the court's decision, it's worth noting that Browner and the Clinton EPA had plenty of opportunity to grant the petition and commence a rulemaking to regulate carbon dioxide from autos. But for whatever reason, the Clinton EPA chose not to take action despite believing, as Browner admitted on "The News Hour," that the EPA already had the legal authority to act.

It was particularly ironic that Browner repeatedly and arrogantly slammed the Bush administration for not acting on the petition while sliding over her own failure to act.

Despite the court's dramatic recitation of the dogma of global warming alarmism at the opening of its decision, its ruling will have little impact on the global warming debate simply because the debate has moved way beyond the EPA.

In 1999, environmentalists were just about the only special-interest group clamoring for greenhouse gas regulation and such regulation—that is, straightforward, mandatory emissions reductions under the Clean Air Act—is what they wanted given that the Senate wasn't going to ratify Kyoto without the participation of China, India and other developing nations.

Since that time, however, the spectrum of special interests clamoring for global warming regulation has significantly expanded, most importantly to big businesses that are now driving the debate—in Congress and not at the EPA.

Through its legislative power, Congress can not only mandate emissions reductions, but more importantly, it can also dole out the global warming pork.

Wall Street firms such as Goldman Sachs, Lehman Brothers and Morgan Stanley want Congress to establish a so-called cap-and-trade system so that they can profit from the trading of greenhouse gas emissions permits.

Industrial giants such as Dupont and Alcoa want Congress to give them "carbon credits"—essentially free money—for greenhouse gas emissions reductions already undertaken. Solar and wind energy firms, as well as the ethanol lobby, want Congress to award them subsidies and tax breaks.

All the new climate piggies that want to gorge themselves at the public trough have crowded out the environmentalists, transforming the global warming issue from an ostensibly serious save-the-planet crusade into a financial orgy complete with taxpayer piñata.

Despite that the Supreme Court remanded the environmentalist petition back to the EPA for reconsideration, the reality is that Congress is where the real action (money) is.

While EPA action tends to cause businesses pain, Congress tends to dole out pleasure; moreover, given that it took eight years from petition-filing to Supreme Court decision, few in the vast global warming lobby will want to risk another protracted and uncertain EPA rulemaking with its attendant litigation risks.

The value of the court decision to the global warming lobby, it appears, is merely psychological, to be used in public relations efforts.

No doubt from now on, global warmers will spin the court's actual decisions—limited to whether Massachusetts had standing to sue the EPA and to whether the EPA complied with the Clean Air Act in rejecting the petition—into spurious declarations that the court ruled that man-made global warming is real and that something must be done about it.

But even that is of limited value. Congress is already furiously working away on climate legislation, trying to juggle the various political interests and picking economic winners and losers.

The fate of global warming legislation will depend on the ultimate balance of power between the Congress' designated winners and losers. It's difficult to see how the Supreme Court decision will even slightly matter in this Darwinian legislative free-for-all.

QUESTIONS FOR CONSIDERATION

1   Policymaking almost invariably involves compromise, since the interests of affected parties often clash. Environmental policymaking, given the diversity of stakeholders, is especially challenging, since, as in this case, the consequences of scaling down the expected result may be dire. Several questions suggest themselves:

a   Is enacting an environmental policy that has less certain, or more modest, results better than "going for broke" and perhaps securing nothing?

b   Does settling for less preserve important options for better choices in the future (when, perhaps, the political prospects are more favorable), or does it indefinitely relieve the immediate political pressure to act?

c   How are the answers to these questions affected when one is addressing an environmental threat that is rapidly accelerating to a point of no return, and whose consequences are irremediable, like global climate change?

2   Is it "rewarding" polluters for bad behavior to grant them emission allowances or credits if that is what is necessary to secure a cap-and-trade agreement?

3   In general, which of the following do you regard as the most effective regulatory protocol: a) command and control, wherein the regulator sets standards of performance and penalizes those who do not meet them; b) a tax on pollution emission levels, which implicitly rewards the good actors (the lower the emissions, the lower the tax) while punishing bad actors (higher emission levels mean a higher tax); or c) cap-and-trade, wherein the regulator sets an increasingly stringent standard, but allows the universe of emitters to swap pollution allowances among themselves?

4   At the core of the cap-and-trade protocol is the notion that air pollution can be best controlled by market forces. Is there something fundamentally wrong with treating air pollution as a commodity?

5   Neither business nor environmentalists uniformly support, or oppose, S-2191. What are the elements or characteristics of this bill, or the cap-and-trade protocol in general, that accounts for its splitting usually cohesive alliances?

Chapter 5

The Food and Energy Security Act of 2007

(The Farm Bill of 2007)

Primary Documents

The Food and Energy Security Act of 2007 (The Farm Bill of 2007)

5.1. US Department of Agriculture Proposals: "Agriculture Secretary Mike Johanns Unveils 2007 Farm Bill Proposals," January 31, 2007

5.2. "Whose Subsidy Is It Anyway?" David Moberg, *In These Times*

5.3. "American Farm Bureau Federation Position Paper on the Farm Bill of 2007"

5.4. "A Safety Net, Not a Security Blanket," Scott Faber, Environmental Defense

5.5. "Reform Coalition Unveils 'Fairness in Farm and Food Policy' Amendment Members Taking Farm Bill Reform Proposal to the Floor"

5.6. "Conservation and the 2007 Farm Bill," Traci Bruckner, Center for Rural Affairs

5.7. "Farm Bill Policy Statement," National Family Farm Coalition

5.8. "Letter to the Chairman and Minority Members of the Senate Committee Deliberating on the Farm Bill, Re: Strengthening the Farm Bill to Reduce Childhood Obesity, and Improve our Environment and the Nation's Health"

5.9. "National Anti-Hunger Organizations Statement on the Nutrition Title in the 2007 Farm Bill"

5.10. "Immigration, the 2007 US Farm Bill, and the Transformation of our Food and Fuel Systems," Backgrounder, Food First

5.11. "Senator Tom Harkin, Chair of the Senate Agriculture, Nutrition, and Forestry Committee: Farm Bill Energy Title Makes Investments in the Nation's Energy Security"

5.12. "Senate Passes Farm Bill: Good for Special Interests, Bad for Consumers and Taxpayers," Competitive Enterprise Institute, News Release, December 14, 2007

BACKGROUND

The Food and Energy Security Act of 2007, commonly referred to as the Farm Bill of 2007, was introduced and debated during the last half of 2007. The current bill is the latest in a succession dating back to the 1930s, when the first farm bill was enacted in the Depression era to protect farmers from the vagaries of climate and the economy. Since that time, farm bills have become the principal formulators of our nation's food and farm policy, all the while accumulating an increasing number of purposes and stakeholders and, of course, becoming more expensive.

Historically, farm bills have had five-year "sunsets" and require reauthorization at those intervals to accommodate changes in domestic and international conditions, politics, and economic circumstances. The wisdom of reviewing food and farm policy at regular intervals has never been more evident than in 2007. Even since May of 2002, when the previous farm bill was enacted, a number of new circumstances, conditions, and social concerns emerged that require different perspectives on our agricultural policies and bring new stakeholders to the table. The result is that farm bills, with relatively narrow objectives, have morphed into sprawling pieces of omnibus legislation whose reach is from World Trade Organization forums to the lunch trays of schoolchildren. All of which has made the debate over the pending bill more contentious and complex than ever.

Specifically, the bill addresses several key components of the 2002 and previous laws. The overarching competition for funding is between two factions of the agricultural industry, and their battle subsumes a number of other political factors. All previous farm bills have given subsidies provided by farm legislation to growers of what are called "commodity" crops—corn, soybeans, wheat, rice, and cotton—sending more than half of all farm spending to just seven states. The subsidy formulas favor those crops. Moreover, the Congressional agriculture committees have been controlled for many years by representatives of the rural states where commodity agriculture is a dominant economic force. But there seems little doubt that those payments will be reduced, though the traditional "farm block" will prevent substantial erosion. The regional and political tilt in favor of commodity crop subsidies has been undercut in recent years by their association with what has been derisively dubbed in many quarters as "big agriculture," the province of food processing giants. Further, in a turnaround since 2002, this sector has enjoyed huge profits, making their case for subsidies more difficult.

The other faction of the industry, growers of what are called "specialty crops"—fruits, vegetables, tree nuts, and nursery plants—have not previously been treated generously by Congress. They are neither politically savvy, nor have they been well organized. However, they have by and large prospered without subsidies though they now need help. Accordingly, they have organized in preparation for the new bill and will enjoy some real gains. Outbreaks of food-borne illness, particularly among imported produce, have pointed to a need for more research. Also, these crops have been buoyed by the medical community's warnings about increasing rates of obesity, especially among children. The sugars and fats that commodity crops like corn and soybeans deliver have been implicated with a whole range of adverse health effects, to say nothing of the degradation of land they cause by heavy use of pesticides and fertilizers. Specialty farmers also seek funding to promote consumption of their wholesome products, especially for a program to include fruits and vegetables in school lunches. While they have not, and will not as a result of the 2007 bill, receive direct payments, they will almost surely get increased assistance for their particular needs.

Environmental interests have also gotten involved in the farm bill deliberations. Their principal interest has been in shifting funds from subsidies to conservation programs. These programs help farmers and ranchers protect environmentally vulnerable land by applying funds that would ordinarily be dedicated to production to the retirement of land from production, and promote environmentally sensitive cultivation. Of marginal environmental value, the bill appropriates funds dedicated to the production of biofuels.

Food stamp and nutritional programs are actually accorded most of the money in the farm bill. They provide low-income families with money to buy food. Provisions to fund these programs were, in fact, supported by the large agricultural interests, who sought to broaden their political base by bringing in urban and suburban district legislators.

Finally, this farm bill, like its predecessors, has an international dimension as well. It sponsors and funds the Food for Peace Program, whereby the government buys food in the US and donates it to aid and relief organizations abroad. Funding for the program is in the billion dollar range.

The deliberations among this broad array of advocates during the winter of 2007 have resulted in different bills reported by the respected Houses, setting the stage for reconciliation by a Conference Committee, to be convened early in January 2008. Given the sharp differences between them, and the wide diversity of interests they reflect, that process will almost surely be contentious. What will make their task even more difficult is the threatened veto of the President if their resulting compromise does not meet his budgetary limitations.

DOCUMENTS

At the outset of 2007, Agriculture Secretary Mike Johanns set out his proposal for a reauthorized farm bill. It is an interesting study of the legislative process to compare his objectives with what ultimately becomes law.

5.1. US Department of Agriculture Proposals: "Agriculture Secretary Mike Johanns Unveils 2007 Farm Bill Proposals," January 31, 2007

WASHINGTON, Jan. 31, 2007–. . . "We listened closely to producers and stakeholders all across the country and took a reform-minded and fiscally responsible approach to making farm policy more equitable, predictable and protected from challenge," said Johanns. "We started with the 2002 farm bill and propose to improve it by bolstering support for emerging priorities and focusing on a market-oriented approach."

USDA began preparations for the 2007 farm bill in 2005 by conducting 52 Farm Bill Forums across the country. More than 4,000 comments were recorded or collected during forums and via electronic and standard mail. These comments are summarized in 41 theme papers. USDA economists, led by Dr. Keith Collins, studied the comments and authored five analysis papers.

The proposals unveiled today represent the final phase of a nearly two year process. Each detailed proposal provides information about why a change is needed, the recommended solution, and relevant background information about the impacted program or policy.

Highlights of the proposals include (funding reflects ten year totals):

- Increase conservation funding by $7.8 billion, simplify and consolidate conservation programs, create a new Environmental Quality Incentives Program and a Regional Water Enhancement Program.
- Provide $1.6 billion in new funding for renewable energy research, development and production, targeted for cellulosic ethanol, which will support $2.1 billion in guaranteed loans for cellulosic projects and includes $500 million for a bio-energy and bio-based product research initiative.
- Target nearly $5 billion in funding to support specialty crop producers by increasing nutrition in food assistance programs, including school meals, through the purchase of fruits and vegetables, funding specialty crop research, fighting trade barriers and expanding export markets.
- Provide $250 million to increase direct payments for beginning farmers and ranchers, reserve a percentage of conservation funds and provide more loan flexibility for down payment, land purchasing and farm operating loans.

- Support socially disadvantaged farmers and ranchers by reserving a percentage of conservation assistance funds and providing more access to loans for down payments, land purchasing and farm operating.
- Strengthen disaster relief by establishing a revenue-based counter-cyclical program, providing gap coverage in crop insurance, linking crop insurance participation to farm program participation, and creating a new emergency landscape restoration program.
- Simplify and consolidate rural development programs while providing $1.6 billion in loans to rehabilitate all current Rural Critical Access Hospitals and $500 million in grants and loans for rural communities to decrease the backlog of rural infrastructure projects.
- Dedicate nearly $400 million to trade efforts to expand exports, fight trade barriers, and increase involvement in world trade standard-setting bodies.
- Simplify, modernize, and rename the Food Stamp Program to improve access for the working poor, better meet the needs of recipients and States, and strengthen program integrity.

The Administration's 2007 farm bill proposals would spend approximately $10 billion less than the 2002 farm bill spent over the past five years (excluding ad-hoc disaster assistance), upholding the President's plan to eliminate the deficit in five years. These proposals would provide approximately $5 billion more than the projected spending if the 2002 farm bill were extended.

In These Times is a liberal journal dedicated to informing and analyzing movements for social, environmental, and economic justice. David Moberg's essay, published as the Congress was to begin its deliberations, is an interesting piece providing needed history and setting in place the main issue hanging over the debate: are we supporting industrial agriculture at the expense of the small farmer? This is an indispensable introduction to the interest group statements that follow.

5.2. "Whose Subsidy Is It Anyway?" David Moberg, *In These Times*

The farm bill, which Congress will likely vote on this fall, will affect environmental, consumer, industrial, trade and anti-poverty policies as well as the prices and subsidies farmers receive for producing commodity crops such as corn, wheat and soybeans. Legislators are now conducting hearings and readying proposals, but the outcome is "more up in the air than it has been in 30 to 40 years," says senior policy analyst Dennis Olson at the Minneapolis-based Institute for Agriculture and Trade Policy. A small opening exists for a new progressive farm policy based on some old principles.

The Winners

Conventional wisdom says that the villains in farm policy are American farmers, who have in recent years collected about $20 billion a year in subsidies. But the government provides the subsidies because commodity prices have been so low that most farmers would have gone bankrupt without them. And prices have been low because legislators have written farm policy to drive those prices down to aid big business rather than farmers—or anyone else.

"The important thing for policymakers and the public to be clear on is that the people who get checks written for them under the farm bill are generally not the beneficiaries of those programs," says Timothy Wise, deputy director of the Global Development and Environment Institute at Tufts University. "So the obvious question is: 'Who benefited?' "

Consider for a moment Big Chicken—not the tacky 56-foot high tourist attraction near Marietta, Ga., but the industry that turns out more than 16 million tons of poultry each year. Once highly diversified, with nearly every farm producing chickens, the industry is now highly concentrated: The top four processors, led by giant Tyson Foods, control more than 56 percent of production.

Tyson and other giants have consolidated their power by purchasing chicken feed for, well, chicken feed. As soybean and corn prices dropped 21 percent and 32 percent, respectively, after the passage of the 1996 farm bill, the chicken industry effectively collected a subsidy of $1.25 billion a year, according to Tufts researchers Elanor Starmer, Aimee Witteman and Wise. The subsidy—worth $2.59 billion to Tyson from 1997 to 2005—represents the savings for the industry compared to paying for the full cost of producing the grain in its feed.

The cheap, subsidized grain also gave big factory farm operations an edge over diversified family farmers. By feeding animals their own grain rather than buying government-subsidized grain on the market, these farmers have to pay the full cost of producing grain they feed to their livestock. Politically, however, it remains "hard for farmers to make the case that they're not the welfare cases," says National Family Farm Coalition Executive Director Katherine Ozer, "but it's Tyson and Cargill that are the real welfare cases."

Big Chicken is not alone. International grain traders (like Cargill), industrial users of food and fiber products (ranging from the biggest users, the livestock and meat industry, to processors like Archer Daniels Midland and the vast array of junk food manufacturers), and the corporate producers of seed, fertilizers, equipment and other farm inputs all profit from overproduction and low commodity prices. Even after a long history of consolidation, tens of thousands of independent farm operators still must compete with highly concentrated agribusiness corporations that have the power to set both prices of products sold to farmers and prices paid for farmers' products.

"You're talking about a huge savings in a huge industry that never is getting a subsidy check written to it," says Wise. Until biofuel demand recently drove up prices, most farmers sold corn or soybeans for less than it cost to produce. Government subsidies covered only some of their financial loss, and many had to take jobs off the farm to make up for their farm losses.

Grain traders then sold that corn and soybeans abroad at below-cost prices. Such dumping drives millions of peasants off their land. The displaced peasants flood urban labor markets and thus depress wages. Their exodus from the land also fuels waves of immigration to more developed countries, including the United States—where many get low-wage jobs processing chicken.

Workers, Small Farmers and Consumers

Farmers who produce 90 percent of all chickens in the United States work under contracts with the big processors. The processors own the chickens and dictate how they are raised. They also require that the farmers make major investments, suffer most of the market risks and typically make poverty-level incomes. Farmers also face the danger of losing their contracts on a whim. Mississippi poultry growers Roy and Nelda Gatlin, for example, claim that in 1997 Sanderson Farms, Inc., unfairly terminated their contract on the basis of a complaint that proved untrue, destroying the Gatlins' business.

Most workers on the farm and in chicken processing plants, increasingly new immigrants, lack union representation and earn around $8 an hour, for jobs that pose grave threats to their health and safety. But workers and other victims of agribusiness are fighting back. The United Food and Commercial Workers continue to organize at a giant Smithfield pork processing plant in North Carolina, despite widespread company violations of labor laws. The Coalition of Immokalee Workers recently forced McDonald's to guarantee higher pay for tomato pickers (see "Doing It For Themselves," p. 33). The Campaign for Contract Agriculture Reform, a group of more than 200 local and national farm and agriculture groups, is lobbying to change this year's farm bill to protect rights of contract farmers, who now account for 36 percent of all agricultural production.

Consumers count as partial winners: They get cheap chicken, even if much of it is contaminated with salmonella, antibiotics and other undesirable pollutants. As the world's biggest chicken producer, the United States is also the leading exporter of chicken, particularly those parts other than the breast meat that Americans prefer, which is sold overseas at rock-bottom prices. Those dumped exports in turn decimate the chicken industry in many developing countries.

Tally it up. Losers: farmers, farm laborers, food processing workers, rural communities, the environment, poor country peasants, many developing country agricultural industries, urban laborers in both developed and developing countries facing wage competition from rural migrants and US taxpayers. The winner: corporate agribusiness.

History of the Farm Bill

During the Great Depression, the federal government adopted many of the ideas of Franklin D. Roosevelt's progressive secretary of agriculture, Henry Wallace. Wallace argued that the farm market is different from other markets and requires regulations that manage how much land is planted or kept in reserve. Managing supply, with the aid of an inventory of stored commodities, conserved the environment and smoothed price hikes and slumps.

The farm market is different because it's so basic to people's lives. Demand is only modestly affected by prices—one can only eat so much. And thousands of independent producers make a decision, which can't be changed once a crop is planted, and then depend on weather to determine their success. When prices drop, farmers may shift crops, but they rarely take land out of production, as a manufacturer might close down a production line in slow times. If market slumps drive some farmers out of business, other farmers will simply buy up their land and expand.

In the mid-1960s, the government began to abandon supply management. Nixon's Secretary of Agriculture, Earl Butz, promised unlimited exports for farmers who planted "fence row to fence row." Then, the 1996 farm bill ended the old policy of managing both prices and production through a system of loans, target prices and stored surpluses. Instead, it provided subsidy payments to farmers that were "decoupled" from production. The intent was to wean farmers steadily from all support. But when prices crashed, pressure for subsidies was politically irresistible and continued with the 2002 legislation, despite criticism from other countries that such subsidies violated global free trade agreements.

What's Next?

Progressive farm experts and advocates say that the government should return to supply management and at the same time bring anti-trust lawsuits against corporate agribusiness. They want to expand measures to protect the environment, encourage better nutrition and help farm workers. Unfortunately, on Capitol Hill, corporate agribusiness lobbyists and campaign donations rule.

The Bush administration has proposed to leave the basic farm bill principles intact, but reduce subsidies. Rep. Collin Peterson (D-Minn.)

and Sen. Tom Harkin (D-Iowa) will take the lead in pulling together Democratic alternatives in the House and Senate. Neither legislator is likely to fully embrace the Food From Family Farms Act, developed by the National Family Farm Coalition and supported by many progressive groups, but some of the core progressive ideas may enter the legislation.

The surge in biofuels, pushing up prices of corn and soybeans, "has really shifted the whole debate," Olson says. Most agribusiness interests want to push prices back down. They could do that by eliminating the tariff on ethanol imports. Cheap Brazilian ethanol would undercut the domestic industry, reducing demand for, and thus the price of, corn.

On the other hand, the Congressional Budget Office projects no need to budget for subsidies, assuming that agricultural commodity prices will stay high. But Congress made a similar, incorrect assumption about higher prices in 1996, and simply eliminating subsidies now without guaranteeing a floor for grain prices could be disastrous.

Olson says that Congress could write the farm bill to subsidize the development of a new sustainable cellulosic ethanol market, which would encourage the construction of farmer- or community-owned ethanol plants that would guarantee fair prices for farmers. The government could expand conservation programs and at the same time encourage production of sustainable crops, like perennial grasses, for ethanol. It could also create a reserve for both food and fuel needs. Such a strategy could stabilize prices for both farmers and consumers at a reasonable level.

Clearly, the field must not be left to the agribusiness and energy giants. Should that happen, the biofuel boom could turn out to be a variant of the story of Big Chicken: good for big business, bad for everyone else. It depends on whether the 110th Congress recognizes that farming is too important to leave to the whims of the market and the power of agribusiness.

www.inthesetimes.com

The American Farm Bureau Federation is the national voice of the agriculture industry. It presents the consolidated position on all matters relevant to farmers and ranchers to Congress and the media. Interestingly, in hailing the Senate's approval of the bill, it gave special praise to its energy (biofuel) provisions.

5.3. "American Farm Bureau Federation Position Paper on the Farm Bill of 2007"

Issue

The 2002 Farm Bill must be renewed or extended prior to September 30, 2007. The current bill's conservation provisions represent the "greenest"

Farm Bill ever. In addition, USDA's nutrition programs have since been reauthorized, improving their efficiencies in providing food to the most vulnerable members of our society. The next Farm Bill must provide balanced funding levels between the commodity title and other titles. In April, Farm Bureau released a Farm Bill proposal with a goal of maintaining balance and benefits to all farm sectors, while remaining fiscally responsible.

Background

The fiscal constraints confronting the nation's budget and the diminishing baseline for the commodity programs is a huge factor in the Farm Bill debate. The current baseline funding is $7 billion per year for the commodity title and $4.4 billion per year for the conservation title. Farm Bureau's proposal is based on four key principles: 1) the proposal is fiscally responsible, 2) the basic structure and funding of the 2002 Farm Bill is maintained, 3) all sectors of American agriculture share in program benefits, and 4) world trade rulings and negotiation leverage are taken into consideration.

Commodity Title

Farm Bureau supports the continuation of the "three-legged stool" safety net structure of the current commodity title (i.e. direct payments, counter-cyclical support and marketing loan payments). Direct payments and loan rates should be frozen at the 2002 levels of support. However, the counter-cyclical program should be modified to have the trigger for payments based on a shortfall in state crop revenue rather than a shortfall in the national average price. A state counter-cyclical revenue (CCR) program gets more money to farmers in years when they need it and less to them when revenues are high enough to minimize their need for support. A CCR program can deliver protection against low prices or low yields. Farm Bureau supports elimination of the fruit and vegetable planting prohibition. This support of elimination only applies to the direct payment program and not counter-cyclical payments.

Standing Catastrophic Assistance

Farm Bureau supports a standing catastrophic assistance program based on county losses for all crops including forage. (Livestock is not included.) A standing catastrophic assistance program payment would be triggered when a county is declared a disaster and actual county yields are less than 50 percent of the five-year Olympic average of county yields. Farm Bureau supports elimination of the catastrophic crop insurance program (CAT) and the Non-insured Assistance Program (NAP) once a standing catastrophic assistance program is enacted.

Dairy

Farm Bureau supports continuation of the Milk Income Loss Contract (MILC) program or another form of counter-cyclical payments. The dairy support program should be changed to reflect the prices of butter, non-fat powder and cheese instead of fluid milk.

Conservation

Farm Bureau supports strong conservation programs with an emphasis on working lands rather than land retirement programs. Farm Bureau's proposal supports reserving selected CRP acreage for grasses raised for cellulosic feedstuff production.

The Environmental Quality Incentive Program (EQIP) should be expanded by $250 million to aid fruit and vegetable producers and by $125 million annually for hog and broiler operations.

Exports

Funding for the Foreign Market Development (FMD) Program and the Market Access Program (MAP) should be maintained at their current levels of $34.5 million and $200 million per year, respectively. Farm Bureau opposes requiring food aid be given as "cash only" instead of allowing nations to continue to provide actual food directly as an emergency and developmental assistance program. We support expansion of the $2 million Technical Assistance for Specialty Crops (TASC) program to mandate an annual level of $10 million. We support a pilot initiative aimed at expanding international understanding and acceptance of the US system of sanitary and phytosanitary (SPS) practices in an effort to boost export opportunities, ensure safe imports and promote adoption of science-based SPS regimes around the world.

Competition

AFBF supports strengthening enforcement activities to ensure proposed agribusiness mergers and vertical integration arrangements do not hamper producers' access to inputs, markets and transportation. AFBF supports enhancing USDA's oversight of the Packers and Stockyards Act (PSA). We also support establishing an Office of Special Counsel for Competition at USDA. AFBF supports efforts to provide contract protections to ensure that production contracts clearly spell out what is required of producers. In addition, we support prohibiting confidentiality clauses in contracts so that producers are free to share their contracts with family members or outside advisors, lawyers or lenders. Farm Bureau supports allowing meat and poultry inspected under state programs, which are equal to federal inspection and approved by USDA, to move in interstate commerce. Farm Bureau supports voluntary country-of-origin labeling.

Farm Bureau supports the establishment and implementation of a voluntary national animal identification system capable of providing support for animal disease control and eradication.

Energy

The Commodity Credit Corporation (CCC) Bioenergy Program, the Biodiesel Fuel Education Program, the Biomass Research and Development Program and the Value-Added Agricultural Product Market Development Grants program should be re-authorized. We support $5 million in funding for demonstration projects to streamline the collection, transportation and storage of cellulosic crop residue feedstocks.

Research

We encourage Congress to establish clearer priorities for agricultural research programs based on increased input from key stakeholders such as farmers. Congress should prioritize: 1) research initiatives to commercialize technologies to make ethanol from cellulosic biomass, 2) research on modifications of dried distillers grains (DDGs) and other byproducts to expand their use, especially in non-ruminant animals, 3) research on development of renewable energy sources, such as power generation using manure, 4) increased funding for research on mechanical production, harvesting and handling techniques for the fruit and vegetable industry, 5) provide increased funding for research on methyl bromide alternatives, and 6) an in-depth USDA study of the agricultural air quality issue.

Nutrition

Farm Bureau supports expansion of the School Fruit and Vegetable Snack Program to ten schools in every state. This should only cost about $7.5 million annually but will provide significant benefits to fruit and vegetable producers, while promoting healthy eating habits among children. We support the administration's proposal to provide an additional $50 million a year for the purchase of fruits and vegetables for the school lunch program.

AFBF Policy: Farm Bureau supports extending the concepts of the current

Farm Security and Rural Investment Act of 2002 into the next farm bill. However, if changes are necessary, consideration should be given to the following:

1   Reduced complexity while allowing producers increased flexibility to plant in response to market demands;
2   Maintenance of a farm income safety net while encouraging efficiency, including consideration of an energy escalator clause because of high prices of fuel and fertilizer;
3   Driven by the needs of production agriculture;
4   Be compliant with WTO agreements;
5   Provide a "green box" compliant compensation program for fruit and vegetable growers. We recommend that the specialty crop industry be given consideration in the farm bill with emphasis focused on fundamental research, food safety, nutrition, marketing and promotions, and investment in the competitiveness and sustainability of the US specialty crop industry;
6   Trade-distorting domestic support (amber box) may be reduced in exchange for an economically proportionate increase in agricultural market access and elimination of export subsidies. Such reduction in US "amber box" supports should be offset by a transfer to fully funded "green and blue box" eligible programs. This could be accomplished though working lands conservation programs, risk management, the Market Access Program (MAP), enhanced crop insurance, the concept of a revenue-based safety net program, or government programs that increase producer profitability that may include direct payments and/or tax credits; and
7   Inclusion of a commodity loan program.

Environmental Defense is one of the nation's preeminent environmental advocacy organizations. In the piece below, ED critiques the farm bill as outdated and excessive, especially in light of the general prosperity of the agricultural sector. It vigorously supports the Fairness in Farm and Food Policy amendment.

5.4. "A Safety Net, Not a Security Blanket," Scott Faber, Environmental Defense

We need a farm safety net as modern and as entrepreneurial as our farmers.

A farm safety net crafted in response to the Dust Bowl and the Depression is no longer needed when farmers have not only joined the middle class but have also joined the investor class.

Farmers are enjoying record prices and have average household income of more than $80,000 a year—or nearly twice as much as the average

American household. The large commercial farmers who collect the lion's share of farm subsidies have farm household income greater than $270,000 a year. According to USDA, the net worth of our largest commercial farms is, on average, more than $2.2 million.

Unfortunately, the safety net proposed by the House Agriculture Committee ignores these and other important developments, such as a federal ethanol mandate that has caused corn and soybean prices to soar.

Spending $26 billion on "direct" subsidy payments—which are linked to past production, not market prices—provides many large commercial farmers a security blanket, not a safety net. And, linking farm subsidies to rising and falling prices ignores the impacts of droughts, floods and other events that reduce yields.

Helping farmers when they need help—and reducing second helpings from the federal farm trough such as direct payments—should be the foundation of farm policy.

But, the proposal developed by the House Agriculture Committee and embraced by many Democratic leaders would provide unlimited subsidies to 99.9 percent of America's farmers, regardless of need. The means test proposed by Chairman Peterson would deny subsidies to roughly 3,000 farm owners and operators—out of 1.6 million.

What's more, the Peterson proposal would renew "direct" subsidy payments—which were created to wean farmers off subsidies but have been an entitlement—for a third time and would raise price supports for many program crops.

The safety net proposed by House reformers like Reps. Ron Kind and Paul Ryan, by contrast, would provide farmers a safety net, not a security blanket.

Their Fairness in Farm and Food Policy Amendment would reform the farm safety net to be linked to farm revenue, not prices, and to set price supports below the market average. Their proposal, developed by USDA and endorsed in concept by many farm organizations would help farmers when they need help in times of low prices and low yields. Price supports would be subject an annual cap of $250,000 per person, and farmers with net farm income of more than $250,00 would be denied any support.

The centerpiece of the Fairness amendment is gradually reducing direct payments.

As the Ruminant [ED's blog] has noted before, direct payments were supposed to be the methadone, not the heroin. Under the Fairness amendment, direct payments would be reduced by $10.4 billion over five years to help meet urgent priorities, including more funds for food stamps, conservation, and rural development. Americans represented by nearly 350 members of the House would fare better if the Fairness amendment is adopted.

Most of our farmers are as comfortable with a spreadsheet as they are spreading manure. We need a safety net as modern as they are.

The Fairness in Farm and Food Policy Amendment, introduced by Representative Ron Kind and a bipartisan group of eight colleagues, represented the most direct and comprehensive challenge to the House bill from within the Congress. It sets price supports rather than subsidies, and phases out federal assistance, serving, as ED above ardently advocates, "a safety net, not a security blanket." However, it did not survive the legislative process; amendments were cut off by a parliamentary procedure. Because it incorporates so many of the recommendations of other interest groups, as well as the United States Department of Agriculture, it merits close scrutiny as a potential direction that future farm bills will take.

5.5. "Reform Coalition Unveils 'Fairness in Farm and Food Policy' Amendment Members Taking Farm Bill Reform Proposal to the Floor"

"This coalition succeeded in elevating the debate about the future of farm policy in America and pushed the Agriculture Committee to make some changes to our commodity programs," Rep. Kind said. "Unfortunately, the changes they made include loopholes large enough to drive a combine through. They failed to address the real problems with our current farm programs: they direct billions in taxpayer dollars to a few but very wealthy producers in a handful of congressional districts at the expense of programs that truly help family farms; they distort the market; and they make us susceptible to WTO challenges. The Fairness Amendment would change that—making farm spending more equitable and fiscally responsible, and reinvesting the savings in rural America through conservation, nutrition, and rural development." Last week, the House Agriculture Committee passed a Farm Bill that makes very minimal changes to commodity programs, making the US even more susceptible to WTO challenges. The bill included an income "limit" of $1 million, which preserves loopholes that will still allow the wealthiest farmers to collect subsidies, and expanded direct payment entitlements at a time when commodity prices are at near-record highs. "Market conditions and the current political environment have created a unique opportunity for Congress to make serious, meaningful reforms to our farm policy," Rep. Flake said. "If we squander this opportunity now, we may be stuck with this antiquated policy for many more years." A unique coalition in the House converged in favor of reform including members of Congress from both sides of the aisle. Earlier this year, the bipartisan group of lawmakers brought the reform debate to the forefront with a legislative package that made significant changes to agriculture policy, FARM 21. In response to feedback on FARM 21 from members, constituents, and others, Reps. Kind and Flake developed the Fairness Amendment, which retains important aspects of the farm safety net that producers have come to know, but will reform them to work better and more equitably. Many of the proposals mirror the ideas advocated by the United States Department of Agriculture and others.

"Because the Farm Bill directly affects the economy, the environment, farmers across the country and everyone who eats every day, it is past time for serious reform," said Rep. Blumenauer. "I have been working to change the Farm Bill since the last reauthorization in 2002 because every American community, whether urban or rural, has a stake in it. The Farm Bill proposed by the Agriculture Committee sadly contains reforms more in name than in substance. The amendment we're proposing today would not only implement reforms to commodity programs but provide resources for local producers and nutrition programs. Make no mistake: the status quo bill proposed by the Agriculture Committee is not only a lost opportunity for reform, but it is a direct threat to the majority of America's farmers and ranchers." The Fairness Amendment will save about $12 billion over five years by making commonsense reforms to commodity programs that will make them more equitable and geared toward family farms instead of a few very large and wealthy entities producing five crops. "The government's farm assistance program should be a safety net for family farmers in times of need—not corporate welfare with million-dollar payoffs," Rep. Paul Ryan said. "With this amendment, we address the abuses and distortions of the current system and set up a better alternative to help struggling family farms during tough times."

Key Reforms

- A fair and modern safety net for production agriculture—replaces depression-era price guarantees with a modern revenue-based safety net developed by USDA experts that better protects family farmers from declines in crop prices and crop yields. Savings: $1 billion over five years.
- Support working family farmers—denies subsidies to large commercial farmers with average annual adjusted gross income greater than $250,000 and limits annual subsidies to $250,000 per person.
- Reform crop insurance—reforms our government-subsidized crop insurance program to fairly share the costs and risks with crop insurance agents and companies. Savings: $2 billion over five years.
- Gradually reduces automatic direct payments—gradually reduces direct payments, created to wean farmers off subsidies, which has become an entitlement program that will cost more than $26 billion over five years. Limited resource farmers would be exempted from cuts, and modest incentives would encourage farmers to invest payments in rainy day accounts. Savings: At least $7 billion over five years.

New Investments (mandatory spending over five years, above the Committee's proposal):

- Domestic hunger assistance—Increases hunger assistance by at least $5.6 billion for domestic programs to feed more deserving people, especially hungry children and seniors.
- Stewardship—increases voluntary conservation programs by $3 billion.
- Fruit and vegetable producers and healthy food choices—more equitably supports fruit and vegetable producers and promotes healthy food choices with an increase of $1.2 billion.
- Minority farmers—provides an additional $500 million to support minority farmers and makes overdue changes to make USDA programs more accessible.
- Rural prosperity—increases by $200 million the grants and loans available for the development of new rural enterprises.
- Deficit reduction—reduces the deficit by $2 billion over five years and by roughly $10 billion over 10 years.
- School lunches overseas—increases by $1.1 billion the McGovern-Dole program to provide school lunches to hungry children in developing countries.

The Center for Rural Affairs is a non-profit organization dedicated to rebuilding rural America by reforming federal policy. This white paper argues that conservation payments are the best kind of farm subsidy because they encourage farmers to manage the country's land as a public resource.

5.6. "Conservation and the 2007 Farm Bill," Traci Bruckner, Center for Rural Affairs

Background

The Conservation Title of the 2007 Farm Bill should focus on rewarding good stewardship of the land by placing a greater emphasis on working lands, communities and fostering a new generation of conservation-minded farmers and ranchers. Although each of us has a moral obligation to leave the land at least as well as we receive it, the public also has an obligation to share in the cost of protecting the land and water on which all of us—current and future generations—rely for survival. The 2002 Farm Bill recognized this obligation and made great strides in this regard. For example, it increased the funding level devoted to conservation programs; developed a whole new approach to conservation programs through the creation of the Conservation Security Program and the Partnerships and Cooperation Initiative; and called for a special initiative through conservation programs for beginning farmers and ranchers. We propose the following for the 2007 Conservation Title:

Conservation for Working Lands

To effectively protect the environment, the farm bill must address working lands as well as land retirement. The Conservation Security Program established by the 2002 farm bill is the basis on which to build. It has several key strengths. It rewards farmers and ranchers who practice environmental stewardship year in and year out. That is far better than only paying the worst actors to change, placing the nation's best environmental stewards at a competitive disadvantage in competing for land and conservation funds. The outcome of the later approach is to shift landownership toward those who care little about stewardship and practice it only when paid. CSP takes a far better approach of both rewarding those who have always practiced stewardship as well as those making improvements. That will yield more far-reaching and lasting environmental gains.

CSP is good for farmers and ranchers. If it's implemented correctly, it will base payments on how intensively the operator manages the land to protect the environment. Payments based on what farm and ranch operators do are far more likely to remain in their pockets than payments based on how much land they operate. The latter payments are inevitably bid into higher cash rents and land prices and thereby transferred to the landowner. Payments based on the operator's management are far more likely to remain with the operator. The CSP has faced enormous implementation and funding challenges, which created an uncertain and shaky start for the program. Therefore, we propose that the new farm bill must include stronger, more decisive language that will:

- Fully fund the program, giving it nationwide status and available to all eligible farmers and ranchers for 2007 and beyond.
- Disallow the Secretary of Agriculture to create ranking or category systems (such as NRCS used for CSP under the 2002 Farm Bill as a means to prioritize distribution of funds).
- Address resource conserving crop rotations—define it and indicate that the Secretary shall include this as an enhancement practice. Specifically indicate that the Secretary of Agriculture shall use a soil analysis model that levels the playing field for all agricultural systems. The soil model that would live up to this standard is the Soil Management Assessment Framework (SMAF) and requires resource conserving crop rotations for Tier III participation.

Community and Conservation

The next farm bill should strive to make better use of conservation programs to make rural communities more attractive places to live and visit. The rural communities that have grown are largely those with environmental amenities—lakes and mountains. In the future, uncrowded natural space may become a key environmental amenity, one many farm and ranch communities could provide. What if, for example, our land retirement based conservation programs provided bonus payments for enrollments that allowed public access as part of a community development plan. It could provide the basis for some tourism-based small businesses— such as bed and breakfasts and other agri- and eco-tourism enterprises. We had hoped that the Conservation Partnerships and Cooperation Program in the 2002 farm bill would serve these purposes, but its statutory language was very general and never implemented by USDA. They instead implemented their own version that did not reflect the original intent of the provision. We propose it be reauthorized as the Cooperative Conservation Partnerships Initiative (CCPI). The CCPI should be implemented on a competitive basis through intermediaries including producer associations, non-governmental organizations, conservation districts, watershed councils, educational institutions, and state and local agencies. The CCPI should be a mandated initiative and be funded through existing state allocations for the full range of farm bill conservation programs. Up to 20 percent of a state's allocation should be available for cooperative conservation projects, with considerable flexibility to match program funding streams and mechanisms to tackle specific local problems and/or projects. Preference should be given to projects that involve partnerships of producers, local governments and local organizations focused on making rural communities attractive places to live and visit by providing landscape and habitat amenities, addressing community needs such as flood control through environmental restoration, or restoring resources and then providing for public access for recreational activities. To ensure this preference, we recommend the inclusion of the following language: The Secretary shall make bonus payments of up to 50% for enrollments in the Conservation Reserve Program, Wetlands Reserve Program and the Grassland Reserve Program under the following conditions:

- the enrollment is certified by a state or local unit of government or Resource Conservation and Development District as consistent with its plan to develop natural space and habitat as a community development asset;
- the land is restored to native plant species and habitat for native animal species; and
- the landowner provides public access to the enrolled land.

Conservation and Beginning Farmers and Ranchers

Beginning farmer and rancher programs need to be a critical part of the new farm bill and conservation programs can play an important role. Present trends and current obstacles are working against the very existence of a new generation of farmers and ranchers: Farm entry rates have declined; the farmer "replacement" rate has fallen to below 50 percent; there are twice as many farmers over 65 as under 35 years old; nearly half of all farm operators in the US are over 55 years in age and nearly three-fifths of all farm assets are owned by those 55 and older.

The 2002 Farm Bill contained a provision to make federal conservation programs more available and accessible to beginning farmers and ranchers and other targeted groups (Indian tribes and limited resource agricultural producers). A provision such as this will achieve two important public policy goals simultaneously—help get new farmers and ranchers started while encouraging them to adopt strong conservation systems from the outset. Unfortunately, USDA failed to implement this special provision. The new farm bill should again include this provision and include the following language:

The Secretary shall create a special initiative for beginning farmers and ranchers, limited resource producers and Indian tribes that will:

- Provide technical service, mentoring programs and educational training that focus on sustainable agricultural farming practices and systems as well as related marketing issues.
- Provide strong conservation planning and technical assistance through NRCS field staff and resource specialists as well as through the development of cooperative agreements between NRCS and extension and non-governmental organizations.
- Provide an option for immediate upfront or advanced payments to beginning farmers and ranchers through multi-year contracts entered into for federal conservation programs such as CSP, WRP, WHIP. This would provide the beginning farmer and/or rancher a more significant cash flow. For example, the contract would provide the beginning farmer a five-year payment stream in return for a legally binding commitment including an easement.
- Offer a financial incentive such as a 25% bonus for beginning farmers and ranchers to develop whole farm/ranch conservation plans under EQIP and CSP. Farmers and ranchers can get a good start with conservation practices through EQIP. By encouraging them to work towards a whole farm/ranch conservation plan, conservation will be furthered and it will enhance their participation in the Conservation Security Program by reading them to participate at the highest and most lucrative level, Tier III.
- Create an incentive such as a 25% bonus payment for landowners under CSP, WRP, WHIP and EQIP to encourage them to rent to beginning farmers and ranchers on a longer-term, multi-year basis in

connection with adoption and installation of conservation structures and management practices.

- Graduate the cost-share portion attributable to the beginning farmer or rancher over a period of years under EQIP with higher cost-share in the beginning and lower at the end of the contract as a means to provide a better cash flow. For example, provide 100% in year one and two and 50% in year three.
- Encourage retirees or non-farming heirs holding Conservation Reserve Program contracts set to expire to make arrangements to transfer the land to beginning farmers and ranchers by offering a rental rate bonus during a transition period, such as a 20% bonus per year for three years.
- Provide a special initiative through the CSP that focuses on keeping land in grass by providing financial incentives such as a 40% payment bonus for beginning farmers and ranchers to develop and improve grazing lands. Encourage farmland preservation transition initiatives focused on whole farm planning. Under such a proposal, farmland enrolled in the Farmland Preservation Program could provide 25% bonus payments to a retiring farmer or ranchers for transferring land and the easement to a beginning farmer or rancher that has established a whole farm conservation plan.

Conservation Cost-Share Programs

The 2002 Farm Bill grandly expanded funding for the Environmental Quality Incentives Program (EQIP). In combination with the increased funding, we also witnessed a dramatic increase in the payment limitation, going from $50,000 in the 1996 Farm Bill to $450,000 under the 2002 Farm Bill. This allows a substantial portion of the program dollars to flow towards large-scale livestock operations. The new farm bill needs to address this issue and re-establish the $50,000 payment limitation and target program dollars towards conservation measures that promote agricultural diversity and a new generation of agriculturalists rather than those measures that encourage the continued consolidation of agriculture and the environmental degradation of rural communities. The EQIP should be funded at no less than $400 million per year.

"Testimony of the American Corn Growers Association," before the Senate Agriculture, Nutrition, and Forestry Committee, Larry Mitchell, CEO

. . . We wish it noted that our farm bill proposal for the crop title of the next farm bill is much more than a corn proposal. We have always attempted to represent the interests of not only corn farmers, but also all those in agriculture. We believe that all family farmers must work together to find a farm policy that restores prosperity to family farmers and ranchers of all types.

We also understand that corn is the most widely grown crop in the US and has by far the largest production volume of any commodity. It has the largest livestock feed usage, and the largest industrial usage. Therefore, we recognize that feed grain policy has a huge impact on all commodity prices, and also directly impacts the structure of the dairy and livestock industries. The commodity title also impacts our rural communities, our environment, our food system and our federal budget more than any other sector of the overall farm bill.

This is why we have been working with scores of other farm, rural, religious, international, environmental, and wildlife groups over the past year to advance the Food from Family Farm Act (FFFA) with the National Family Farm Coalition and some 60 other organizations. We will present the basic concepts of the FFFA today and ask for your consideration and support for the plan as you advance your endeavor in drafting this year's farm bill. But first, we are obliged to request your consideration of a broader review of which direction we should choose in the next farm bill.

In addition to our support for the FFFA, we take this opportunity to state that ACGA also supports the following farm bill provisions:

- Retention and expansion of the Conservation Reserve Program (CRP),
- Full funding and deployment of the Conservation Security Program (CSP),
- Expansion of the Energy Title of the farm bill,
- Establishment of a standing disaster program,
- Development of a Cellulosic Reserve Program,
- Extension of the Milk Income Loss Contract (MILC),
- Inclusion of a competition title similar to Senator Tom Harkin's Agricultural Fair Practices Act,
- Implementation of the current Country of Origin Labeling (COOL) provision of the 2002 farm bill, and
- Improved delivery and full funding of programs targeted toward limited resource and socially disadvantaged farmers and ranchers.

www.cfra.org

The National Family Farm Coalition speaks for grassroots groups on farm, food, trade, and rural economic issues. It is especially concerned that rural communities are economically threatened by the growing corporate control of agriculture.

5.7. "Farm Bill Policy Statement," National Family Farm Coalition

Public policy must be fashioned to protect and strengthen the future of our food supply, environment, public health, and rural communities. A new US farm bill and international trade agreements must reverse the current policy that uses taxpayer dollars as a substitute for income not provided to farmers through the low prices paid by multinational corporations for products from our nation's farms and ranches. Family farms must help prevent global warming and be an essential source of renewable energy with respect for local control. Low commodity prices and high taxpayer expenses combine to exacerbate the nation's budget and trade deficit, create cheap feed that encourages destructive industrial production of livestock, and spread the curses of unhealthy diet and low farm income abroad while destroying economic opportunity on family farms and in rural communities here at home.

Our nation's food security and food sovereignty require in the new farm bill:

- Establishment of food security reserves, commodity price floors, fair wages and working conditions for all workers in the food system.
- Support for new generations of diversified, sustainable family farmers.
- Encouragement of fair and open competition and enforcement of existing rules pertaining to competition and anti-trust to address the rampant concentration in the food industry.
- All farm and food policies to fully serve the diversity of our nation's family farmers through accessible USDA programs.
- Stewardship of land and water through improved conservation programs.
- Encouraged economic development through new markets for healthy, sustainably produced food.
- A democratic policymaking process that protects the future of our environment and encourages healthy rural communities.

The Specialty Crop Farm Bill Alliance is a coalition of more than 120 specialty crop organizations representing 350 individual specialty crops. This coalition provides what specialty crop growers have never had—an organized political lobby to advocate for their cause. Heretofore, as noted, virtually all subsidies have gone to commodity growers, each crop having its own advocate. This coming together of what has been a disorganized and politically impotent sector of the industry no doubt accounts for their better treatment in 2007.

The 2007 Farm Bill

The fresh fruit and vegetable industry represents a vitally important segment of American agriculture and brings crops to market that are essential to the health of all Americans. While the produce industry does not grow fruits and vegetables in every Congressional district, our industry is important to the good health of all Americans, as well as to our government's efforts to prevent disease, reduce obesity and improve the well-being of our citizens. The federal government and Congress must consider all solutions to help the fruit and vegetable industry remain world leaders in food production and competitiveness. . . .

The Specialty Crop Farm Bill Alliance succeeded in the 109th Congress to work with key members in Congress to develop a comprehensive farm bill package that provided the necessary framework to enhance the competitiveness of the specialty crop industry. In the 109th Congress, Senators Larry Craig (R-ID) and Debbie Stabenow (D-MI) introduced the Specialty Crop Competition Act of 2006, a marker bill aimed at strengthening the competitiveness of the specialty crop industry through enhancing current federal nutrition programs, funding for invasive pest and disease programs and expanding the popular specialty crop block grant program. As a marker bill, the Specialty Crop Competition Act gained bipartisan support in the US Senate. Meanwhile, Reps. Richard Pombo (R-CA), Adam Putnam (R-FL), Dennis Cardoza (D-CA), and John Salazar (D-CO), introduced H.R. 6193, the Equitable Agriculture Today (EAT) for a Healthy America Act. Also intended as a marker bill, the 109th EAT Healthy America Act was supported by 77 co-sponsors, representing over 20 states. Most importantly, the legislation addressed the need for long-term investments that are critical to promoting consumption and demand for our agricultural products. EAT Healthy America Act highlighted our industry's efforts to adapt to changes in the business environment and provided us with the tools necessary to succeed. . . .

Literally hundreds of physicians and health care professionals signed the following letter to the Chairman and ranking Minority members of the Senate committee deliberating on the Farm Bill. Such a document is relatively unusual, since medical professionals are not disposed to partake in political affairs. Their participation testifies to the salience of the health dimension of the issue.

5.8. "Letter to the Chairman and Minority Members of the Senate Committee Deliberating on the Farm Bill, Re: Strengthening the Farm Bill to Reduce Childhood Obesity, and Improve our Environment and the Nation's Health"

We, the undersigned, are physicians and healers, public health and other health professionals, not farmers. But we eat, we have patients and families who eat, and so we care about what farmers grow. We want to see the 2007 Farm Bill become a "Healthy Food Bill."

Obesity and unhealthy eating constitute a national crisis, with $117 billion per year in estimated treatment and indirect costs. The epidemic of child obesity, however, promises a worse crisis in the making—these children will have more heart disease, diabetes, cancer and stroke, in some cases not long after they become adults.

Today's agricultural policies are inconsistent with healthy eating. They help flood our communities, including our schools, with high-calorie, nutrient poor, highly-processed foods made from cheap starches, sweeteners and oils derived from grains and soybeans. These foods are a big part of the health problems we face. We must do better.

US agricultural policy helps to make unhealthy foods some of the cheapest, "most affordable" to buy. It also contributes to a population deficient in healthful omega-3 fatty acids, with likely impacts on inflammation and other chronic disease—heart disease, stroke, and diabetes. We must do better.

We also care about how farmers grow our food. Current farm policy promotes agricultural methods that deplete water resources, and use pesticides and fossil fuels intensively, with impacts on consumers, communities and our climate. By underwriting the industrial-scale production of animals raised on grain, our farm policy also supports significant air and water pollution.

Grain-fed animals raised under confinement can be more disease-prone than those raised in traditional pasture-based systems. These animals are routinely fed human antibiotics to counter disease and to promote more rapid growth. The Institutes of Medicine confirm this practice hastens the spread of antibiotic resistance, while in medicine we are losing our arsenal of antibiotics that work. We must support healthier agriculture.

With the 2007 Farm Bill, our government has the opportunity to invest taxpayer dollars in a food system that promotes rather than hinders individual health. Farmers, communities, and the health of our environment would benefit as well.

We urge you to make sure this Farm Bill advances Americans' health and well-being. The Farm Bill should:

Give all Americans better access to healthy foods (fresh fruits and vegetables, whole rather than refined grains, and better fats) and especially to locally produced foods that will support farmers and strengthen the economic and environmental health of our communities.

Help ensure better school access to healthy foods, making the diets of schoolchildren more consistent with the Dietary Guidelines for Americans.

Take proactive steps to make fresh produce and other healthy foods more affordable relative to unhealthy foods, as well as to help build the infrastructure needed to get these foods into even our lowest-income communities. . . .

A coalition of anti-hunger advocacy, food bank, and emergency feeding organizations working to reduce hunger in America, constituted as National Anti-Hunger Organizations (NAHO), issued a statement strongly supporting the Nutrition Title in the 2007 Farm Bill. The Food Stamp Program and other nutrition assistance programs have been among the most popular and important to be funded by the farm bill. These organizations want to insure that the farm bill continues to provide the resources necessary to reduce hunger in our country. Members reach into every Congressional District in the country, which accounts for its continued federal support.

5.9. "National Anti-Hunger Organizations Statement on the Nutrition Title in the 2007 Farm Bill"

We are deeply concerned about the many people in our communities who, for lack of resources, are not consistently able to put food on their tables for themselves or their families. Indeed, the most recent USDA/Census Bureau survey of food security documents that more than 35 million people in the United States live in households that face a constant struggle against hunger. Thus, it is essential that the 2007 Farm Bill address the pressing problem of hunger amidst plenty by strengthening the nation's food assistance programs.

Our organizations' top priority in the 2007 Farm Bill reauthorization is a strong Nutrition Title that reauthorizes and improves the Food Stamp Program, the nation's first defense against hunger, and bolsters the efforts of the emergency food assistance system. We strongly urge that the 2007 Farm Bill and the Fiscal Year 2008 Budget Resolution reflect those urgent national priorities and ask you to consider the following recommendations.

The Food Stamp Program, the nation's first defense against hunger, is a crucial and effective program that has nearly eliminated malnutrition from the national landscape and helps prevent the problem of hunger from becoming worse in our communities. Food Stamp Program participation closely tracks economic trends, responding quickly to increases in need, whether due to local or national economic circumstances or to disasters, as seen in the aftermath of Hurricane Katrina.

Food stamps help strengthen families and the American communities where those families reside—rural, urban and suburban. More than 80 percent of food stamp benefits go to families with children, allowing their parents to obtain food at grocer stores for meals at home. Much of the remainder goes to seniors and persons with disabilities. Through the nationwide use of Electronic Benefit Transfer (EBT) cards, program utilization has been streamlined for transactions for consumers and store clerks, and EBT has quantifiably reduced the chances of program abuse.

Food Stamps pay dividends for consumers, food producers and manufacturers, grocery retailers and communities. As food stamp purchases flow through grocery checkout lines, farmers' markets and other outlets, those benefits generated almost double their value in economic activity, especially for many hard-pressed rural and urban communities desperately in need of stimulus to business and jobs.

The Food Stamp Program's basic entitlement structure must be maintained while greater resources are provided to the program to more effectively fight hunger in our communities. Areas for program investment include:

Adequacy of Benefits Must Be Improved   The first step to reducing hunger in the US is to ensure that everyone in the Food Stamp Program has the resources to assist them in purchasing and preparing a nutritionally adequate diet. Neither the average food stamp benefit level of $1 per person per meal, nor the $10 monthly minimum benefit is sufficient to help families purchase an adequate diet. This dietary shortfall negatively impacts recipients' health and impedes the ability of children to learn and adults to work. Another key element to securing an adequate diet will be finding ways to improve access to affordable and healthful foods for food stamp households in low-income neighborhoods;

Access to the Program Must Be Expanded   Too many people in our communities are in need of food stamps but cannot get them. Only 33 percent of the people in food bank lines are enrolled in food stamps. Those people in need of food but excluded from the Food Stamp Program include working poor families with savings slightly above decades old and outdated resource limits, many legal immigrants, and numerous indigent jobless people seeking employment;

Program Simplification and Streamlining for Caseworkers and Clients Must Continue   While food stamp outreach and nutrition education are making important inroads, these efforts need more resources, and enrollments are hampered by shortfalls in state technology and supports. Too many eligible people—especially working poor and elderly persons—are missing out on benefits.

In addition to the necessary improvements to the Food Stamp Program, the 2007 Farm Bill also will provide Congress with an opportunity to assist the front-line agencies that deal with the problem of hunger every day. The nation's food banks, food pantries, and soup kitchens are stretched to serve more and more people whose food stamps have run out mid-month or whose income and resources put them just above the food stamp eligibility threshold. Currently, more than 25 million unduplicated people are accessing emergency food annually through food banks. In any given week, some 4.5 million people access food through pantries and soup kitchens throughout the United States. Requests for emergency food assistance are outstripping the resources provided through The Emergency Food Assistance Program (TEFAP) and the Commodity Supplemental Food Program (CSFP). In TEFAP alone, surplus commodity deliveries have declined more than 50 percent in the past year, at the same time that requests for emergency food have increased.

Therefore, we urge the 2007 Farm Bill and FY 2008 Budget to invest significant new resources to make food stamp benefit allotments sufficient to real world needs, to open eligibility to more vulnerable populations, to connect more eligible people with benefits, and to adequately support emergency feeding programs.

We are fortunate to live in a nation with an abundant and varied food supply. In the upcoming Farm Bill reauthorization, we strongly urge the Congress to help connect more vulnerable people with that food supply and move our nation closer to a hunger-free America.

The Institute for Food and Development Policy/Food First seeks to effect social change by changing how people think about the root causes of global hunger, poverty, and ecological degradation. Here the Institute argues that the Farm Bill addresses the symptoms, but not the root causes, of the immigration problems.

5.10. "Immigration, the 2007 US Farm Bill, and the Transformation of our Food and Fuel Systems," Backgrounder, Food First

The current immigration legislation attempts to balance the fears of a post-9/11 electorate with the management of the largest single migration in the modern history of the Americas. At this writing, this bill focuses on symptoms rather than causes and faces strong opposition from all sides.

Rather than immigration reform, sweeping reform of our national and international food and agricultural policies could do much to address the underlying causes of immigration—grinding poverty that drives people to abandon home and family.

For decades the US Farm Bill has used taxpayer subsidies to keep grain prices low, causing overproduction that benefited big grain companies who then dumped cheap grain abroad at below the cost of production. This subsidized overproduction—coupled with free trade agreements and the devastating polices of the International Monetary Fund—forced millions of small farmers in the Global South out of farming. Many of the 1.1 million immigrants crossing the US's southern border each year are these farmers, who can no longer afford to farm. In the US, overproduction of grain encourages overconsumption of cheap, processed, unhealthy foods. It has concentrated market power in the agribusiness sector, making farmers worldwide dependent on a handful of corporate giants for their inputs and their markets.

Though the economic power of the agri-foods industry (and their lobbyists) is strong, many observers maintain that conditions for far-reaching agricultural reform in the US have never been better. This is because our food systems are in a profound state of flux and transformation.

First, as the Food First Backgrounder, *Biofuels: Myths of the Corporate Agro-Fuels Transition* explains, the "agro-fuels boom" is transforming our food and fuel systems worldwide, bringing both under one enormous industrial roof. There will be big winners and losers in this transition. The question is not whether agro-fuels have a place in our future—they are inescapable—but whether or not we allow a handful of global corporations to determine the future of our food and fuel systems.

Another major element transforming our food systems is the global liquidity crisis: money is backing up in the world's banks. Globalization has efficiently concentrated enormous wealth over the past 20 years. We now have 500 billionaires and over a million millionaires in the world—while the number of people living in poverty continues to grow. Banks are driven to loan; otherwise they are stuck paying interest, with no income to offset that interest . . . Extractive sectors including agro-fuels, oil and mining are prime investment opportunities because of their capacity to absorb large sums of investment capital quickly. Multilateral development banks, including the World Bank and the Inter-American Development Bank, provide governments with loans to re-structure laws, markets, and local infrastructure to favor corporate investment—often at the price of local food security. Two pending 2007 Food First Development Reports will detail how the World Bank's territorial restructuring in favor of mining corporations is driving farmers from the land, channeling precious natural resources to foreign businesses, and undermining food security in Ghana and Guatemala.

At the same time, activism in the US and worldwide on food, environment and social justice issues is at an all-time high. From underserved neighborhoods of people of color fighting to ensure health and nutrition, to slow food advocates seeking quality food, to farmers producing for the local market, people are taking back their local food systems from the corporate agri-foods industry. Paul Hawken, author of *Natural Capitalism and Blessed Unrest, How the Largest Movement in the World Came into Being and Why No One Saw It Coming* claims that there are a minimum of 130,000 registered civil society organizations working for social and environmental justice on the planet—there may be as many as one million. These organizations are reacting to the negative changes in our food systems and then advancing alternatives, shaping outcomes, and building parallel systems serving millions of people. They have held the largest anti-war demonstrations in the history of the world and the largest immigrant rights demonstrations in the US since the Civil Rights Movement in the 1960s. They are taking matters into their own hands by setting up thousands of gardens in schools and on vacant lots, challenging government on food regulations and strengthening local food systems through farmers markets, community supported agriculture (CSA), and by educating themselves about where food comes and how much energy it takes to transport it to market. They are creating markets and extending the meaning of organic, fair trade, and direct trade, and are rebuilding local economies by reinvesting the food dollar in local production, local processing and local distribution systems.

All of these actions are pieces of an international movement that is organizing and putting pressure on government officials for food sovereignty—the right of people to control their own food system. The struggle for food sovereignty is the struggle for control over the transformation of the world's food and fuel systems.

The 2007 Farm and Food Bill could advance the process of agricultural reform in favor of food and fuel sovereignty. There are a number of "marker bills" before the Agricultural Committee in Congress with provisions to ensure a fair price to family farmers, put a cap on subsidies, encourage fruit and vegetable production, resource conservation, research in organic agriculture, and the rebuilding of local food systems in underserved communities. . . .

Senator Tom Harkin, Chair of the Senate Agriculture, Nutrition, and Forestry Committee, has taken a lead role in the biofuels component of the Farm Bill. In the following statement, he discusses its details and its goals.

5.11. "Senator Tom Harkin, Chair of the Senate Agriculture, Nutrition, and Forestry Committee: Farm Bill Energy Title Makes Investments in the Nation's Energy Security"

Washington, DC—Senator Tom Harkin (D-IA), Chairman of the Senate Committee on Agriculture, Nutrition and Forestry, today discussed the importance of the farm bill's energy title at a press conference on Capitol Hill.

"Good morning. With regular gasoline prices back above $3 a gallon and with oil prices closing in on $100 a barrel, there is no longer any debate about the need to ramp up production of home-grown, renewable energy in a very robust way. That's exactly what the new farm bill does.

"I included the first-ever energy title in the last farm bill back in 2002. But, relatively speaking, that was just baby steps. Current biofuels production capacity is approximately six billion gallons annually. The new farm bill will put us on a path to producing ten times that—60 billion gallons annually—by 2030.

"The farm bill's energy title allocates $1.1 billion over five years for new investments in farm-based energy.

"The good news is that we have strong agreement between Congress and the White House on the need to emphasize cellulosic biofuels and bioenergy—energy derived from cellulosic feedstocks such as switchgrass and wood pulp. Indeed, this is exactly what the President called for in his State of the Union Address early this year.

"However, we confront a classic chicken-and-egg dilemma: Entrepreneurs won't build cellulosic bio-refineries in the absence of a reliable supply of feedstocks. And producers won't grow the cellulosic feedstocks unless and until there are bio-refineries to purchase them.

"Well, in this bill, we address this dilemma very aggressively. On the supply side, we allocate $130 million over five years to the Biomass Crop Transition Program. We know it takes a few years to get crops like switchgrass started and established. So farmers are going to need financial assistance during the transition. And that's what we provide in the Senate bill.

"On the demand side, we allocate $300 million to support grants for bio-refinery pilot plants, loan guarantees for commercial bio-refineries, and support for repowering existing corn-ethanol plants and other facilities so they can process cellulosic biomass.

"In addition, we continue the CCC bioenergy program with $245 million to support feedstock purchases for advanced biofuels production. And, we're including about $140 million for biomass research and for biomass crop experiments.

"Let me just note two reasons why the future of biofuels lies in the use of cellulosic feedstocks. One, cellulosic is more energy efficient than corn ethanol. And, two, it can be produced in most parts of the United States, which will expand biofuels production beyond our major corn-producing regions, and to places closer to where the fuels are blended and consumed.

"I'll make this prediction: If we can preserve the Senate energy provisions in conference—and maybe get some additional funding for them, which we'll certainly try to do—I predict that within five years we are going to see cellulosic biofuel refineries sprouting like mushrooms all across the country.

"The bottom line is that when we draw our energy from farm fields and other renewable sources here in the US, and reduce our dependence on the oil fields of the Middle East, that is a win, win, win for America. It is good for our national security. It is good for the environment. And it's good for farmers and the rural economy.

"That's why I find it unconscionable that the Administration is threatening to veto this bill. The energy provisions in this bill are critically important to the national security of this country. There is no time to waste. And it is extremely unfortunate that this bill is in jeopardy of being killed by a Presidential veto.

The Competitive Enterprise Institute is a non-partisan public policy group promoting the principles of free enterprise and limited government. CEI has argued that the Farm Bill is financially irresponsible, rewarding the rich at the expense of "consumers, taxpayers, and the poor."

5.12. "Senate Passes Farm Bill: Good for Special Interests, Bad for Consumers and Taxpayers," Competitive Enterprise Institute, News Release, December 14, 2007

Yesterday the Senate passed the 2007 Farm Bill, the first major revision of agricultural policy in five years. "The $286 billion Senate version of the Farm Bill is a good deal for farmers, but a shabby one for taxpayers who foot the bill for this Congressional largesse," said Competitive Enterprise Institute Adjunct Fellow Fran Smith.

Now the House and Senate conferees will get together and resolve their differences. "Those differences are in the details, but the broad scope of both bills continues and even expands the bloated farm support programs begun in the Great Depression," said Smith. "Consumers, taxpayers, and the poor will be the ones paying out of their pockets to swell the coffers of special-interest farmers," she said.

To cut off possible filibusters by Southern Senators, the Senate pulled a parliamentary trick so that each of the 40 amendments allowed to be offered needed 60 votes to win. "That supermajority vote meant that any reform attempt at this late stage was doomed to failure," said Smith.

Even some amendments offering small reforms, for example, to cap the amount of payments a farmer could receive. One of the amendments offered would have limited farm subsidies to $250,000 per year for a married couple, a reduction from the current $360,000 limit. Another would have limited payments to people actively engaged in farming, rather than to long-distance and wealthy owners who receive some hefty farm payments.

Smith said, "The House-Senate conferees have a last chance to fix some of the more egregious problems with both bills. The sugar program would be a prime candidate. Both versions of the Farm Bill would make the program even worse—by increasing the price supports for sugar producers, restricting imports, and even using taxpayer dollars to purchase excess sugar for ethanol production."

"We urge them to stand up for their true constituents—taxpayers and consumers."

QUESTIONS FOR CONSIDERATION

1   Does omnibus legislation such as this farm bill, which embodies a variety of only marginally related, sometimes even conflicting, programs, result in good public policy, or is it simply a political expedient. Shouldn't these important public purposes be considered independently of one another given that some could not secure passage on their own?

2   When the first farm bill was enacted, approximately 25% of the population lived on farms, or were involved in one or another aspect of its infrastructure. Today, that figure is a tiny fraction of that, perhaps 2%. Does this erosion of the agriculture sector render a farm bill of the kind we've seen over the years an anachronism, especially in light of the consolidation of the farming industry? Is industrial agriculture under threat, and is it joining more "progressive" interests to salvage at least its base?

3   Given the number of alternate food/dietary regimens—organics, slow food, vegetarian and vegan diets, localism—do you expect to see even more erosion of industrial agriculture in the future, or is the global need to feed more people "big" agriculture's insurance policy?

4   Agricultural extension services, established, sponsored and funded by states, have historically provided free technical assistance to small farmers and independent entrepreneurs. Are these disappearing from the landscape, or do they remain a valuable resource for "specialty crop" growers? Why do you suppose they are not included among the beneficiaries of farm bills?

5   The government continues to provide pre-emptive financial support for farmers, though the mix of that assistance varies, as we have seen. Yet, no other professional or occupational group or industry is so favored by our government. Is there a solid justification for this, or is our agrarian heritage and our intimate relationship to land so fundamental to who we are that we cannot contemplate its demise?

6   Is the succession of farm bills testament more than anything else to the awesome political power of long-tenured committee chairs who jealously guard their turf?

Chapter 6

The Healthy Forests Restoration Act and Federal Wildfire Policy

Primary Documents

The Healthy Forests Restoration Act and Federal Wildfire Policy

6.1. "Healthy Forests: An Initiative for Wildfire Prevention and Stronger Communities," White House Public Statement

6.2. Press Release: "President Bush Signs 'Healthy Forests Restoration Act' into Law"

6.3. "President Bush Signs 'Healthy Forest Restoration Act' into Law: Remarks by the President at Signing of H.R. 1904, The Healthy Forests Restoration Act of 2003"

6.4. "Remarks Prepared for Delivery by the Honorable Gail Norton, Secretary of the Interior," on behalf of the Western Governor's Association, at the Forest Summit, June 19, 2003

6.5. "Healthy Forest Bill an Important First Step," Society of American Foresters

6.6. "Letter to the US House of Representatives: Support H.R. 1904, the Healthy Forests Restoration Act of 2003," May 19, 2003

6.7. "Tree-Huggers or Fire-Huggers? The Environmental Movement's Confused Forest Policy," Thomas M. Bonnicksen, Ph.D on behalf of the Center for Public Policy Research

6.8. "The 'Let Our Forests Burn Policy' is Criminal and Stupid—It Must be Re-examined by the Scientists of This Nation," Bill Wattenburg, Research Foundation at California State University at Chico, August 18, 1998

6.9. "The Fires This Time," Roger Sedjo, The Property and Environmental Research Center

6.10. "Issue Paper, May 2003," The Natural Resources Defense Council

BACKGROUND

The Healthy Forests Restoration Act (HFRA), signed into law on December 3, 2003, represents the latest in a series of major shifts in federal wildfire policy. For almost 100 years, the nation has struggled to forge a fire management strategy that would accommodate the competing claims of public safety, private property protection, and ecological sustainability. Our historic inability to settle on a consistent forest management protocol that has wide and consistent support reflects the complexity of the issues involved and the number and diversity of stakeholders with interests in such a protocol: the USDA Forest Service, the federal agency charged with developing and implementing forest resource management policies; residents and business owners whose property, especially on the wildland-urban interface, is most vulnerable to fire; environmentalists, who regard wildfires as long-term benefits to ecological viability; local and state governments, whose economies are dependent on thriving enterprises and tourism; timber companies, who are the principal logging and thinning contractors in return for commercial quality timber; and, of course, firefighters themselves, hundreds if not thousands of whom have, over the years, been casualties in carrying out firefighting operations.

The competing claims of these interest groups notwithstanding, the impetus to change direction in 2003 was attributable to the growing recognition that the current plan was not succeeding. The complex of fires in 2000 made it one of the worst fire seasons in history, and the record-setting fires in 2002 veritably overwhelmed fire managers. That season, wildfires burned more than seven million acres of public and private land, and the cost of their suppression was unprecedented. In all, 21 firefighters were killed, tens of thousands of residents were evacuated, and thousands of buildings were destroyed. The Healthy Forest Initiative, an administration plan to regain control over these destructive forces, was propelled by a sense of urgency.

As noted earlier, this new initiative was only the most recent plan to deal with forest fires. From the late 1800s to the 1970s, it was official government policy to extinguish all fires as soon as possible. Wildfires were clearly treated as destructive forces to be suppressed expeditiously. The protection of personal property, as well as forest resources, was the priority. In 1972, a revised Park Service policy

recognized fire's ecological role. The newly adopted "let it burn" policy gave officials the discretion to allow fires ignited by natural forces to burn, if they posed
only minimal threat to life or property. It is widely accepted among scientists
that such fires promote the regeneration of vegetation, and, in so doing, support
diverse animal life. They can also clear brush and other fuels that burn easily.
Finally, they can create firebreak corridors that reduce the risk of catastrophic
conflagrations. Ecological considerations were a key component of the management protocol in the 1970s and 80s, but their benefits were more long-term and
more in tune with nature.

But the 90-year suppression policy did result in the accumulation of decayed
dead wood, a veritable tinderbox over periods of low-humidity, drought, and heat.
Those were, in fact, the mix of forces that ignited the celebrated Yellowstone
National Park fires in 1988. Clearly, a more nuanced strategy was in order, and
some combination of logging, mechanical thinning, brush removal, and careful
observation became the order of the day. The Healthy Forests Restoration Act,
based on the 2000 Initiative, is an attempt to do just that.

Substantive issues aside, there are beneficiaries of each of these protocols.
Total suppression of wildfires obviously benefits local property owners and
businesses, and, more obliquely, rebuts the implicit notion that Eastern environmentalism should trump Western welfare. For its part, the environmentalist community can characterize the administration's efforts as a thinly veiled boon to
the timber industry, which collects not only sagebrush but commercially valuable
trees. And the Forest Service itself, it is alleged, requires funding to carry out its
mission beyond what public funding can be raised and needs to outsource some
of its work. What makes the policy debate interesting is that there is no single
answer, no unimpeachably best strategy. It's a problem that has no obvious
solution.

On the broadest level, the issue is a classic man v. nature battle. But, unlike other
natural disasters—volcanoes, earthquakes, floods, droughts, and heat waves—
wildfires are events over which we think we can have some control; humans can
intercede and affect the results. Moreover, they are emotionally engaging. They are
spectacularly photogenic, capturing front pages of newspapers and TV screens
whenever they strike, exerting pressure from a public both mesmerized and
shocked by them. None of these make policymaking in this area any easier.

Perhaps more problematic are factors that promise to exacerbate the problem, factors that have already begun to manifest themselves. Global climate
change will almost surely increase droughts and other atmospheric conditions
that promote such blazes. A second factor is the westward migration that has
been taking place over the past several decades. The population of western
states is growing exponentially, and areas proximate to wilderness are at once
the most attractive and the most vulnerable. Already, 2006 was the worst fire
season in history with 100,000 fires and 10 million acres burned. And 2007 is
already ahead of the pace set in 2006. The Healthy Forests Restoration Act is
already being sorely tested.

DOCUMENTS

The Healthy Forest Initiative was completed and published in August of 2002, and serves as the blueprint for the "Healthy Forests Restoration Act" enacted the following year. Two prominent features of the Initiative and subsequent act should be noted. First is the frequency with which the word "health" is used to describe the ideal toward which human efforts to control forest fires must be directed. It seems clear that "forest health" is the Administration's rhetorical response to ecologists, who regard many, if not most, natural forest conflagrations as ecologically desirable in the long term. The second feature of the initiative, as well as the following Administration promotional speeches, is the order of priorities in the goals of the protocol—"people, property, and ecosystem health." The "Communities" in the Initiative's title reinforces the people-centeredness of the proposal and act. The Executive Summary of the extensive report follows. The complete report is accessible at http://www.fs.fed.us/r8/texas/publications/mande_2003_final/04_02_03_exec_sum.pdf

6.1. "Healthy Forests: An Initiative for Wildfire Prevention and Stronger Communities," White House Public Statement

Executive Summary

This fire season is already one of the worst in modern history.

Catastrophic fires are caused by deteriorating forest and rangeland health.

These deteriorated forest and rangeland conditions significantly affect people, property, and ecosystem health.

Enhanced measures are needed to restore forest and rangeland health to reduce the risk of these catastrophic wildfires.

The American people, their property, and our environment, particularly the forests and rangelands of the West, are threatened by catastrophic fires and environmental degradation. Hundreds of millions of trees and invaluable habitat are destroyed each year by these severe wildfires. These unnaturally extreme fires are caused by a crisis of deteriorating forest and rangeland health, the result of a century of well-intentioned but misguided land management. Renewed efforts to restore our public lands to healthy conditions are needed.

This Fire Season is Already One of the Worst in Modern History

Already more than 5.9 million acres of public and private land have burned this year, an area the size of New Hampshire and more than twice the average annual acreage, with more than a month of fire season remaining. Fires have burned 500,000 acres more than they had at this time during the record-setting 2000 fire season.

Hundreds of communities have been affected by these wildfires. Tens of thousands of people have been evacuated from their homes, and thousands of structures have been destroyed. With more people living near forests and rangelands, it is becoming increasingly difficult to protect people and their homes. Land managers must do more to address the underlying causes of these fires.

Catastrophic fires are caused by deteriorating forest and rangeland health.

America's public lands have undergone radical changes during the last century due to the suppression of fires and a lack of active forest and rangeland management. Frequent, low-intensity fires play an important role in healthy forest and rangeland ecosystems, maintaining natural plant conditions and reducing the build-up of fuels. Natural, low-intensity fires burn smaller trees and undergrowth while leaving large trees generally intact. Natural fires also maintain natural plant succession cycles, preventing the spread of invasive plant species in forests and rangelands. This produces forests that are open and resistant to disease, drought, and severe wildfires.

Today, the forests and rangelands of the West have become unnaturally dense, and ecosystem health has suffered significantly. When coupled with seasonal droughts, these unhealthy forests, overloaded with fuels, are vulnerable to unnaturally severe wildfires. Currently, 190 million acres of public land are at increased risk of catastrophic wildfires.

These Deteriorated Forest and Rangeland Conditions Significantly Affect People, Property, and Ecosystem Health

Fuels have accumulated so significantly that fires no longer burn at natural temperatures or rates, making them dangerous to fight and difficult to control. Catastrophic wildfires grow extremely quickly, making them difficult to control if they are not stopped immediately. For example, the Rodeo fire in Arizona grew from 800 acres to 46,000 acres in just one day.

Nearly 83 percent of firefighters surveyed identified the need for fuels reduction as the top priority for improving their safety.

Catastrophic wildfires burn at much higher temperatures than normal fires, causing long-lasting and severe environmental damage. A large, catastrophic fire can release the energy equivalent of an atomic bomb. Rather than renewing forests, these fires destroy them. While most natural fires burn at ground level and at relatively low temperatures, these catastrophic fires burn at extreme temperatures, destroying entire forests and sterilizing soils. These extreme fires can even kill giant sequoia trees that have survived centuries of natural fires. It can take as long as a century for forests to recover from such severe fires.

Enhanced measures are needed to restore forest and rangeland health to reduce the risk of these catastrophic wildfires.

Federal, state, tribal and local governments are making unprecedented efforts to reduce the build-up of fuels and restore forests and rangelands to healthy conditions. Yet, needless red tape and lawsuits delay effective implementation of forest health projects. This year's crisis compels more timely decisions, greater efficiency, and better results to reduce catastrophic wildfire threats to communities and the environment.

The Healthy Forests Initiative will implement core components of the National Fire Plan's ten-year Comprehensive Strategy and Implementation Plan. This historic plan, which was adopted this spring by federal agencies and western governors, in collaboration with county commissioners, state foresters, and tribal officials, calls for more active forest and rangeland management. It establishes a framework for protecting communities and the environment through local collaboration on thinning, planned burns and forest restoration projects.

The following two documents clearly set forth the rationale for enactment of the Healthy Forests Restoration Act.

6.2. Press Release: "President Bush Signs 'Healthy Forests Restoration Act' into Law"

- On December 3, 2003, President Bush signed into law the Healthy Forests Restoration Act of 2003 to reduce the threat of destructive wildfires while upholding environmental standards and encouraging early public input during review and planning processes. The legislation is based on sound science and helps further the President's Healthy Forests Initiative pledge to care for America's forests and rangelands, reduce the risk of catastrophic fire to communities, help save the lives of firefighters and citizens, and protect threatened and endangered species.

- The Healthy Forests Restoration Act:

  o Strengthens public participation in developing high priority forest health projects;

  o Reduces the complexity of environmental analysis allowing federal land agencies to use the best science available to actively manage land under their protection;

  o Provides a more effective appeals process encouraging early public participation in project planning; and

  o Issues clear guidance for court action against forest health projects.

- The Administration and a bipartisan majority in Congress supported the legislation and are joined by a variety of environmental conservation groups.

The Need for Common-Sense Forest Legislation

- Catastrophic fires, particularly those experienced in California, Arizona, Colorado, Montana and Oregon over the past two years, burn hotter and faster than most ordinary fires.
- Visibility and air quality are reduced, threatening even the health of many who do not live near the fires.
- The habitat for endangered species and other wildlife is destroyed.
- Federal forests and rangelands also face threats from the spread of invasive species and insect attacks.
- In the past two years alone, 147,049 fires burned nearly 11 million acres

  o 2002: 88,458 fires burned roughly 7 million acres and caused the deaths of 23 firefighters.
  o 2003 (thus far): 59,149 fires have burned 3.8 million acres and caused the deaths of 28 firefighters.
  o Nearly 6,800 structures have been destroyed in 2003 (approximately 4,800 in California).
  o The California fires alone cost $250 million to contain and 22 civilians have died as a result.

6.3. "President Bush Signs 'Healthy Forest Restoration Act' into Law: Remarks by the President at Signing of H.R. 1904, The Healthy Forests Restoration Act of 2003"

THE PRESIDENT: Thanks for coming. Thanks for finally inviting me to the Department of Agriculture; it's an honor to be here. I'm really glad to be here as our government takes a major step forward in protecting America's forests.

Almost 750 million acres of forest stand, tall and beautiful across the 50 states. We have a responsibility to be good stewards of our forests. That's a solemn responsibility. And the legislation I sign today carries forward this ethic of stewardship. With the Healthy Forest Restoration Act we will help to prevent catastrophic wildfires, we'll help save lives and property, and we'll help protect our forests from sudden and needless destruction. . . .

[Expresses appreciation for attendance of Cabinet Secretaries and officials, California firefighters, members of Congress, state and local officials, and even a Rolling Stone member who is a tree farmer—all both as a courtesy but also to highlight the broad base of support]

For decades, government policies have allowed large amounts of underbrush and small trees to collect at the base of our forests. The motivations of this approach were good. But our failure to maintain the forests has had dangerous consequences and devastating consequences. The uncontrolled growth, left by years of neglect, chokes off nutrients from trees and provides a breeding ground for insects and disease.

As we have seen this year and in other years, such policy creates the conditions for devastating wildfires. Today, about 190 million acres of forest and woodlands around the country are vulnerable to destruction. Overgrown brush and trees can serve as kindling, turning small fires into large, raging blazes that burn with such intensity that the trees literally explode.

I saw that firsthand when we were flying over Oregon, magnificent trees just exploding as we choppered by. The resulting devastation damages the habitats of endangered species, causes flooding and soil erosion, harms air quality, oftentimes ruins water supplies. These catastrophic fires destroy homes and businesses; they put lives at risk, especially the lives of the brave men and women who are on the front line of fighting these fires.

In two years' time, fires throughout the country have burned nearly 11 million acres. We've seen the cost that wildfires bring, in the loss of 28 firefighters this year alone. In the fires that burned across Southern California this fall, 22 civilians also lost their lives, as whole neighborhoods vanished into flames. And we ask for God's blessings on the family members who grieve the loss and on the friends who mourn for their comrades.

We're seeing the tragic consequences brought by years of unwise forest policy. We face a major national challenge, and we're acting together to solve the challenge. The Healthy Forest Initiative I announced last year marked a clear and decisive change in direction. Instead of enduring season after season of devastating fires, my administration acted to remove the causes of severe wildfires. We worked within our existing legal authority to thin out and remove forest undergrowth before disaster struck. We emphasized thinning projects in critical areas. And since the beginning of 2002, we've restored almost five million acres of overgrown forest and rangeland.

And that's pretty good progress. But it's not enough progress. And so, thanks to the United States Congress, thanks to their action, and thanks for passing the Healthy Forest Restoration Act—we now can expand the work to a greater scale that the dangers of wildfires demand. In other words, we were confined. The Congress acted in a bipartisan spirit in order to enable this administration to work harder to do what we can do to prevent wildfires from taking place.

The bill expedites the environmental review process so we can move forward more quickly on projects that restore forests to good health. We don't want our intentions bogged down by regulations. We want to get moving. When we see a problem, this government needs to be able to move. Congress wisely enabled a review process to go forward, but also wisely recognizes sometimes the review process bogs us down and things just don't get done.

The new law directs courts to consider the long-term risks that could result if thinning projects are delayed. And that's an important reform, and I want to thank you all for that. It places reasonable time limits on litigation after the public has had an opportunity to comment and a decision has been made. You see, no longer will essential forest health projects be delayed by lawsuits that drag on year after year after year.

This Act of Congress sets the right priorities for the management of our nation's forests, focusing on woodlands that are closest to communities and on places where the risk to wildlife and the environment is the greatest. It enforces high standards of stewardship so that we can ensure that we're returning our forests to more natural conditions and maintaining a full range of forest types. It enables collaboration between community groups and private stewardship organizations and all levels of government before projects are chosen. This law will not prevent every fire, but it is an important step forward, a vital step to make sure we do our duty to protect our nation's forests.

The principles behind the Healthy Forest Initiative were not invented in the White House, and truthfully, not invented in the Congress. They are founded on the experience of scientists, forestry experts, and, as importantly, the firefighters who know what they're talking about. Chief Tom O'Keefe, of the California Department of Forestry, is among those who have seen the consequences of misguided forest policy. He put it this way: "A lot of people have been well-intentioned. They saved trees, but they lost the forest." We want to save the forests.

This bill was passed because members of Congress looked at sound science, did the best they could to get all the politics out of the way for good legislation. Members from both parties came together, people from different regions of the country. A broad range of people who care about our forests were listened to, whether they be conservationists, or resource managers, people from the South, people from the West, people from New York. You see, we all share duties of stewardship. And today we shared in an important accomplishment. . . .

The Western Governors' Association is a strong and active political force for states in the region. They play an important role in the deliberation on issues affecting their jurisdictions, as they did, for example, on the Endangered Species Act reform proposals. Here, however, the Secretary of the Interior documents the ways in which the Association works hand-in-glove with the federal government, both administratively and technologically.

6.4. "Remarks Prepared for Delivery by the Honorable Gail Norton, Secretary of the Interior," on behalf of the Western Governor's Association, at the Forest Summit, June 19, 2003

Exactly one year ago yesterday, the Rodeo fire started in the White Mountains of Arizona.

A reporter for the *Arizona Republic* described the first sighting of the fire as a thin veil of white-gray smoke curled on itself in a half-dozen twisted knots and wafting northeast with the late afternoon breeze.

In the time it took firefighter Gary Thompson to call the Bureau of Indian Affairs dispatch office in White river, brilliant orange flames punched through the gray smoke.

Two firefighting crews headed for the Red Dust Rodeo grounds in Cibecue. More crews had to be called in, but wouldn't arrive for three hours.

The newspaper reporter wrote:

> "In that short time, the Rodeo fire exploded, gobbling tinder and trees at an astonishing pace. By midnight, the docile plume of knotted gray smoke Thompson spotted would devour 300 acres."
>
> "The wonder now isn't that the fire grew so quickly, but that it didn't grow even faster."
>
> "Humidity was staggeringly low. Temperatures were dangerously high. The air around Cibecue was poised to suck up flames and spew them hundreds of yards into lush undergrowth that experts say was thicker and drier than almost any time in the past century."

At one point the fire was a six-mile wall of flames, 400 feet high generating 2,000-degree temperatures. You know the rest of the story of the Rodeo fire. It merged with the Chediski fire, created a 50-mile wall of flame and eventually burned more than 450,000 acres. Thousands were evacuated and more than 400 structures were destroyed.

This horrific scene was repeated across the West last year. The fire season was among the worst in the past four decades burning an area the size of New Jersey and Rhode Island put together.

Three states—Oregon, Colorado and Arizona registered the worst fires in their history. This year, the fire season has just begun in several states that are at substantial risk of wildland fire.

The mid-June report showed very high to extreme fire indices in Arizona, Colorado, Nevada, New Mexico, Texas, Western Montana and Utah. The Missoula area was added on Monday. As Gov. Napolitano noted, fires are already burning in Arizona.

You have designated this section of your program as: "ACCEPTING THE CHALLENGE AND GETTING RESULTS."

The challenge is clear from the Rodeo-Chediski fire and all the others that burned last year. Interior and Agriculture have accepted the challenge. President Bush himself is very personally interested in this issue. In many ways the Western Governors' Association was a catalyst.

We reached consensus with the WGA and other partners in May of 2002 on a ten-year Comprehensive Strategy Implementation Plan. We have taken it very seriously. Within five weeks of signing the Agreement, we completed detailed work plans to address the 23 implementation tasks identified in the plan.

Overall, the ten-year plan set four goals. The first was Improving Fire Prevention and Suppression.

We have worked on a bipartisan basis to increase the resources available for fire fighting and fuels treatment work. The result: Interior and Agriculture dollars available in 2003 to fight fires have increased 55 percent since 2000.

These dollars mean more firefighters, helicopters, airtankers and heavy equipment to fight fires. This has allowed us to continue to do an outstanding job of fire fighting, controlling more than 99 percent of the wildfires on initial attack.

The plan's other goals were reducing hazardous fuels, restoring fire-adapted ecosystems and promoting community assistance.

Those three goals are embodied in the President's Healthy Forest Initiative. Last month the President recalled his visit to the Squires Peak Fire in Oregon.

He introduced the Washington DC press corps to the fact that thinned forests survive fires.

President Bush said: "On one side of a dirt road, where small trees and underbrush had been removed before the fire rolled through, the forest was green and alive. On the other side of the road, where a similar thinning project had been stalled by lawsuits, the landscape was charred and the trees looked like matchsticks. The contrast between these two sides of the forest was startling, and it was tragic."

The President said active forest management could have saved both areas; and he encouraged Congress to move legislation on the Healthy Forests Initiative.

The House of Representatives has passed a measure by Rep. Scott McInnis of Colorado, and the Senate will have a hearing on a similar bill by Sen. Domenici next Thursday.

When I took office, the lessons learned from 2000 were just beginning to be implemented. There was no method, no plan for making fuels treatment work. There were no priorities, no database to keep track of the work.

That has changed. We have issued a series of directives and we now have a system for setting priorities. We are beginning to see results in high priority areas.

Some 62 percent of the dollars spent are going into the Wildland Urban Interface areas.

The projects chosen are fully collaborative with our State partners.

Interior will meet or exceed budget targets this year. As of June 12th, we have already treated 800,000 acres. That is 70,000 more acres than were treated in all of 2001.

We are already on track to treat more than a million acres in fiscal year 2004.

But the federal forests have an estimated 190 million acres that are in the overgrown condition described earlier in the Rodeo fire story.

We have implemented a number of improvements and are looking at more to help facilitate the Healthy Forest Initiative.

Without changes, we obviously can't make a dent in the untreated acres.

We are in the field now with 15 model environmental assessment projects. These projects are testing guidance set up by the Council on Environmental Quality to streamline the NEPA process to allow more efficient planning for fuels reduction.

The goal was to follow the process in the National Environmental Policy Act that instructs us to be thorough but brief in our analysis. It reinforces NEPA and stresses the required components of environmental analysis.

Interior has ten of these model projects in Western states. One is already out for public comment and six of the ten will be out for public comment by the end of the month. These projects show a range of ecosystems—Pinyon/juniper and salt cedars from 15–20 feet tall.

Also under the National Environmental Policy Act there is a "categorical exclusion" that we would like to use for fuel reduction projects. Categorical exclusions have been used for decades on a broad range of land management activities. It simply means there is a category of action that in the past consistently has had findings of no significant environmental impact.

We should not have to recreate the wheel for every similar project. This should save time and allow professional foresters to exercise their judgment. They need to be able to respond to insect and disease infestations.

We also have issued guidance under the Endangered Species Act for managers to expedite consultation under Section 7 by putting similar projects together in a batch, collaborating early on with agencies on project design and improving dispute resolution.

The Fish and Wildlife Service and the National Marine Fisheries Service have directed their field offices to consider the balance between short-term adverse impacts and significant long-term gains during Section

7 consultation on hazardous fuels treatment. For example, restoring fire-adapted ecosystems ultimately will benefit many listed and sensitive species and their habitat.

Finally under the ESA we are proposing a regulation on an alternative consultation process under Section 7 for forest management projects within the scope of the National Fire Plan. The alternative process will eliminate the need to conduct informal consultation on actions determined "not likely to adversely affect" on any listed species or designated critical habitat.

One of the greatest tools we have open to us now—thanks to action by the Congress—is stewardship contracting. Both the Bureau of Land Management and the Forest Service have this authority through the year .2013. It allows contracts with private or public entities to clean-up lands in exchange for the value of timber or other wood products removed from public lands.

We need to emphasize public/private partnerships that are self-sustaining and can endure for decades.

This brings me to the crux of my message today: The importance of biomass in stewardship contracting.

I am announcing today that the Interior, Agriculture and Energy Departments have signed a memorandum of understanding on woody biomass utilization. Its purpose is to focus efforts by the Departments and their partners. We know that using woody biomass by-products can be an effective restoration and hazardous fuel reduction tool that delivers economic and environmental benefits and efficiencies.

Biomass provides a net reduction in greenhouse gases. Dr. Richard Bain of the Energy Department's National Renewable Energy Lab says biomass gives us a 34 percent gain in carbon sequestration.

The President's Healthy Forests Initiative, the National Fire Plan and the ten-year implementation plan all call for biomass and wood fiber use. The recent House-passed bill has a title on biomass that promotes developing and expanding markets.

The use of biomass also meets an objective in the President's National Energy Policy. Both Interior and Energy have been working for more than a year on renewables on public lands. This is just one aspect of that work.

The problem has been that markets for biomass and small wood are sporadic and marginally economic, in most western states. Stewardship contracting for the next ten years presents the opportunity for a steady supply, new markets and product uses. This can include Indian Tribal projects and promote jobs on reservations.

Thinning for biomass allows for wildlife habitat improvement with wildlife biologists designing the projects. These projects go on all the time on private land and are profitable for the environment, energy and the landowner. A million acres have been thinned in the last 25 years for biomass use and 800,000 of those acres were private. Many of you saw yesterday on our field trip some of the new technology that is available to harvest woody products and still protect the mass of the forest.

I'm going to take you one step further into the future of technology in the forest.

How many of you remember the all terrain Armored Transport or AT-AT walker from the first Star Wars movie? It was a four-legged transport and combat vehicle used exclusively by the Imperial ground forces. It was ungainly but resembled a gigantic beast and it was intimidating.

[Walking machine clip.]

Now take a look at this clip. This machine may be the future of thinning wood. It treads lightly on the forest leaving virtually no trail behind it.

This equipment from Plustech is being developed in Finland. It is a six-legged machine that fells, de-limbs, crosscuts and piles. It is designed to adapt to the forest environment by going backwards, forwards, sideways, diagonally and up and down. It can step over obstacles and leaves a minimum impact on the land. It even tests and shifts its weight in order to do minimum soil compaction.

This only goes to show that truth is often stranger than fiction and that the technology of the future will allay many of the concerns about the methods for achieving forest health.

The degree of cooperation between the state and federal governments on forest health issues is virtually unprecedented.

The Society of American Foresters is a non-profit organization that represents more than 17,000 professional foresters and natural resource professionals. It is the scientific and educational association representing the profession of forestry in the United States. The Society's primary objective is to advance the science, technology, education, and practice of professional forestry for the benefit of society.

6.5. "Healthy Forest Bill an Important First Step," Society of American Foresters

This bill is an important step in a long-term effort that is needed to allow forest managers to begin to address the forest health crisis on our nation's forests," says Michael T. Goergen, executive vice-president and CEO of the Society of American Foresters. "With more than 190 million acres of forests at risk of wildfire and millions more threatened by insects, disease, and invasive species, this legislation will allow us to begin work to address the complex and difficult challenge ahead."

According to Goergen, "Foresters can improve forest conditions and reduce the risks of wildfire, insects, disease, and invasive species through forest management. The Healthy Forest Restoration Act gives professional forest managers additional tools to improve conditions on the national forests and private lands, while maintaining both environmental protections and public participation."

"Foresters have been frustrated with the impediments to action that have arisen over the past decade. It is frustrating to watch the conditions of many of our forests decline, when we know we can make a difference," says Goergen. "It's encouraging for us to see that Congress shares our sense of urgency about the health of our nation's forests. We look forward to continuing to work with Congress and the Administration to craft other solutions to the challenges facing our forests."

The US Chamber of Commerce (US Chamber) is the world's largest business federation, representing more than three million businesses of every size, sector, and region.

6.6. "Letter to the US House of Representatives: Support H.R. 1904, the Healthy Forests Restoration Act of 2003," May 19, 2003

May 19, 2003
Member of the House of Representatives:

In 2002, the United States experienced some of the most extreme forest fires in recorded history. Thousands of homes and businesses were evacuated, and hundreds were destroyed. The federal government spent some $1.6 billion to contain these devastating blazes and many local and regional economies experienced tremendous financial losses.

Yet even today, on the heels of last year's devastating fire season, nearly 200 million acres of federal lands are at high risk to catastrophic wildfire, with another 72 million acres at extremely perilous risk. However, federal land managers treat only approximately 2.5 million acres of land vulnerable to wildfire annually; because of the overly burdensome and unnecessary regulatory scheme they must navigate to do so. It may take several years for any one given forest health project to receive ultimate approval. Meanwhile that area teeters on the verge of destruction, vulnerable to a single spark.

Congressmen Scott McInnis and Greg Walden's Healthy Forest Restoration Act (H.R. 1904) will streamline the procedural and bureaucratic morass a forest management project is subject to, without eliminating rigorous environmental analysis or administrative and legal challenges. This legislation merely condenses the timeframe in which the review and challenges take place, so as to not extend the risk of wildfire any longer than necessary. The bill will also give priority to projects near communities and codify the public participation process, both as advocated by the Western Governor's Association.

The US Chamber of Commerce urges you to vote for H.R. 1904.

The National Center for Public Policy Research is a conservative think tank that believes in free-market solutions to public policy problems. Here, Dr. Bonnicksen decries the ecologist argument for allowing fires to burn while making the case for allowing the private sector to promote forest "health."

6.7. "Tree-Huggers or Fire-Huggers? The Environmental Movement's Confused Forest Policy," Thomas M. Bonnicksen, Ph.D on behalf of the Center for Public Policy Research

The drumbeat for prescribed fire has never been louder. The Sierra Club and other environmentalists say this is the way to solve the wildfire crisis: fire is natural and therefore good for forests. Yet, the Sierra Club has a "zero cut" policy. It wants to protect trees from loggers but it does not mind killing millions of trees with fire.

Environmentalists cannot have it both ways. Are they tree-huggers or fire-huggers?

Widespread burning would make sense in a different century. However, it is 2002, not 1802.

If we looked back 200 years, we would see fires burning regularly in 91 percent of our forests. These were mostly gentle fires that stayed on the ground as they wandered around under the trees. You could walk over the flames without burning your legs.

In a historic forest, gentle fires burned often enough to clear dead wood and small trees from under the big trees. They might flare up in a pile of logs or a patch of thick trees, but would quickly drop back to the ground. Such hot spots kept forests diverse by creating openings where young trees and shrubs could grow.

These were sunny forests that explorers described as open enough to gallop a horse through without hitting a tree. Open and patchy forests like this also were immune from monster fires like those that scorched Arizona and Colorado this year.

Our forests look different today. They are crowded with trees of all sizes and filled with logs and dead trees. You can barely walk through them, let alone ride a horse. That is why the gentle fires of the past have become the ravenous beasts we know today.

Environmentalists blame foresters for creating thick forests by putting out fires. However, environmentalists want thick forests. They lobbied for years to convert forests to old-growth, which they define as dense, multi-layered, and filled with dead trees and logs. Now they also want to keep 58 million acres of forest roadless and unmanaged. They are using treehugger arguments to set up our forests to burn. Then they use fire-hugger arguments to justify the infernos they create.

It is naïve to believe we can have thick forests and gentle fires. Even carefully planned prescribed fire is unsafe in today's forests. Each 20,000 acres of prescribed burn is likely to produce one escaped fire. That means there could be 243 escaped fires a year. This is unacceptable. There are 94,000 homes at risk in California's Sierra Nevada alone.

Environmentalists also overlook what it was like when fires burned freely. Explorers often complained in their journals about the pall of smoke hanging over mountains and valleys. Today, health hazards and air pollution restrictions make extensive burning difficult and unpalatable.

In addition, most forests require thinning before prescribed burning, and 73 million acres need treatment. Therefore, the initial treatment would cost about $60 billion during the first 15 years. Maintenance costs of about $31 billion for subsequent 15-year periods would last forever since fuels continue to accumulate. This does not include money spent to fight escaped fires, rebuild destroyed homes, control erosion and plant trees to replace burned forests.

Taxpayers will not pay this enormous cost. Likewise, the public will not stand for smoky skies from prescribed fires and burned homes from inevitable escapes. We must find a better solution.

Restoration provides the best hope for returning health to our forests because it uses forest history as a model for management. The forests that explorers found were beautiful, diverse, filled with wildlife, and resistant to monster fires.

Restoring historic forests is easy, but success requires working with the private sector. People who make their living from forests have the skill and desire to help. It would take little public funding since restored forests would come close to supporting themselves from the sale of wood products. Restoration is a cost-effective and safe way to protect our forests and solve the wildfire crisis.

Dr. Bill Wattenburg, a Research Scientist with the Research Foundation at California State University at Chico sets out a scientific critique of the "Let It Burn" policy, obviously stimulated by the Yellowstone National Park Fires.

6.8. "The 'Let Our Forests Burn Policy' is Criminal and Stupid—It Must be Re-examined by the Scientists of This Nation," Bill Wattenburg, Research Foundation at California State University at Chico, August 18, 1998

A major focus of the environmental movement and ecology studies is supposed to be the preservation of our natural resources. But many self-proclaimed ecologists in high academic and government positions actively promote a policy of "let forest fires burn" which they know can result in the total incineration of many of our forests and all living things therein. Many other good scientists and experienced foresters who have seen the consequences consider this blanket policy to be grossly irresponsible, if not often outright insane, considering the explosive condition of our forests today. Forest fires do promote forest renewal, but only when the fires do not destroy far more than can be renewed. There was a time when most of our forests were fire tolerant. That is not the case today, as described below. The "let forest fires burn" dogma can at best be called a religion because there is no science that says that a forest totally destroyed is better for the ecology long-term than a forest that continues to live.

The 1988 fire that destroyed almost 40 percent of the Yellowstone forest and its once rich ecology is a ghastly example of horrible judgment that the "let forest fires burn" promoters are still trying to rationalize (with tens of millions of dollars of scarce government research funds). The recent monstrous fires in Florida are another good example of what will eventually happen in all of our forested areas unless we mount a national campaign to clean up our forests and return them to fire safe conditions. The US Interior Department has spent more money in the last ten years to rationalize what its National Park Service dogma of "let fires burn" did to Yellowstone in 1988 than would have been required to construct protective fire breaks and conduct controlled burns that could have saved both the Yellowstone and Florida forests.

I am a scientist who grew up in our national forests. I have fought forest fires at dangerous times and helped manage controlled burns at proper times for the last forty years. I was one of ten thousand called upon, too late, to try to stop the burning of the Yellowstone forests in 1988. Defiant National Park Service bureaucrats, humming their religious "let it burn" mantra, ordered that hundreds of lightening fires be allowed to rage unchecked during the most dangerous fire season in decades. Experienced government firefighters and knowledgeable scientists alike pleaded with the park officials to stop these fires before they joined up and became an unstoppable fire storm. The park service officials wouldn't listen. They insisted that there was some divine difference between a fire started by a man-made match and a fire ignited by a lightening strike.

Any thinking person can easily understand and respect the vast difference between the "natural fires" of a hundred years ago and the all-consuming forest fires of today. When our forests were in fire equilibrium, frequent forest-cleansing ground fires (usually caused by lightening) reduced the combustible fuel load on the forest floor. Native Americans often torched brushy areas that nature did not clean up in time. These natural fires periodically burned the brush, debris, and excessive numbers of small trees. This was mother nature's way of cleaning house—without burning down the house. Anyone who walks through an old-growth forest can see the burn marks on the lower trunks of many big trees as evidence that the natural fires of long ago seldom reached the lower limbs of big trees which would cause them to ignite and in turn create a fire storm that incinerates everything else in the forest. Unfortunately, a fire storm is what usually happens in forest fires during peak fire season today.

Very few natural fires can occur today because most of our forests are not in equilibrium. Man stopped most natural forest fires a hundred years ago. Incendiary conditions now prevail because of decades of accumulated brush, debris, and thickets of small trees on the forest floors. This unnatural fuel load creates intensely hot forest fires that ignite the big trees and destroy every living thing in the forest. Massive amounts of precious top soil is then washed away from hillsides before new root structure can save it. Failure to recognize this difference between the consequences of natural fires of a century ago and unchecked forest fires of today can be disastrous for our forests, as the 1988 Yellowstone fire demonstrated.

Nevertheless, officials in charge of our national parks and forests actually espouse the theory that there is something divine about lightening-caused fires as compared to man-caused fires. They approve stopping a runaway campfire, but won't allow firefighters to extinguish lightening fires. This is what happened in Yellowstone in the summer of 1988. Can anyone even suggest with a straight face that the progress of a raging forest fire is dictated by whether man or nature provided the first spark? There is not a shred of evidence that mother nature preferentially directs its lightening bolts at forested areas that deserve to be burned—as the "let fires burn" religion seems to believe.

The cruel irony is that any camper who lets an uncontrolled campfire burn even a few square meters of national forest will be charged with a criminal act, while a government agency that deliberately incinerated 320,000 hectares of our most beautiful national park is then allowed to spend tens of millions of dollars of scarce research funds to cover up its acts of horrendous negligence based on unforgivable ignorance of the consequences of inappropriately applying their "let forest fires burn" dogma. Anyone who doubts this should take a look at the forest of blackened carcasses and scorched landscape that still typifies most of the burned areas in Yellowstone today and assess for themselves whether what was done in 1988 by park officials was an act of divine wisdom—or an act of such incredibly low-grade stupidity that it must be covered up at all cost by National Park Service officials.

Many experienced foresters and scientists believe that a long-term program of constructing fire breaks and conducting controlled burns during off-peak fire season is the only way we can clean up and protect our national forests and avoid their eventual destruction by "unnaturally" intense forest fires during peak fire season.

Ironically, many national groups that call themselves environmentalists opposed a bill in congress that would build fire breaks in three large national forests in northern California as the primary objective of sustained-yield timber harvesting operations on these forests. This plan is called the Quincy Library Group plan. It was formulated by local environmentalists, the US Forest Service, and timber industry representatives meeting in Quincy, California, over several years. A bill to implement this plan was approved overwhelmingly in the House of Representatives by both parties. In press reports, the President praised the plan as an example of what he wanted when he asked for compromise, not confrontation over the issue of managing our national forests. Nevertheless, national environmental groups such as the Sierra Club have lobbied selected US Senators such as Barbara Boxer from California to stop the bill in the Senate because these groups claim that approval of any activity by man in our national forests will lead automatically to expanded exploitation of the forests. But they, the self-styled environmentalists, are quite willing to watch these same forests go up in smoke! They know that all our forests, even the few remaining old-growth forests that they claim they are protecting, eventually will be burned to blackened stumps if there is no way to stop unnatural forest fires or at least limit their extent during peak fire season.

To protect our national forests and parks until they can be returned to fire equilibrium, firefighters must have defensive fire breaks. Adequate fire breaks require only thinning excessive numbers of small trees and reducing the fuel and debris on the forest floor, not removing the big trees, just as nature once did with natural forest fires. Then controlled burns can be safely attempted in isolated sections and lightening fires can be allowed to burn in off-peak times because they will be limited in area by surrounding fire breaks. Eventually, the entire forest becomes a fire break because it has returned to fire equilibrium. This is the only sensible and sane "let forest fires burn" policy that congress should allow. This is the Quincy Library Group plan.

Fortunately, the Quincy Library Group plan was finally approved by in the Senate in the fall of 1998. However, there are already indications that the Clinton White House will buckle under to the power-hungry so-called environmental organizations, such as the Sierra Club, and resist implementation of the law.

All scientists who care about our national parks and forests must demand a national debate and assessment of the "let forest fires burn" policy. Otherwise, more of our most precious natural resources such as the Yellowstone forest will be senselessly sacrificed as guinea pigs for poorly supported ecological theories that are not consistent with the conditions of today. I think any scientist should take great offense to the implication that only those who anoint themselves as modern "fire ecologists" are fit to judge what is sensible policy for the management of our forests. Any thinking person, scientist for sure, can easily understand the basics of this subject and the consequences of fire in any given forest today. Letting forest fires burn during high fire season with the present incendiary conditions of our forests is as stupid and irresponsible as telling people to build campfires next to the gas pumps at service stations.

The Property and Environmental Research Center prides itself as the pioneer of free-market environmentalism, which is based on the following principles: private property rights encourage stewardship of resources; market incentives spur conservation; and government subsidies often degrade the environment. In the following report, Roger Sedjo talks about the evaporation of the Forest Service's original purpose, to "forestall a timber famine," and has outlived the mission of its founder, Gifford Pinchot. His recommendation is to return forest management to local control.

6.9. "The Fires This Time," Roger Sedjo, The Property and Environmental Research Center

Summer is approaching, and wildfires are already raging through parts of New Mexico, Colorado, and Georgia. Yes, there is drought again this year, but it is increasingly clear that the US Forest Service is in a poor position to act decisively. It can throw more money at fire suppression, but this only postpones the inevitable fire crises. The fires will return. They are tragic, but they are just a symptom. The federal agency must regain its ability to manage its land.

The Forest Service is an agency without a mission. Thus, it moves with the current fashion, and currently the politically correct fashion is the preservation of biodiversity, to use a phrase of former Forest Service chief Jack Ward Thomas.

The Forest Service was created because of a misunderstanding at the end of the 19th century. Logging companies were cutting a wide swathe across the upper Midwest, and many people anticipated a timber famine. Theodore Roosevelt, among others, expected that an uncontrolled private market would wipe out the nation's timber. The federal government created forest preserves to provide a continuous supply of timber. Yet the timber famine never arrived.

The private sector turned out to be decent managers. Today, the United States is the world's largest producer of commercial wood, accounting for over one-quarter of the world's total output. Less than five percent of this timber comes from federally owned forests.

So the original purpose of the Forest Service has disappeared. Timber harvests from national forests have fallen by about 85 percent since the 1980s, from over 12 billion board feet to less than 2 billion. To many this is a waste as well as a hardship on communities dependent on timber production. Perhaps most important, it contradicts good management. Mature, crowded, and insect-infested trees burn, and they burn hot and fast.

How did this happen? In its early years, the Forest Service at least had a clear mandate: to produce timber, protect water, and make sure that the forests were maintained. Ironically, one of its great successes was in curtailing destructive forest fires, which peaked around 1930. In 1952, a *Newsweek* story praised the agency in glowing terms, featuring Smokey the Bear on the cover. The agency managed to satisfy the interest groups that paid attention to it, the timber industry, the nascent environmental movement, hunters, and people living near the forests. Most decisions were made locally.

During the 1970s and 1980s, however, large environmental groups gained power. They pushed for more preservation and more old-growth forest. They succeeded in nationalizing public forest issues. Voters in New England proved to be passionate, and influential, about the environment in Montana.

The battle over the northern spotted owl, a small bird listed under the Endangered Species Act and residing in the old-growth forest of the Pacific Northwest, epitomized the conflict. When the dust cleared, an estimated 17 million acres of forest, a large portion of it old-growth, had been removed from the national forests timber base. The national environmental groups had won.

This was a pyrrhic victory, however. Such decisions including the subsequent set-aside of 60 million acres by the Clinton administration have created a tinderbox throughout the national forests. Although environmentalists point out the benefits of small fires in reducing fuel loads, 70 years of fire suppression have created conditions ripe for large catastrophic fires. In these cases, creating healthy, resilient forests is more safely done by careful timber management than by uncontrolled fire.

Today, the Forest Service faces several choices. One is to return to the multiple-use objectives of the past getting back into the timber business while supporting recreation and some preservation. This seems unlikely.

Environmental groups push for a different alternative, custodial management and hands off approach. Yet this policy threatens even more fire.

Active ecosystem maintenance and restoration is another option, but there is no consensus on what ecosystems the forests should be restored to. Pre-Columbian forests? This would be very costly, probably impossible, and there is no compelling logic for electing any particular period in history.

Another choice is to begin to return management to local control. The Forest Service would allow the people in each forest region to influence forest planning to respond to local conditions. The Quincy Library Group, a coalition in northern California, has tried this approach, attempting to inject more local input into management plans. They haven't gotten very far. All such approaches face a hard time because of bitter opposition by self-interested national environmental groups. But unless the Forest Service moves forward in some direction, it, too, like its timber base, might well go up in flames.

The Natural Resources Defense Council (NRDC.org) is a preeminent environmental advocacy organization. In this Issue Paper of May, 2003, it summarizes what it regards as the best available science and analysis on Western wildfires and woodland community protection. Notably, it introduces the argument that the proposed legislation would violate existing environmental law, especially the National Environmental Policy Act (NEPA).

6.10. "Issue Paper, May 2003," The Natural Resources Defense Council

This May, the House Resources Committee is considering legislation by Rep. Scott McInnis (R-CO) that promotes hasty, aggressive and ill-considered logging of Western forests in the name of fire prevention. The legislation shares essential features with President Bush's Healthy Forests Initiative. Its adoption would be a bonanza for the timber industry, a major loss of accountability for federal agencies and a severe setback for public forestlands.

The bill's supporters seek to exploit understandable fear of fire to repeal essential forest protections, including statutorily guaranteed public appeal rights and the heart of environmental review under the National Environmental Policy Act (NEPA). The bill also seriously interferes with federal courts. It hands over to agencies determinations that have long been at the core of our judicial system. It orders federal officials to report judges to Congress if they choose to protect forests from logging for more than 45 days while deciding challenges to logging projects.

No one disagrees that fire poses a serious threat to many Western communities. Real, proven protection for forest communities, however, has been abandoned, lost in political posturing over proposals like the McInnis bill.

Why the West burns: Even Smoky the Bear can't prevent forest fires—in fact, now he's making them worse.

Fire is an inevitable part of all Western forests. Human action may change the timing or intensity of forest fires, but when the requisite conditions exist, they burn. Many forests normally burned—and still burn—infrequently and at high or mixed intensity. Others, principally dry pine forests on flat, south-facing or westerly slopes at low- to mid-elevations, naturally burned frequently and lightly. Human management miscalculations and excesses have changed this pattern in many dry pine sites. The major culprits have been logging, livestock grazing and fire suppression.

When it initially started suppressing fires, the US Forest Service faced opposition from woodland residents—and even timber companies—who saw frequent, low intensity fires as beneficial. By 1930, it had become apparent to Forest Service officials that when fires were artificially extinguished, flammable material built up in the woods and subsequent fires were hotter and more difficult to control. But fire fighting was rapidly becoming institutionalized at federal agencies, and by 1935 the Forest Service had adopted a "10 a.m. policy" that aimed to suppress all forest fires by mid-morning on the day after they started. The popular face of this policy was Smoky the Bear, the Forest Service cartoon character who warned the public, "Only you can prevent forest fires." Wildland fires (in rangelands as well as forests) that burned 140 million acres annually in pre-industrial days, dropped to 30 million acres a year in the 1930s and to between two and five million by the 1960s. In the 1990s, however, as fuels continued to build up and suppression became ever more difficult, this trend began to reverse, with wildfires burning eight million federal acres in 2000.

Today, we face two distinct challenges in responding to wildfire risks: 1) Fire threatens homes and communities in an increasing percent of the West, as people move to the forest; and 2) away from structures, many dry pine stands are at risk from abnormally hot fires owing to an extensive build-up of woody material, including small trees, brush and litter on the forest floor. While great uncertainty surrounds how and whether human intervention can alleviate this latter problem, we know quite well how to safeguard homes and communities. Immediate action is needed to do this now, to safeguard people and homes and also to allow better, less crisis-driven decision making about when to suppress future fires and when to let them burn. But instead of taking steps to solve the problem, the administration and members of Congress are poised to make another catastrophic mistake.

Firewise: Protecting Homes and Communities

Loss of homes and threats to communities from wildfire is a serious problem that can and must be dealt with in a serious, results-oriented, and non-politicized fashion. Job #1 must be to protect homes and communities.

Forest Service research has found that the most effective way to protect homes is to focus on the houses themselves and their immediate surroundings. Two simple measures give homes considerable wildfire survivability: installing fire resistant roofing and clearing flammable vegetation from the immediate vicinity . . . Homeowners need immediate help with information, technical support and financial assistance to protect their homes and communities. Unfortunately, federal funds for these activities have not kept up with the demand or need. The government should be doing more.

Investigations by the US General Accounting Office (GAO) and US Department of Agriculture's Office of Inspector General have found no evidence that the Forest Service has been allocating National Fire Plan funds as Congress has directed—to the highest risk communities and ecosystems. According to the Forest Service, in Fiscal Year 2002 only 39 percent of thinning acreage was planned in wildland-urban areas. In Fiscal Year 2003, the agency plans to raise the number to only 55 percent. The Forest Service and Bureau of Land Management should devote maximum resources to treatments in the immediate vicinity of homes and communities. This includes financial assistance to help homeowners and communities act directly to protect themselves.

Thinning the Backcountry: Code for Taxpayer Funded Corporate Subsidies

Rather than concentrating its energies on helping homeowners in need, the Bush administration and its allies in Congress and the timber industry are trying to capitalize on the fear of fire. They are proposing to restore forests by thinning commercially valuable trees. Unfortunately, "thinning," when such trees are involved, is a codeword for commercial exploitation that is subsidized by taxpayers.

According to a 1999 GAO report, "Most of the trees that need to be removed to reduce accumulated fuels are small in diameter and have little or no commercial value." But the timber industry and its allies continue to push for logging of large, commercially valuable trees in remote areas in the name of fire suppression. Forest Service officials admit they tend to "(1) focus on areas with high-value commercial timber rather than on areas with high fire hazards or (2) include more large, commercially valuable trees in a timber sale than are necessary to reduce the accumulated fuels."

Thinning the Backcountry: A Recipe for More Catastrophic Fires

The Forest Service and the Bureau of Land Management are poised to commit another catastrophic mistake by expanding mechanical thinning of commercially valuable trees, which can actually increase fire risk. While thinning of small trees and brush may reduce fire risk, how to do so in a way that maintains forest health while reliably achieving wildfire goals remains highly speculative:

- A recent federal interagency report on wildland fire conceded that "information on the relative effectiveness and consequences of different fuel treatment methods is being developed but is not yet available."
- Researchers for the federal government's Joint Fire Science Program pointed out last year that "[t]he lack of empirical assessment of fuel treatment performance has become conspicuous."

Removing larger trees, rather than just thinning out small undergrowth, could make fires worse:

- According to Forest Service research, "timber harvest can sometimes elevate fire hazard by increasing dead-ground fuel, removing larger fire-resistant trees, and leaving an understory of ladder fuels."
- A 2000 report of the Secretaries of Agriculture and Interior to the president warned that "the National Research Council found that logging and clearcutting can cause rapid regeneration of shrubs and trees that can create highly flammable fuel conditions within a few years of cutting."
- A group of prominent fire ecologists wrote the president last fall that "removal of small diameter material is most likely to have a net remedial effect [a]nd their removal is not so likely to increase future fire intensity, for example from increased insulation and/or the drying effects of wind."
- Thinning remote areas often results in road construction, which increases the likelihood of man-made fires.

One needs look no further than summer 2002's Rodeo/Chediski fire in Arizona to see that logged areas are vulnerable. The blaze spread throughout a landscape that had been logged and which has a road density among the highest in the nation. Another example: In a photo op to dramatize the announcement of his Healthy Forests Initiative, President Bush stood on the site of last year's Squires Fire in Oregon. Ironically, the fire actually illustrates the opposite of the president's intent. Photographic evidence and firsthand accounts show that in numerous places thinned areas burned more intensely than other parts of the landscape that were not logged.

Fanning the Flames of Politics: The Folly of Politicizing Wildfires

In its effort to politicize and exploit fire worries, the Bush administration and its allies in Congress and statehouses have tried to scapegoat environmental laws and conservationists, claiming that appeals and litigation have blocked efforts to protect communities. For example, as a fire last summer burned near the Giant Sequoia National Monument in central California, claims were made that environmentalist appeals were to blame. But according to the local Forest Supervisor, not a single Forest Service hazardous fuels reduction project within the burn area had been blocked by conservation groups in the past six years.

Conservationists strongly support the kinds of risk reduction activities right around structures that are proven by Forest Service research to safeguard homes and communities. Nearly all appeals occur when the government tries to advance the most controversial projects, those involving logging of larger trees in sensitive areas or in violation of environmental laws.

University researchers have concluded that the report was flawed because of the incomplete and selective use of data. They have constructed a database of Forest Service appeals, which is now being analyzed. In a preliminary report, one of the researchers concluded that: "members of Congress and the administration demoniz[ed] environmental groups through the use of rhetoric, synecdoches, and the repetition of unconfirmed data."

Legal Loopholes: An End-Run Around NEPA

The Healthy Forests Initiative and McInnis bill would set the worst kind of precedent by interfering with our bedrock environmental laws and the independent judicial review that is a cornerstone of American democracy. Efforts to waive laws like the National Environmental Policy Act (NEPA) are particularly egregious because they often involve the lands most in need of protection. NEPA was intended to resolve controversy and balance competing public needs by increasing public input and access to the best available scientific information about risky and uncertain government activities.

The Environmental Protection Information Center (EPIC) is a group of community activists with the mission to protect and restore ancient forests, watersheds, coastal estuaries, and native species throughout Northwest California, utilizing an integrated, science-based approach, combining public education, citizen advocacy, and litigation.

6.11. " 'Healthy Forests Initiative': A Campaign of Severe Forest Policy Rollbacks," Scott Greacen, Environmental Protection Information Center

As massive fires raged in Southern California, the Bush Administration's attempts to establish the "Healthy Forests Initiative" were fueled by the flames.

Congress' passage of "healthy forests" legislation marks the triumph of a propaganda campaign to change the debate over public forest policy.

Though sold as a compromise by politicians and press, the bill gives the Bush Administration—and the logging industry—pretty much what it asked for. Thus, the law adds force to a radical program of forest policy changes already underway, and already sweeping in its implications.

The law conflicts with sound science and common sense, failing to provide increased protection from fire for human communities. However, in the Senate, all but 14 environmental votes abandoned forest defense in the furor over huge fires in Southern California. Those fires burned primarily in windswept, fire-adapted chaparral invaded by suburbs, miles from any National Forest. They devastated places where the "healthy forests" bill, tied to National Forests, could never and will never have any effect at all. Human tragedy, death, and property destruction were used as political props to pass a law that will pry open our remnant backcountry forests to industrial logging and development.

It is disturbing that the Administration's federal forest policy has been advanced by Democratic support. With Oregon's Wyden and Montana's Baucus, California's Senator Feinstein abandoned a commitment to stand firm for genuine protection, instead negotiating a "compromise" with industry's allies that gives the Bush Administration nearly everything it wanted from Congress. The Administration's forest policy initiatives are in effect a package of giveaways for industry and handcuffs for citizen activists.

The next few years will be a critical time in federal forest policy. Taken together, the law and the laundry list of unlegislated changes swept up in the "Healthy Forests Initiative" will make citizen advocacy on National Forest issues no easier and even more necessary. As environmental groups like EPIC document, debunk, and put on public display the Forest Service's actual plans for public lands, the Bush Administration and the timber industry may yet be held accountable in the court of public opinion.

The natural threats to the health of forest ecosystems are real, but our National Forests now face further threats from the timber industry and the Forest Service, acting under the Bush Administration's Healthy Forests Initiative. The legislation just passed is as disheartening as the deception used to pass it. Now it is more important than ever to monitor, and challenge when necessary, the Forest Service's management of our public lands. The timber industry and its allies have a great deal to lose, and they know they're on the wrong side of public opinion, science, and Mother Nature. It's up to us to make sure they're on the wrong side of history as well.

The Legislation

Like the even harsher version of the Healthy Forest Restoration Act passed in the House, the Senate bill was touted as a means to reduce wildfire threats to human communities. One of its principal sponsors, Oregon's Sen. Wyden, claimed that the bill was a "balanced, bipartisan compromise" that would provide the first legislative protection for old growth and "streamline the appeals process to eliminate its worst abuses."

Environmental analysts warn, however, that the law will lead to more cutting of mature and old-growth forests, further damage to wildlife habitat, greater risk of destructive fires, and little additional assistance to communities. They point out that the bill:

- Fails to provide increased protections or funding for homes or communities, or indeed any non-federal land, at risk of wildfire, and defines "community protection" so broadly that it can justify backcountry logging;
- Creates sham protections with obvious loopholes that would allow logging of old-growth trees, including a two-year window for the Forest Service to adjust its rules, and exemptions for insect and storm damage that mean virtually every stand of old growth could legally be cut;
- Fails to ensure that "fuel reduction" projects will actually target the unprofitable underbrush, very small trees, and logging slash that create the greatest risk of destructive fires, while allowing logging that will dry out forests and promote more underbrush;
- Provides no protections for roadless areas (already targeted by effective repeal of the Roadless Rule), regulations protecting "uninventoried areas," and policies protecting potential wilderness;
- Cuts the heart out of the National Environmental Policy Act (NEPA) by restricting the alternatives analysis to a few choices defined by the agency's agenda;
- Deprives the public of its right to participate in public lands-decisions by shielding many decisions from public review and restricting citizen input and appeals rights on many others;
- Interferes with the courts, setting a thumb on the scales of justice by instructing federal courts to give even greater weight to agency positions, and restricting the duration of injunctions on logging projects. No other industry is accorded this type of special treatment.

Changing the Rules: Regulatory and Judicial Angles

The Bush Administration is moving aggressively on every possible front to maximize timber production in our National Forests at the expense of environmental protection. The comprehensive campaign proceeds on political, regulatory, and judicial fronts, as well as legislatively.

Within hours of George W.'s oath of office, the Bush White House began chopping away at forest policy and public lands regulations enacted during the Clinton Administration, including the Roadless Area Conservation Rule and rules written by the Forest Service to interpret the National Forest Management Act (NFMA) and guide its management of National Forests.

Among the NFMA regulations targeted are the critical "viable populations" rule, key appeals provisions, and the planning regulations revised in 2000 which, had they gone into effect, would have made protecting ecosystem integrity the primary goal of National Forest management. (EPIC has recently joined a legal challenge to the Bush version of the planning rules.) The Administration has also introduced a series of new changes to rules implementing the National Environmental Policy Act (NEPA), shielding from public review whole categories of actions taken in the name of "thinning," "fuel reduction," and "forest health," no matter what the likely environmental consequences.

Policies have been changed both overtly and, where necessary, by inviting lawsuits from former colleagues in industry, eliminating the public's input. A series of important policy issues, including the roadless rule, key protections for threatened and endangered species, and wilderness policy, have been excluded from public oversight in this way.

Then, in the fall of 2002, against the backdrop of the landscape-scale Biscuit Fire in Southwest Oregon and Northwest California, the Bush White House launched its effort to decimate the Northwest Forest Plan. Under the new management's vision, the still-evolving mechanism for ecosystem restoration in the public forests from Mendocino to the Canadian border will be retooled as a machine for producing timber and burying environmental dissent.

Mother Jones Magazine *is the most widely read progressive publication in the United States. It is an independent, non-profit magazine rooted in progressive political values. The following, appearing on its companion website, alleges that "forestry experts have long known that commercial logging increases the risk of forest fire" and suggests that they ignore that fact to reward loggers.*

6.12. "Fighting Fire With Logging?" Dan Oko and Ilan Kayhatsky, "MotherJones.com," August 1, 2002

As wildfires continue to burn across the American West, from Colorado to California, a debate is heating up over how the Bush administration has implemented the federal government's fire-prevention plan.

Spurred into action by the catastrophic wildfires of 2000, which burned more than eight million acres, Congress approved a National Fire Plan in the fall of that year. In the initial draft of the plan, Clinton administration officials called for a multi-pronged approach to protecting communities near fire-prone forests. Among other things, that initial plan advocated the limited thinning of forests considered to be at high risk of fire—particularly forests in which logging or earlier fires had claimed large trees, allowing highly flammable small trees and shrubbery to take over.

Still, forestry experts warned in the 2000 plan that logging should be used carefully and rarely; in fact, the original draft states plainly that the "removal of large merchantable trees from forests does not reduce fire risk and may, in fact, increase such risk."

Now, critics charge that the Bush administration is ignoring that warning. Neil Lawrence, a policy analyst with the Natural Resource Defense Council, claims that Washington has taken a far more aggressive approach to incorporating commercial logging in its wildfire prevention plans. As a result, Lawrence and other critics say, the National Fire Plan is becoming a feeding ground for logging companies. Moreover, critics claim the administration's strategy, far from protecting the lives and homes of those most at risk, could actually increase the likelihood of wildfires.

"The plan consists mostly of complaining about forest fires and ginning up more money for logging," Lawrence says.

To oversee the plan, for which Congress has approved some $2.27 billion, the Bush administration has formed a new cabinet-level Interagency Wildland Fire Leadership Council. The panel is co-chaired by Undersecretary of Agriculture Mark Rey, who happens to be a former timber-industry lobbyist. That money is paying for hiring an additional 5,000 firefighters nationwide, and for a broad range of fire-prevention efforts, including what is called "hazardous fuels reduction"—the removal of trees and other flammable material from forests.

While most environmentalists do not argue with the basic approach, they charge that too many old, large trees are being cut down under this rubric of "fuels reduction," and that federal land managers are allowing commercial logging operations to cut too many large trees too far from cities or towns, where the clearing has no real impact on human safety.

As a recent Sierra Club report explains: "(L)ogging operations are likely to remove the trunks for lumber while leaving behind mountains of slash that can ignite into a raging bonfire, or they leave behind clearcuts littered with tinder across which wildfires can race and grow . . . [W]hen thinning is used as a method of fire prevention, the dense and flammable brush that leads to intense fires is not sufficiently removed."

Lloyd Queen, director of the National Center for Landscape Fire Analysis in Missoula, Montana, argues that environmentalists are exaggerating the degree to which the fire plan promotes logging and the fire risk posed by commercial logging. Using satellites and computer mapping, Queen is helping the Forest Service and other agencies to determine what federal forests are most at risk during wildfire season. He estimates that roughly

40 million acres across the country need some sort of thinning—either through logging or so-called "prescribed fires," small wildfires set by forest managers.

"There's a broad consensus that we need to treat these areas," Queen says. "I just don't see federal managers as being able to use the plan as justification for just cutting trees."

The results of an internal audit conducted by the Agriculture Department last fall, however, suggest that Queen's faith may be misplaced. That audit found that nearly $2.5 million in funds designated for rehabilitation and restoration projects in Montana's Bitterroot National Forest were instead spent on preparations for commercial logging projects. Environmentalists at the Center for Biological Diversity in Tucson, Arizona, say forest managers are taking similar steps in the Southwest. One federal forestry project, ostensibly an attempt to reduce the risk of fire in Arizona's Sitgreaves National Forest through commercial thinning, was allowed to lapse into a wholesale logging bonanza, center officials claim. Another such project, in New Mexico's Gila National Forest, resulted in the unplanned commercial logging of dozens of acres of large trees, center officials say.

In California, the John Muir Project reports that more than 95 percent of the $15.5 million earmarked for fire plan projects in the Sierra Nevada national forests has been diverted to fund commercial logging. Merri Carol Martens, Forest Service spokesperson, confirms that logging is indeed called for in the projects funded by that $15 million, but is only one component of them. Another Forest Service spokesperson, Mary Farnsworth argues that, in some cases, commercial logging is a reasonable tool that can help improve forest health and avoid wildfires. And, she adds, in cases where it provides some local economic benefit, it's a very attractive approach.

"But you have to keep in mind, it's just one approach, we're using," Farnsworth says, noting that prescribed burns, non-commercial logging, and other approaches are also under consideration. "But you can't deal with the removal of large or small standing material as effectively with a prescribed burn, and we have plenty of science that says the fuel has got to come out of the woods."

Still, environmentalists maintain that the Forest Service's enthusiasm for "fuels reduction" is doing little more than fueling commercial logging. And they argue that, by allowing for commercial logging as part of the plan, forest officials are actually ignoring the very science Farnsworth cites.

"It's a classic bait-and-switch," says Timothy Ingalsbee, director of the Western Fire Ecology Center, an Oregon-based advocacy group. "They want to do commercial logging and call it fuels reduction."

The Cato Institute is a libertarian think tank founded on the principles of limited government, individual liberty, and free markets. Accordingly, Randal O'Toole claims that the Bush plan, and our historic plans to manage wildlife fires, send the wrong signals and provide the wrong incentives. He would decentralize federal forest and other federal lands, and have forest managers fund their activities out of user fees.

6.13. "Bush's Fire Plan Won't Work," Randal O'Toole, The Cato Institute

President Bush recently announced his "healthy forests initiative," which calls for thinning 2.5 million acres of federal forests a year for ten years while relaxing environmental standards that might slow down the process. The less excess biomass in the forests, the thinking goes, the less fuel for the sort of monster fires that have devastated the West over the past couple of years. Yet the very fires that have forced him to act prove that the plan won't work.

For instance, the president announced his initiative at the site of the Squires Peak fire near Medford, Oregon. The Bureau of Land Management (BLM) had thinned 400 acres of forest in the area, but environmental regulatory delays forced them to leave 80 acres untreated. A fire started in those 80 acres and burned uncontrollably, eventually covering 2,800 acres and costing $2.2 million to suppress.

The lesson the administration apparently learned from the Squires Peak fire is that environmental delays are bad. That's the wrong lesson. The real lesson is: Unless you thin every acre, you might as well not thin any at all.

The federal government reports that 70 million acres of federal lands need immediate thinning and another 140 million acres must be thinned soon. The president's plan to thin 25 million acres in the next ten years will cost $4 billion yet leave nearly 90 percent of these acres untreated. Unfortunately, that will leave forest homes and communities as defenseless as they are today.

There is a better way to defend those communities. Forest Service researchers have shown that homes and other structures are safe from wild-fire if their roofs are non-flammable and the landscaping within 150 feet of the buildings is made relatively fireproof. A recent Forest Service report estimates there are just 1.9 million high-risk acres with homes and other structures near federal lands, nearly all of them private.

To defend homes and communities, we should treat those acres and fireproof the homes. This could be done in just one or two years at a tiny fraction of the cost of treating federal lands.

Once homes and communities are protected, the Forest Service and other federal agencies should simply leave the fires alone, which is what fire ecologists agree they should do. Fire crews should make sure fires do not cross onto private lands but otherwise let nature take its course. This would save taxpayers billions of dollars, protect firefighters lives, and improve the health of forest ecosystems.

To understand why this isn't being done, you only have to look at recent Forest Service budgets. Before 2001, declining timber sales forced many national forests to cut staffing. But after the fires of 2000, Congress suddenly doubled fire budgets.

The real problem with forest fire fighting is not a shortage of funds, but too much money. Congress has given the Forest Service a virtual blank check to put out fire and is now giving it a near-blank check to thin forestlands. When you have a blank check to do something, that becomes the only thing you want to do even if something else would work better at a far lower cost.

Similar perverse incentives can be found in the Forest Service timber program. Federal programs indirectly reward forest managers for losing money on timber sales while penalizing them for making money or doing good things for the environment. As long as these perverse incentives are in place, we can't trust the Forest Service to sell timber without the environmental safeguards that President Bush wants to remove.

No hard-and-fast rules can apply to all 600 million highly diverse acres of federal land. Commercial timber sales could improve forest health in some areas. Complete fire suppression may make sense in other areas. Yet the current incentives push the Forest Service to make the wrong decisions in most places.

The solution is to decentralize the national forests and other federal lands so that forest managers can make the right decisions free of political pressure or centralized control. The best way to do this is to stop the flow of budgetary appropriations to the Forest Service. Instead, require that forest managers fund their activities out of their own receipts—including timber, recreation, and other user fees. Congress could supplement those receipts to pay for activities, such as habitat protection, that cannot generate user fees.

While well intentioned, President Bush's plan to thin millions of acres of federal land will not protect homes and communities from wildfire. His proposal to lift environmental safeguards without fixing the incentives will do more harm than good. Before giving the Forest Service more blank checks, Congress needs to look at alternatives that will save money, promote forest health, and truly protect communities.

Dissident Voice unabashedly describes itself as "a radical newsletter that challenges the distortions and lies of the corporate press and the privileged classes it serves." It here offers a compelling critique not only of the Bush administration plan, but the unwitting complicity of the environmental community. The author sees only eco-terrorism as an antidote.

6.14. "Chainsaw George Bush Fire Plan: Log It All," Jeffrey St. Clair, *Dissident Voice*

George W. Bush, fresh off a brush clearing operation at his Crawford ranch, snubbed the Earth Summit in Johannesburg for a trip to Oregon, where he vowed to fight future forest fires by taking a chainsaw to the nation's forests and the environmental laws that protect them.

In the name of fire prevention, Bush wants to allow the timber industry to log off more than 2.5 million acres of federal forest over the next ten years. He wants it done quickly and without any interference from pesky statutes such as the Endangered Species Act. Bush called his plan "the Healthy Forests Initiative." But it's nothing more than a giveaway to big timber, that comes at a high price to the taxpayer and forest ecosystems.

Bush's stump speech was a craven bit of political opportunism, rivaled, perhaps, only by Bush's call to open the Arctic National Wildlife Refuge for oil drilling as a way to help heal the nation after the attacks of September 11. That plan sputtered around for awhile, but didn't go anywhere. But count on it: this one will.

Bush is exploiting a primal fear of fire that almost overwhelms the crippling anxiety about terrorists. In a one of the great masterstrokes of PR, Americans have been conditioned for the past 60 years that forest fires are bad . . . bad for forests. It's no accident that Smokey the Bear is the most popular icon in the history of advertising, far outdistancing Tony the Tiger or Capt. Crunch.

But the forests of North America were born out of fires, not destroyed by them. After Native Americans settled across the continent following the Wisconsin glaciation, fires became an even more regular event, reshaping the ecology of the Ponderosa pine and spruce forests of the Interior West and the mighty Douglas-fir forests of the Pacific Coast.

Forest fires became stigmatized only when forests began to be viewed as a commercial resource rather than an obstacle to settlement. Fire suppression became an obsession only after the big timber giants laid claim to the vast forests of the Pacific Northwest. Companies like Weyerhaeuser and Georgia-Pacific were loath to see their holdings go up in flames, so they arm-twisted Congress into pouring millions of dollars into Forest Service fire-fighting programs. The Forest Service was only too happy to oblige because fire suppression was a sure way to pad their budget: along with the lobbying might of the timber companies they could literally scare Congress into handing over a blank check.

In effect, the Forest Service fire suppression programs (and similar operations by state and local governments) have acted as little more than federally-funded fire insurance policies for the big timber companies, an ongoing corporate bailout that has totaled tens of billions of dollars and shows no sign of slowing down. There's an old saying that the Forest

Service fights fires by throwing money at them. And the more money it spends, the more money it gets from Congress.

"The Forest Service budgetary process rewards forest managers for losing money on environmentally destructive timber sales and penalizes them for making money or doing environmentally beneficial activities," says Randal O'Toole, a forest economist at the Thoreau Institute in Bandon, Oregon. "Until those incentives are changed, giving the Forest Service more power to sell or thin trees without environmental oversight will only create more problems than it solves."

Where did all the money go? It largely went to amass a fire-fighting infrastructure that rivals the National Guard: helicopters, tankers, satellites, airplanes and a legion of young men and women who are thrust, often carelessly, onto the firelines. Hundreds of firefighters have perished, often senselessly. For a chilling historical account of how inept Forest Service fire bureaucrats put young firefighters in harms way read Norman Maclean's (author of *A River Runs Through It*) last book, *Young Men and Fire*. In this book, Maclean describes how incompetence and hubris by bureaucrats led to the deaths of 13 firefighters outside Seeley Lake, Montana in the great fire of 1949. More recently, mismanagement has led to firefighters being needlessly killed in Washington and Colorado.

Since the 1920s, the Forest Service fire-fighting establishment has been under orders to attack forest fires within 12 hours of the time when the fires were first sighted. For decades, there's been a zero tolerance policy toward wildfires. Even now, after forest ecologists have proved that most forests not only tolerate but need fire, the agency tries to suppress 99.7 percent of all wildfires. This industry-driven approach has come at a terrible economic and ecological price.

With regular fires largely excluded from the forests and grasslands, thickets of dry timber, small sickly trees and brush began to build up. This is called fuel loading. These thickets began a breeding ground for insects and diseases that ravaged healthy forest stands. The regular, low-intensity fires that have swept through the forests for millennia have now been replaced by catastrophic blazes that roar with a fury that is without historical or ecological precedent.

Even so the solution to the fuels problem is burning, not logging. The Bush plan is the environmental equivalent of looting a bombed out city and raping the survivors. The last thing a burned over forest needs is an assault by chainsaws, logging roads and skid trails, to haul out the only living trees in a scorched landscape. The evidence has been in for decades. The proof can be found at Mt. St. Helens and Yellowstone Park: Unlogged burned forests recover quickly, feeding off the nutrients left behind dead trees and shrubs. On the other hand, logged over burned forests rarely recover, but persist as kinds of biological deserts, prone to mudslides, difficult to revegetate and abandoned by salmon and deep forest birds, such as the spotted owl, goshawk and marbled murrelet. They exist as desolate islands inside the greater ecosystem.

Even worse, such a plan only encourages future arsonists. The easiest way to clearcut an ancient forest is to set fire to it first. Take a look at the major fire of the West this summer: the big blazes in Arizona and Colorado were set by Forest Service employees and seasonal firefighters, another big fire in California was started by a marijuana suppression operation, fires in Oregon, Washington and Montana have been started by humans.

In Oregon more than 45,000 acres of prime ancient forest in the Siskiyou Mountains was torched by the Forest Service's firefighting crews to start a backfire in order to "save" a town that wasn't threatened to begin with. The fires were ignited by shooting ping-pong balls filled with napalm into the forest of giant Douglas-firs. By one estimate, more than a third of the acres burned this summer were ignited by the Forest Service as backfires. That's good news for the timber industry since they get to log nearly all those acres for next to nothing.

Far from acting as a curative, a century of unrestrained logging has vastly increased the intensity and frequency of wildfires, particularly in the West. The Bush plan promises only more of the same at an accelerated and uninhibited pace. When combined with global warming, persistent droughts, and invasions by alien insects species (such as the Asian-long-horned beetle) and diseases, the future for American forests looks very bleak indeed.

Predictably, the Bush scheme was met with howls of protest from the big environmental groups. This is part of Bush's irresponsible anti-environmental Agenda," said Bill Meadows, president of the Wilderness Society. "The truth is that waiving environmental laws will not protect homes and lives from wildfire."

But they only have themselves to blame. They helped lay the political groundwork for the Bush plan long ago. And now the Administration, and its backers in Big Timber, have seized the day and put the environmentalists on the run.

The environmentalists have connived with the logging-to-prevent-fires scam for political reasons. First came a deal to jettison a federal court injunction against logging in the Montana's Bitterroot National Forest designed to appease Senator Max Baucus, friend of Robert Redford and a ranking Democrat. More than 14,000 acres of prime forest inside formerly protected roadless areas are now being clearcut. Then last month came a similar deal brokered by Senate Majority Leader Tom Daschle with the Sierra Club and the Wilderness Society that allows the timber industry to begin logging the Black Hills, sacred land of the Sioux, totally unfettered by any environmental constraints.

Grassroots greens warned that such willy-nilly dealmaking with Democrats would soon become a model for a national legislation backed by Bush and Republican legislators that would dramatically escalate logging on all national forests and exempt the clearcuts from compliance with environmental laws. We've now reached that point. And there's no sign the big greens have learned their lesson.

The latest proposal comes courtesy of the Oregon Natural Resources Council and the Sierra Club. It's rather timidly called the "Environmentalist New Vision." There's nothing new about the plan, except that it is being endorsed by a claque of politically intimidated green groups instead of Boise-Cascade. It calls for thinning (i.e., logging) operations near homes in the forest/suburb interface. This is a pathetic and dangerous approach that sends two wrong messages in one package: that thinning reduces fire risk and that it's okay to build houses in forested environments.

In fact, there's no evidence that thinning will reduce fires in these situations and it may provide a false sense of security when there are other measures that are more effective and less damaging to the environment.

"Forest Service fire researcher Jack Cohen has found that homes and other structures will be safe from fire if their roof and landscaping within 150 feet of the structures are fireproofed," says O'Toole. "A Forest Service report says there are 1.9 million high-risk acres in the wildland-urban interface, of which 1.5 million are private. Treating these acres, not the 210 million federal acres, will protect homes. Firebreaks along federal land boundaries, not treatments of lands within those boundaries, will protect other private property. Once private lands are protected, the Forest Service can let most fires on federal lands burn."

As it stands, the Sierra Club's scheme will only result in more logging, more subdivisions in wildlands and, predictably, more fires. Any environmental outfit with a conscience would call for an immediate thinning of subdivisions on urban/wildland interface, not forests. Don't hold your breath. Too many big-time contributors to environmental groups own huge houses inside burn-prone forests in places like Black Butte Ranch, Oregon, Flagstaff, Arizona and Vail, Colorado.

Of course, there's still resistance to these schemes. When Bush arrived in Portland to make official his handout to big timber, he was greeted by nearly a thousand protesters. On the streets of the Rose City, Earth Firsters anti-war activists shouted down Bush and his plans for war on Iraq and the environment. The riot police soon arrived in their Darth Vader gear. The demonstrators, old and young alike, were beaten, gassed, and shot at with plastic bullets. They even pepper sprayed children. Dozens were arrested; others were bloodied by bullets and nightsticks.

This is a portent of things to come. When the laws have been suspended, the only option to protect forests will be direct action: bodies barricaded against bulldozers, young women suspended in trees, impromptu encampments in the deep snows of the Cascades and Rockies.

Not long ago, the occupation of cutting down the big trees ranked as one of the most dangerous around. Now, thanks to the connivance of Bush, Daschle and the big enviro groups, the job of protecting them will be fraught with even more peril.

Those brave young forest defenders, forced into the woods as a thin green line against the chainsaws, should send their bail requests to the Sierra Club and their medical bills to the Wilderness Society. They can afford it.

QUESTIONS FOR CONSIDERATION

1   Forest fire policy is another public issue that, to a significant degree, reflects a genuine dispute between science and politics. But science and public policy have competing, if not mutually exclusive, goals. How can government sort out the respective claims of human safety and personal property protection in the short term and ecological viability in the long term.

2   Wilderness areas are attractive as residential environments. To what extent are people who settle near forested areas personally responsible for mitigating damages, either by constructing their homes in a more fireproof manner, or by clearing a buffer area around them? And are governments—and ultimately taxpayers—obliged to spend increasing amounts of money to address threats created, or at least exacerbated, by people voluntarily locating near fire-prone areas, sometimes called the wildland-urban interface?

3   Opponents of the new government policy embodied in the HFRA claim that the logging and timber industries (along with the Forest Service) are the real beneficiaries of the new protocol, since they are allowed to take, among other detritus, mature trees in compensation for their work as "clearing contractors." Does their role and "compensation" in "clearing and thinning" activities compromise the integrity of the policy, or does it serve to reduce public costs and relieve the strain on Forest Service expenditures?

4   What claims, if any, does wildlife welfare have on any adopted policy? Ecologists claim that natural fires in fact ultimately increase their food supply and enrich their habitat. If so, how, and to what extent, should they be taken into account? Is assuring that the relevant provisions of the Endangered Species Act and the National Environmental Policy Act are enforced appropriate and sufficient in the face of, say, an uncontrolled multistate fire?

5   One observer frames the debate as one between Eastern ecological ideals and Western welfare. Are forest fires principally a Western concern and, if so, should Western interests play the dominant role in developing a policy to manage them?

6   If this issue is, to a great extent, a scientific one, "whose science" should prevail—that of the foresters and local woodland managers or the acknowledged expertise of environmentalists and ecologists? Sort out the justifiable claims of each.

Index

This relates purely to the United States